MW00587928

Writing Genre Fiction
A Guide to the Craft

H. Thomas Milhorn, M.D., Ph.D.

Universal Publishers
Boca Raton, Florida
USA • 2006

Writing Genre Fiction:
A Guide to the Craft

Universal Publishers
Boca Raton, Florida • USA
2006

ISBN: 1-58112-918-1

www.universal-publishers.com

PREFACE

The title *Writing Genre Fiction: A Guide to the craft* is self-explanatory. It is a book about how to write genre fiction. After many years of writing nonfiction—three books, 12 chapters in books, and over a hundred articles—I decided to write a novel—a medical thriller in the mold of Robin Cook, Michael Crichton, and Michael Palmer. The problem was that, although I knew how to write and had received a number of awards for nonfiction works, I didn't know how to write genre fiction. So, before beginning the manuscript I did a thorough search of the literature, which included reading numerous books and hundreds of website articles. What I discovered was that there simply wasn't one good source from which to learn the craft of writing genre fiction.

Although there were numerous books on writing fiction, none were satisfactory for my purpose. Some were put together by editors, with each chapter being written by a different author. As with all edited books, some chapters were better then others and all the books were incomplete. Other books were written by single authors, but these varied greatly in terms of their actual usefulness for the purpose they were intended and none covered the subject adequately for my needs. For example, none came close to adequately covering the two important areas of emotions and body language—subjects I have devoted two entire chapters to. And none made use of the wealth of information about writing genre fiction that is available on the Internet.

The fact that none of the how-to books I reviewed were written by authors with experience writing nonfiction I believe to be of significance because a how-to book on writing fiction is a nonfiction book. To adequately write such a book logically requires nonfiction-writing skills.

My research resulted in the publishing of my first novel, *Caduceus Awry*, which was a finalist in the Eudora Welty Film and Fiction Festival novel competition.

Writing Genre Fiction: A Guide to the Craft is the book I was looking for when I set out on my quest to learn how to write genre fiction. It is an attempt to share what I learned from my research. It covers the six key elements of genre fiction; the various genres and subgenres; a large number of genre-fiction writing techniques; plot, subplots, and parallel plots; structure; scene and sequel; characterization; dialogue; emotions; and body language. It also covers additional information about copyrighting and plagiarism, where to get ideas, manuscript formatting and revising, and query letters and synopses. In addition, an appendix gives a large number of grammar tips.

Throughout the book, to prevent the frequently repeated use of "he or she," I have used "he" with the understanding that it refers to either sex. Also, to avoid confusion between quotation marks used to indicate that a character is speaking and quotation marks used to indicate a reference is being quoted, I have used quotation marks to indicate character speech and italics to indicate quotes from references.

Tom Milhorn
Meridian, Mississippi

Contents

Chapter I. Key Elements of Genre Fiction   1
Literary Fiction versus Genre Fiction   2
    Literary Fiction   2
    Genre Fiction   2
Fiction Length   3
Key Elements   4
    Plot, Story, and Structure   4
    Setting   6
    Characters   7
    Point of View   11
    Prose   12
    Theme and Subject   14

Chapter 2. Choosing your Genre   19
Action/Adventure   20
Christian   21
Fantasy   21
    Light Fantasy   21
    Arthurian Legend   22
    Heroic Fantasy   22
Gay/Lesbian   23
Historical   24
Horror   24
Mystery/Detective   25
    The Amateur Detective   26
    The Cozy   27
    The Police Procedural   27
    The Private Detective   28
    The Puzzle   29
Romance   29

Contemporary   29
Gothic   30
Regency   30
Other Subgenres   31
Science Fiction   31
Apocalyptic/Post-apocalyptic   32
Cyberpunk   32
First Contact   32
Hard   33
Military   33
Soft/Sociological   34
Space Opera   35
Time Travel   35
Spy/Espionage   35
Thriller   36
Medical Thriller   37
Legal Thriller   37
Technothriller   38
Western   38
Young Adult   39

Chapter 3. Backstory to Description   43
Backstory   43
Direct Methods   43
Indirect Methods   50
Backstory Length   51
Clichés   52
Cliché Phrases   52
Cliché Characters   54
Cliché Situations   55
Description   56
Blending Description   56
Brand Names   57
The Words to Use   57

Chapter 4. Figurative Language to Introspection, Insight, &
Perception   63
Figurative Language   63
Painting Mental Pictures   63
Substituting Words for Sounds   64

Contents

Other Functions   65
Foreshadowing and Flash Forward   66
   Foreshadowing   66
   Flash Forward   67
Form and Structure   68
   Form   68
   Structure   69
Imagery   69
   Levels of Imagery   70
   Suggestions for Using Imagery   71
Information   71
Interlocking Episodes   71
Introspection, Insight, and Perception   72
   Introspection   72
   Insight   73
   Perception   73

Chapter 5. Linking Episodes to Series Novels   77
Linking Episodes   77
Modifiers   78
   Adjectives   78
   Adverbs   79
   Valueless Modifiers   80
Narrative   81
Point of View   82
   First-person Point of View   82
   Third-person Point of view   83
   Multiple Points of View   86
   Second-person Point of View   86
Sentences   87
   Sentence Fragments   87
   Sentence Variety   87
Series Novels   88

Chapter 6. Setting to Special Scenes   91
Setting   91
   Time   92
   Place   92
   Experience   95
   Mood   95

Simultaneity   99
Special Scenes   100
   Action Scenes   100
   Crowd/Battle Scenes   102
   Death Scenes   105
   Love Scenes   105

Chapter 7. Style and Tone to Verb Strength   111
Style and Tone   111
   Style   111
   Tone   112
Symbolism and Allegory   112
   Symbolism   112
   Allegory   112
Telling versus Showing   113
   Telling   113
   Showing   114
Time   115
Transitions   115
   Simple Transitions   116
   Jump-cut Transitions   117
   Chapter Breaks   119
Verb Strength   119
   Active versus Passive Voice   119
   Strong versus Weak Verbs   120

Chapter 8. Plot   123
Plot Structure   123
Parallel Plots and Subplots   125
   Parallel Plots   125
   Subplots   126
Crisis and Challenge   127
   Crisis   127
   Challenge   127
Conflict and Suspense   128
   Conflict   128
   Suspense   132
Coincidence   134
Withholding Information   135
Story Focus   135

Contents

Plot Driven Story 135
Idea Driven Story 136
Character Driven Story 136
Twenty Basic Plots 137
Plot Summary 146
Outlining 147

Chapter 9. Structure 151
Title 152
Categories 152
Importance 153
Prologue 154
Types of Prologues 155
Prologue Test 157
Beginning 157
Story Question 159
Questions Readers Ask 159
Components of the Beginning 161
Wide and Narrow Beginnings 172
Beginnings to Avoid 173
Middle 174
Complications 175
Crisis 177
The Sagging Middle 178
End 181
Climax 182
Resolution 182
Types of Endings 183
Stated Goal versus True Goal 185
Deus ex Machina 186
Symbolic Event 187
Epilogue 188
Structure Chart 188

Chapter 10. Scene and sequel 193
Scene 194
Questions to Answer 194
Cause and Effect 196
Scene Stages 197
Scene Length 200

Sequel   200
    Purposes of a Sequel   201
    Sequel Stages   203
    Sequel Length   208
Variation of Scene-Sequel Structure   208
    Scene Structure Variation   208
    Sequel Structure Variation   209
Ways to Keep the Reader Worried   209
    Scene Ways   209
    Sequel Ways   210
Pacing   210

Chapter 11. Characterization   213
Character Classification   213
    Major Characters   214
    Minor Characters   218
    Major or Minor Characters   219
Character Description   223
    Dominant Characteristics   223
    Tags   224
    Uniqueness   225
    Involvement   227
    Desires and Goals   228
    Compensation   228
    Self-image   229
Character Development   229
    Methods of Creating Characters   230
    Character Change   230
Names   231
Personality Components   233
Examples of Character Attributes   236
How to Bring in a Character   238
Character Chart   239

Chapter 12. Dialogue   245
Conversation versus Dialogue   245
Direct and Indirect Dialogue   246
Uses of Dialogue   246
Types of Dialogue   249
    Directed Dialogue   249

Interpolated Dialogue   250
Misdirected Dialogue   250
Modulated Dialogue   252
Dialogue Techniques   253
Dialogue Conventions   255
Men Talking to Men   255
Bits and Pieces versus Chunks   256
Situational Dialogue   256
Individuality   257
Internal Dialogue   257
Emphasis   257
Sounds   257
Speeches   258
Cursing   259
Rules for Good Dialogue   259
Dialogue Tags   260
Speech Tags   260
Action Tags   261
Creative Dialogue Tag Syndrome   261
Excessive Direct Address   262
Overuse of Modifiers   262
Dialect, Slang, and Jargon   263
Dialect   263
Slang   264
Jargon   264
Slang and Jargon Websites   265
Punctuating Dialogue   265
Statements, Questions, and Exclamations   265
New Speaker   266
More than One Paragraph of Dialogue   266
Nested Quotation Marks   266

Chapter 13. Emotions   269
Characteristics of Emotion   269
Etiology of Emotions   269
Mixed Emotions   270
Range of Emotions   270
Levels of Emotion   270
Emotions and Body Language   271
Table of Emotions   271

Examples of Emotions   276
    Descriptive Phrases   276
    Emotional Situations   277

Chapter 14. Body Language   283
Types of Body Language   284
    Facial Expressions   284
    Gestures   285
    Posture   286
    Spatial Relationships   287
Groups   288
Table of Body Language   289
Examples of Body Language   293

Chapter 15. Additional Information   297
Copyright and Plagiarism   297
    Copyright   297
    Plagiarism   299
Getting Ideas   300
    Sources for Ideas   301
    Record your Ideas   302
Manuscript   302
    Format   302
    Revision   304
Query Letter and Synopsis   309
    Query Letter   309
    Synopsis   312

Appendix. Grammar Tips   319
Comma and Semicolon Use   319
    Lists   319
    Nonessential and Essential Clauses   319
Commonly Confused Words   320
Double Negatives   329
Modifiers   329
    Dangling Modifiers   330
    Nearly, Almost, and Only   330
One Word or Two?   331
Possessives   333
Pronouns   333

Contents

    Case   333

    Noun-pronoun Agreement   334

    Antecedent Agreement   334

Sentence Structure   334

    Comma Splice   334

    Run-On (Fused) Sentences   335

Split Infinitives   335

Subject-Verb Agreement   336

Verbals   338

    Participles   339

    Gerunds   339

    Infinitives   340

    When to Use Verbals   340

Whether or Not   341

Index   343

Chapter 1

Key Elements of Genre Fiction

*F*iction is a literary work whose content is produced by imagination and is not necessarily based on fact. Writing fiction is generally conceded to be a combination of *craft* and *talent*. This is sometimes stated as:

$$\text{Writing Fiction} = \text{Craft} + \text{Talent}$$

The craft part of the equation is the part that can be taught or learned. The talent part is the part that cannot be taught or learned. You were either born with it or you weren't. It's like a lot of other things in life. For instance, all heart-transplant surgeons are taught the same craft, but some are much better at it than others. Why is that, you might ask? It's because they were born with a greater innate ability to do that kind of work, in part due to better eye-to-hand coordination, which is genetically determined.

The same goes for painting, doing mathematics, or playing basketball. You are either born with innate talent in one of these areas or you aren't. It's why Pablo Picasso, Albert Einstein, and Michael Jordon stood out among others in their fields. However, despite being born with innate abilities, these individuals put forth the necessary effort to learn their respective crafts. Without that effort they never would have attained greatness. Until you learn the craft of writing fiction and try your hand at it, you won't know whether you have talent to be a good writer or not. Read on.[1,2,3]

LITERARY FICTION VERSUS GENRE FICTION

Literary Fiction

Literary fiction is said to be the fiction of ideas. Its primary purpose is to evoke thought. The writer's goal is self-expression. Literary fiction is usually considered to be more concerned with style and solid writing, to stress character development and good descriptions, and to be paced more slowly than genre fiction. It is sometimes referred to as "serious fiction," compared to genre fiction, which is considered "commercial."[2,4-6]

Genre Fiction

Genre fiction is the fiction of emotions. Its primary purpose is to evoke feelings. The writer's goal is to entertain the reader. Any consideration of self-expression, if one exists, is usually secondary. Genre fiction is typically characterized by a great deal of dialogue, characters that readers can easily identify with, and plots that are fast paced. As a rule, publishers expect to make a substantial profit from selling a genre fiction book, which is not always true of a literary fiction work.

The most obvious function of genre is as a publishing category; that is, a marketing tool. Calling two different books "science fiction" lets a buyer know that they are similar in some way. If a person enjoyed one book classified as "science fiction," there's a greater chance he will enjoy another book classified the same way than he will one classified as "romance." As a result, genre allows booksellers to group novels in their bookstores in such a way that readers can more easily find the sort of book they want. Genre fiction is sometimes called *popular*, *category*, or *formula fiction.*[2,4-6]

FICTION LENGTH

Depending on length, works of fiction are classified as short stories, novelettes, novellas, and novels.

Short Story. A *short story* is a brief work of fiction, usually considered to be less than 7,500 words, although some extend the length to 10,000. It is more pointed and more economically detailed as to character, situation, and plot than longer works. Well-known writers of short stories include Anton Chekhov (*The Lottery Ticket, The Shoemaker and the Devil*) and O. Henry (*The Gift of Magi, The Blind Man's Holiday*). Ray Bradbury (*A Sound of Thunder, The Illustrated Man*) is a more recent writer of short stories.

A less well defined work of fiction is *flash fiction*—a genre of short story characterized by an even more limited word length, generally less than 2,000 words and tending to cluster in the 250 to 1,000 word range. Flash fiction has roots leading all the way back to Aesop's Fables. The Internet has brought new life to flash fiction with its demands for short, concise works. *Ezines*, periodic publications distributed by e-mails or posted on websites, are a ready market for flash fiction works. Many print magazines publish enzines as well.[2,7]

Novelette. A *novelette* is a work of fiction between short story and novella in length (7,500 and 17,499 words).[2] *Shop Girl* (2001) by Steve Martin is a recent novelette that was made into a movie in 2005.

Novella. A *novella* is a work of fiction shorter than a novel but longer than a novelette (17,500 and 39,999 words). However, some consider the upper limit of a novella to be anywhere from 49,999 to 59,999 words. Two well-known novellas are *Strange case of Dr. Jekyll and Mr. Hyde* (1886) by Robert Lewis Stevenson and *The Heart of Darkness* (1902) by Joseph Conrad.[2,7]

Novel. A *novel* is a long work of fiction of 40,000 words or more, although some consider the lower limit of a novel to be anywhere from 50,000 to 60,000 words. A novel is usually much more complex than the shorter forms of fiction, having more characters, more situations, a more complicated plot, and even subplots and parallel plots.

Most modern-day novels go well beyond the 40,000-60,000 word mark. Dan Brown's highly successful novel *The Da Vinci*

Code (2003), for example, approaches 200,000 words.[2,7,8]

Although *Writing Genre Fiction: A Guide to the Craft* is addressed primarily to those who wish to write genre novels or improve their genre novel-writing skills, most of the techniques discussed apply equally well to the shorter forms of fiction.

KEY ELEMENTS

To create a fictional world that seems real to readers, writers use a minimum of six key elements: (1) Plot, story, and structure; (2) setting; (3) characters; (4) point of view; (5) prose; and (6) theme and subject.

Plot, Story, and Structure

Before beginning a novel it is important to understand the concepts of plot, story, and structure.

Plot

Plot is the sequence of events in a story as the author chooses to arrange them. It is a chain of events, each event the result of some prior events and the cause of some subsequent events. Its purpose is to get readers involved by creating tension so they feel a need to know what happens next. The hero and the villain each keep thwarting the other, forcing each to improvise under pressure. This continues until finally one gains the upper hand.

If the plot is organized around a single central problem, it usually ends when that problem is resolved. If the plot deals with a series of problems, it ends when the last problem is dealt with.[2,9-15] Plot is discussed further in Chapter 8.

Story

Story, unlike plot, is the sequence of events in a work of fiction in the order they actually occur. Story and plot may differ because writers use devices like flashbacks, recollections, introspections, and flash forwards so that the plot does not always

4

proceed in a chronological order. A story persists as long as there are problems to be resolved. [2,9-15]

Structure

Structure is the framework of a novel. It is the way the plot is arranged in both a logical and a dramatic manner to create maximum suspense. In all cases it consists of (1) a title, (2) a beginning, (3) a middle, and (4) an end. In addition, some novels have prologues, fewer have epilogues, and even fewer have both.

Title. You can choose almost anything you want as a *title* as long as it isn't overly long. It certainly can't be too short, since many titles consist only of a single word. [9,15-17]

Beginning. Every *beginning* makes a promise to readers. A romance novel promises to entertain and titillate them, a mystery novel makes a promise to intellectually challenge them, a thriller novel makes a promise to excite and keep them wondering what is going to happen next, and a horror novel promises to scare them. If you as a writer don't live up to our promise in subsequent pages, readers will be bitterly disappointed.

Usually readers are brought into the story at the moment the status quo is threatened. The closer the opening scene is to the precipitating event, the more force and emergency it will have. Ideally, readers should find characters in difficulty in the first chapter, the first page, or even better in the first paragraph. [9,15-17]

Middle. The *middle* increases conflict, further develops the main characters, and introduces other characters. It is composed of *complications* in which things progressively get worse for the hero and a *crisis* in which he must make a decision that can lead to either success or failure in achieving his ultimate goal. With complications, every attempt by the hero to solve a problem usually makes the problem worse or creates a new, more tenacious problem. Even if his situation improves, the forces arrayed against him grow comparably in magnitude. By the end of the middle, all the various forces that will collide at the story's climax should have been put in place. [15,18]

End. The story narrows down as the *end* approaches so the ending can take place clearly and decisively. Any subplots and side issues should have been disposed of. If the novel has parallel plots, they should have already converged into a single plot line.

All the subordinate characters should be "offstage," their work done, to leave the main characters alone in the "spotlight" to do the final battle.

The end consists of a climax and a resolution. The *climax*, also known as the *showdown*, is the decisive event that resolves the conflict. Although a genre novel has a number of high points of tension and action, the climax is the highest point. It is the logical coming together of the facts and events that took place earlier in the novel. It can be thought of as the ultimate surprise, revealing the answer to the central mystery. It is the moment that relieves all the tension that has built up through the beginning and middle of the story.

Once the climax is finished, the falling action leads quickly toward the story's *resolution,* which refers to the final outcome of a plot. It is the final explanation of events. Its function is to wrap up the story. Resolution is also known as the *denouement,* which literally means "unknotting."[14,17,19]

Structure is discussed further in Chapter 9.

Setting

The *setting* of a novel is the background on which the writer builds the plot and characters. It involves the entire environment: (1) time, (2) place, (3) experience, and (4) mood. Setting can be revealed through narration and dialogue and illustrated by the characters' actions, thoughts, and speech patterns.[2,20-22]

Time

Time is important to every story. Is it day or night? Is it just after the Civil War, during the great depression, or 50 years in the future? Does the story take place in New York City in 2006 or in New York City in 1880?

The year in which the story takes place is not the only temporal aspect of setting to consider. The time of year might change the physical setting—winter (snow, ice, leafless trees, and unbearable cold), fall (warm days, cool nights, and an array of color in the trees), spring (sun-shiny days, flowers in full bloom, and birds chirping). In general, the winter is a more gloomy time than other seasons of the year, but not always. Children laughing and frolicking in the snow is certainly a happy scene.[2,20-22]

Place

Place includes the bigger picture (city, county, state, country) and the smaller picture (local businesses, places of residence and work, streets and avenues, and other local details). The place in which the story takes place may be real or fictitious.[2,20-22]

Experience

Setting is "seen" through a character's *experience*. Different characters may perceive the same surroundings in very different ways based on their familiarity with the setting. A man from a small town in the Mississippi Delta who is visiting Brooklyn for the first time might describe it differently than a man who has lived there all his life.[2,20-22]

Mood

The *mood* or *atmosphere* of a story is the impression it creates and the emotions it arouses in readers. Writers create appropriate moods through their choices of specific details, images, and chosen words and phrases. The character's five senses and the weather can be very helpful in establishing mood.

Filtering a scene through a character's feelings can profoundly influence what the reader experiences. For instance, the same setting may portray more than one mood depending on how the writer approaches it. A woman walking across a meadow may experience different feelings (happiness, sadness, anger, or fear) depending on the descriptive words the writer chooses to use.[2,20-22] Setting is discussed further in Chapter 6.

Characters

Characterization is the creation of imaginary people (*characters*) who appear to be real and believable to readers. In most stories, characters and their interactions drive the plot and create the suspense and tension. Readers rely on the characters to draw them into the story.

Characters are usually human, but can be animals, aliens, robots, or anything you want them to be. Characters have names, physical appearances, and personalities. They often wear certain kinds of clothes, speak using slang or jargon, and sometimes have accents. They communicate with each other verbally and nonverbally.

Characters are classified as either major or minor, depending on the magnitudes of their roles in the story. Some characters may be either major or minor, also depending on their roles in the story.[2,10,23-25]

Major Characters

Also known as round characters, *major characters* are three dimensional figures. Their goals, ambitions, and values change as a result of what happens to them. Therefore, they are referred to in literature as *dynamic* characters. A dynamic character progresses to a higher level of understanding in the course of the story. Like real people, they have particular fears, aspirations, strengths and weaknesses, secrets, and sensitivities. They are not all good or all bad. The two major characters in fiction are the protagonist and the antagonist.

The *protagonist* (hero) is the character who dominates the story. He is a complex character who usually has three attributes: (1) A need or a want (prevent the murder, solve the crime, win the heart a loved one, escape from prison, get revenge for his wife's murder), (2) a strong point (courage, wisdom, persistence, kindness) that confers on him the potential for triumph, and (3) a flaw (alcoholism, prejudice, greed, fear of heights or crowds) that, unless overcome, may lead to his downfall.

The *main character* is the person the audience views the story through. Most of the time the main character is the protagonist; at other times the main character is a narrator, and at other times a secondary character. Each gives valuable insights into the protagonist from an outside prospective.

The *antagonist* (villain) is any character who opposes the efforts of the protagonist. He's the bad guy. There wouldn't be much conflict for your protagonist to overcome without the antagonist to throw up roadblocks. Many stories have only a single antagonist, or one main one, while longer works, especially novels, may have more than one.

Like the protagonist, the antagonist is a three-dimensional character, and he must be a worthy opponent. He should be an intelligent, logical character who does what he does because his reasons make sense to him. No one sees himself as mean, evil, or insane; the antagonist doesn't either. To him, his actions and his logic are perfectly sound.[1,13,23-27]

Minor Characters

Also known as flat characters, *minor characters* are almost always one or two-dimensional characters; that is, they only have one or two striking qualities. Unlike major characters, they usually are all good or all bad and intentionally lack depth. Minor characters are sometimes referred to as *static* characters because they don't change in the course of the story. They can be bit players, stock characters, or sacrificial characters.

Bit players can be passing suspects in mysteries, incidental friends, coworkers, neighbors, waitresses, clerks, maintenance people, doormen, and so forth. The more important ones can be given some quirk or bit of color that lifts them somewhat above the masses (a maintenance man who spits snuff into a paper cup, a secretary who always wears black lipstick, a doorman who is always intoxicated).

A *stock character* is a stereotyped character, such as a mad scientist, an absent-minded professor, a spiteful mother-in-law, or a dumb blonde. In general, these characters should be avoided, unless you have a really good reason for using them.

Sacrificial characters (chauffeurs, double agents, crooked policemen, mistresses, and so forth) are killed in the course of the story for various reasons, including to keep them from revealing critical information to the protagonist. Also, the protagonist may kill one or more skilled opponents simply to demonstrate his prowess to the reader.[1,13,23-27]

Major or Minor Characters

Some characters can be either major or minor depending on

their roles in the story. These include foil characters, eccentrics, psychos, memorable characters, and phobics.

A foil is a piece of shiny metal put under gemstones to increase their brightness. *Foil characters* are closely associated with the character for whom they serve as a foil, usually a friend or lover whom he can confide in and thus disclose his innermost thoughts. They serve to bring out the brilliance of the character to whom they serve as a foil. Note that the foil can be a supporter of any of the characters, not just the protagonist. Some foil characters are included for comedy relief; others are included to reinforce the goal or the beliefs of the character they support. Still others are introduced to provide contrast. Foil characters also are known as *confidants, sidekicks,* or *faithful followers.*

Eccentrics follow their own rules of behavior. They know their code is right and everyone else's is wrong. An eccentric might be miserly despite being a multimillionaire, arrange bills by serial number in his wallet, avoid stepping on cracks in the sidewalk, believe the world is flat, or wear earmuffs in August.

The *psycho* character, on the surface, often appears normal, but the reader knows that he is not. In fact, the psycho may be normal in all aspects of his life but one, and that one is strange and bizarre, often hidden from the public. For instance, the psycho might appear to be a mild mannered accountant during the day, but wander through neighborhoods at night killing cats. Or worse, he brutally murders women who look like the old girlfriend who rejected him.

The *memorable character* may wear wildly colored clothes, have an extraordinary height or weight, be a priest who grows pot in the church's rectory, or be an idiot savant. To create a memorable character, writers select some unique aspect of body, mind, or personality. They exaggerate it and make it striking and colorful.

A *phobic character* is one with a persistent, abnormal, and irrational fear of a specific thing or situation that compels him to avoid the object of his phobia despite knowing that it is not dangerous. A character may be afraid of cats, bats, microbes, heights, closed spaces, or almost anything. [1,13,23-27]

Characterization is discussed further in Chapter 11.

Point of View

The *point of view* of a novel is the perspective from which the reader is allowed to view the action and the characters. As a writer, there are a number of points of view to choose from, and each has its advantages and disadvantages. Various authors have categorized them in different ways, but the system used in this book is the most common one. The points of view most often used in genre fiction are first person and third person.

First-person Point of View

With *first-person point of view,* a single character narrates the story from his point of view (*I* pulled the trigger). This point of view is used most often by writers of mystery novels and short stories.[2,28-31]

Third-person Point of View

Third-person point of view is the one most commonly used by writers of genre fiction (*He* pulled the trigger). One problem with this point of view is that the character cannot describe himself physically, unless he describes his image in a mirror, but this has been used so much that it's become a cliché and should be avoided.

A variant of third-person point of view used by most modern-day writers of genre fiction is to use the point of view of a single character, but let that character be different from scene to scene or chapter to chapter. For instance, in one scene the point of view might be that of the protagonist; in the next scene the point of view might be that of the antagonist; in a third scene it might be that of a foil character. A change in point of view in a published novel is usually indicated by skipped lines between scenes or by chapter breaks. In this way confusion is minimized.[2,28-31]

Second-person Point of View

Second-person point of view is rarely used because it is extremely difficult to pull off (*You* pulled the trigger). The reader may feel that he is the one spoken to and will find it difficult to accept that he is doing the things the narrator tells him he is doing. If used, second-person point of view must be done very carefully.[2,28-31]

Point of view is discussed further in Chapter 5.

Prose

Prose is ordinary written language—the language of fiction. It comes in several forms, among them (1) narrative, (2) description, and (3) dialogue. Each of these types of prose has a different function in fiction, and it is necessary to understand how each one works.[23,32]

Narrative

Narrative, in contrast to action and dialogue, is essentially stagnant blocks of information. The character is telling what is happening—giving a summary of dialogue and action. Regardless of how engaging and well written narrative is it won't hold a reader's attention for long because nothing is actively going on in the story. There's no action.

Narrative is useful when acting out the story with dialogue and action would do little to further the reader's understanding of the characters or plot. It is information the reader needs to understand what is happening in the present, but not deemed by the writer to warrant the amount of space that action and dialogue would require. Narrative also can be used to foreshadow a coming major event.

Because narrative is summarizing, it lacks the excitement of dramatization. Therefore writers try to be certain that narrative doesn't drag down their novel's pacing. How do they accomplish this? By breaking it up with dialogue and action.

Narrative of dramatic situations, such as a car chase or a fight scene, is known a *dramatic summary.* With dramatic summary, material that might take several pages of action and dialogue may take only a few paragraphs.[2,18,23,32] Narrative is discussed further in Chapter 5.

Description

Writing *description* is painting a vivid picture with words. It can be used to set the scene, move the plot, set the mood, foreshadow events, give a sense of character, or whatever it has to do to keep the story moving. Without description, characters move about in vague buildings or fuzzy landscapes. However, some writers err in the other direction by including too much description; by doing so they run the risk of boring the reader.

By using description in combination with action and dialogue, writers break the description down into palatable pieces. For instance, instead of stopping a story to describe trees, flowers, and a waterfall in a plush lobby of an upscale office building, writers come up with a reason for this description to be in the story; that is, a reason for the characters to be interacting with that setting through action and dialogue.[33-35] Description is discussed further in Chapter 3.

Dialogue

Verbal communication, known as *dialogue*, generally refers to anything spoken by a character, even if the character is not actually speaking to anyone.

- "What do you mean Vito's disappeared with the money?" Angelo asked.

Sometimes the term is broadened to include the thoughts of a character.

- "If I tell him the truth he'll kill me," Pasquale thought.

Conversation, the way we speak to one another in daily living, isn't dialogue. In real life, whether conversation is dull or interesting has little bearing. The opposite is true of dialogue; it has to be interesting. Dialogue is said to be a special kind of conversation; that is, conversation with drama.[1,2,36,37] Dialogue is discussed further in Chapter 12.

Theme and Subject

Theme and subject are two related concepts that require a little explanation.

Theme

A *theme* is the understanding that the author seeks to communicate through his work. It is the central and unifying idea about which the story is structured. It is the meaning or concept we are left with after reading a piece of fiction.

Examples of themes are "oppression leads to oppression," "managed care is bad for patients," "global warming is over-hyped," and "love is difficult." The theme for L. Frank Baum's *The Wonderful Wizard of Oz* (1900) might be stated "If you believe that you have the strength and ability to accomplish a goal, then you do have that strength and ability." The theme of my novel *Caduceus Awry* (2000) is "Man can overcome personal demons to achieve a desired end."

Theme directs a writer's decisions about which path to take, which choice is right for the story, and which choice is wrong for it. With theme, the writer actually structures his writing on a concept that guides him from start to finish. A theme that best suits the story the writer wants to tell helps him express his central idea more clearly.

In some works the theme is a prominent element and unmistakable; in other works the theme is more elusive. A major theme is an idea the author returns to time and again. It becomes one of the most important ideas in the story. Minor themes are ideas that may appear from time to time, but are less important. All that said, because the major aim of genre novels is to entertain, not to express a point of view, not every genre novel has a theme. [10,11,23,29,38,39]

Subject

The *subject* of a literary work is the topic on which an author has chosen to write, as opposed to the theme which expresses some opinion on that topic. For example, the subject of a story might be "war" while the theme might be the idea that "war is unnecessary" or "war is bad."[23]

References

1. Bishop, Leonard, Dare to be a Great Writer, Writer's Digest Books, Cincinnati, 1992.
2. Silvester, Niko, Creative Writing for Teens, http://teenwriting.about.com/library/weekly/aa111102a.htm.
3. Wayman, Anne, Craft v. Art, Romance Writing Tips, http://groups.msn.com/RomanceWritingTips/craftvart.msnw.
4. Fiction Genre Definitions, Manus & Associates Literary Agency, http://www.manuslit.com/flash/index.html.
5. Meinhardt, Shelly Thacker, Market Savvy for Fiction Writers: Popular Fiction vs. Literary Fiction, http://www.shellythacker.com/marketsavvy.htm, 2004.
6. Zackheim, Sarah Parsons, and Adrian Zackheim, Getting Your Book Published For Dummies, John Wiley & Sons, New York, 2000.
7. Wikipedia, http://en.wikipedia.org/wiki/Main_Page.
8. Brown, Dan, The Da Vinci Code, Doubleday, New York, 2003.
9. Dibell, Ansen, Plot, Writer's Digest Books, Cincinnati, 1999.
10. Elements of fiction, http://www.newton.mec.edu/brown/ENGLISH/eng_elements_of_fiction.html.
11. Elements of fiction, VirtuaLit : Interactive Fiction Tutorial, http://bcs.bedfordstmartins.com/virtualit/fiction/elements.asp.
12. Kilian, Crawford, Advice on novel writing, http://www.steampunk.com/sfch/writing/ckilian/#6.
13. Kittredge, Mary, Hot to Plot! A Plotting "System" that Works, In The Writer's Digest Handbook of Novel Writing, Writer's Digest Books, Cincinnati, 1992, pp 56-61.
14. Lake, Lori L., Plot: Part Two, Navigating dangerous terrain, http://www.justaboutwrite.com/A_Archive_Plot2LL.html, 2003.
15. Swain, Dwight V., Techniques of the Selling Writer, University of Oklahoma Press, Norman, 1974.
16. Article: In the Beginning, Writing and Publishing, Suite101.Comhttp://www.suite101.com/article.cfm/novel_writing/18290/1.
17. Kress, Nancy, Beginnings, Middles & Ends, Writer's Digest Books, Cincinnati, 1999.
18. Hinze, Vickey, Exposition vs. Narrative, http://www.fictionfactor.com/guests/exposition.html.

19. Rasley, Alicia, End Thoughts, Writers' Corner, http://www.sff.net/people/alicia/art1.htm, 1997.
20. Allen, Moira, Four ways to bring setting to life, http://www.writing-world.com/fiction/settings.shtml.
21. Kay, Kim, It's your world: Setting your novel: It's Your Novel, Suite101.com, http://www.suite101.com/article.cfm/novel_writing/13665/1, December 15, 1998.
22. Kelman, Judith, How to write and publish a novel, http://www.jkelman.com/fiction/index.html.
23. Bokesch, Laura, Literary terms, Literary elements, Academy of the Arts, http://www.orangeusd.k12.ca.us/yorba/literary_elements.htm.
24. Masterson, Lee, Casting your characters, Fiction Factor, http://www.fictionfactor.com/articles/casting.html.
25. Swain, Dwight V., Creating Characters, Writer's Digests Books, Cincinnati, 1990.
26. Character function, Basics of English Studies, http://www.anglistik.uni-freiburg.de/intranet/englishbasics/Character02.htm.
27. Character in fiction and drama, http://www.ccsn.nevada.edu/english/lab/CHARACT.htm.
28. Colburn, Jeff, Who Said That? First, Second or Third-Person Point of View, FictionAddiction.net, http://fictionaddiction.net/articles/contributed/colburnpov.html
29. Novel, Microsoft Encarta Encyclopedia, 2003.
30. Rosenberg, Joe, Choosing your storyteller, In The Writer's Digest Handbook of Novel Writing, Ed. By Clark, Tom, William Brohaugh, Bruce Woods, Bill Strickland, and Peter Blocksom, Writer's Digest Press, Cincinnati, 1992.
31. Tritt, Sandy, Point of view and other devices, Elements of Craft, Inspiration for Writers, http://tritt.wirefire.com/tip9.html.
32. Harris, Robert, A glossary of literary terms, VirtualSalt, http://www.virtualsalt.com/litterms.htm, January 4, 2002.
33. Bickham, Jack M., The 38 Most Common Fiction Writing Mistakes, Writer's Digest Books, Cincinnati, 1992.
34. Marble, Anne M., Romancing the keyboard, Writing-World.com, http://www.writing-world.com/columns/romance/marble17.shtml, 2004.
35. Schnelbach, S. and C. S. Wyatt, Tameri Guide for Writers, http://www.tameri.coml, March 14, 2005.
36. Masterson, Lee, Writing dazzling dialogue, Sci Fi Editor, http://www.scifieditor.com/lee1.htm.
37. Chiarella, Tom, Writing Dialogue, Story Press, Cincinnati, 1998.
38. Milhorn, H. Thomas, Caduceus Awry, Writer's Showcase, San Jose,

2000.
39. Reuben, Paul, PAL: Perspectives in American Literature, Appendix G: Elements of Fiction, http://www.csustan.edu/english/reuben/pal/append/AXG.HTML.

Chapter 2

Choosing Your Genre

All genres have conventions—certain things that are understood between reader and writer. Readers purchase specific genre because those are the kinds of stories they enjoy the most. Romance readers don't tend to buy westerns, science fiction readers don't tend to buy historical novels, and horror readers don't tend to buy detective novels.

The mystery genre is a good example of specific genre conventions. By its very nature, a mystery story has to have a mystery in it. In the beginning of the story the protagonist either finds or learns about a dead body, a theft, or whatever the mystery is to be. The story ends when the mystery is solved. The middle part of the story consists of gathering clues.

Some things are more appropriate for one genre than another. Heavy emotional love scenes, for example, are an integral part of romance novels, but they are not appropriate for thriller novels because they diminish the danger and slow the pace.

The fact that the various genres have conventions doesn't mean you have to follow the conventions entirely. It does mean, however, that you, as a writer of a specific genre, must be aware of what the conventions are. In other words, you have to know the rules before you are allowed to break them.

Suspense, the main ingredient of genre novels, is obtained in various ways, depending on the genre being written. In the mystery novel, suspense is achieved by the dispersions of clues and the danger of additional murders. In the romance novel, suspense is achieved by the handicaps and hazards imposed on the lovers before they can come together for a final and total happiness. In the thriller novel, suspense is achieved by the ever present physical danger to the protagonist or other characters.

Genre fiction books are classified as mystery, horror, romance, science fiction, and so forth to make it easier for potential purchasers to find what they are looking for in a bookstore. Using genre as a marketing tool also has distinct disadvantages. It means that a science fiction fan might never venture over into the mystery aisle, despite the fact that there could be any number of books in that aisle that he would like as well or even better.[1,2]

ACTION/ADVENTURE

Action/adventure novels make few demands on the reader. The story lines are simple—good guy versus bad guy. The novels are about action—the adventure rather than the growth of characters. The action usually takes place in some far-off place, such as at the bottom of the sea, at the North Pole, in the desert, or in the mountains. The prize, which both the protagonist and the antagonist are after, can be gold, a lost treasure, national secrets, the Holy Grail, or whatever you want it to be. The protagonist tries to get there first, but even if he does he may still have to fight it out with the antagonist to claim the prize. Not until the story's end is it clear who will win out.[2,3]

In Clive Cussler's *The Golden Buddha* (2003), an organization of mercenaries, known as the Corporation, is headquartered on the ship, Oregon, which is a marvel of science and technology disguised as an ancient, rust-bucket cargo vessel. The Corporation has been secretly hired by the U.S. government to find and acquire an ancient statue known as the Golden Buddha, which was stolen from the Dalai Lama upon his ouster from Tibet by the Chinese in 1959. Making a deal with the Russians and Chinese depends on finding the statue that contains maps and records related to Tibet's oil reserves.[4]

CHRISTIAN

A *Christian novel* involves the Christian faith and often contains a plot revolving around the Christian life, evangelism, or religious conversion.[5]

The Robe (1943) by Lloyd C. Douglas is based on the fictional life of the Roman soldier, Marcellus Gallio, who is the son of a prestigious Senator and a Tribune in the time of Christ. Marcellus is in charge of the group that is assigned to crucify Jesus. He wins Jesus's homespun robe as a gambling prize after the crucifixion. The memory of the crucifixion plunges Marcellus into a deep melancholy, tormented by nightmares and delusions. The robe miraculously heals him as he touches it. Hoping to find a way to live with what he has done, he returns to Palestine to try to learn what he can of the man he helped kill.[6]

FANTASY

Fantasy fiction is any story of the impossible—a tale that has events that could never happen in the real world. Fantasy fiction is based on the belief that some people are special; that is, they can cast spells or travel to parallel universes, while other people cannot. The best fantasy novels blend back and white magic, terrifying evil, and great protagonists and antagonists who meet on the field of battle.

Since magic and unnatural beings are part of the fantasy genre, your first task, if you choose to write a fantasy novel, is to decide what kind of world you are going to create and what rules govern it. Next, decide what sort of creatures inhabits that world.

Fantasy is a questing category; that is, there is a prize to be won, so you have to decide what that prize is—a princess, a shield of gold, a magic ring, or whatever.[3,7-9]

Fantasy subgenres include (1) light fantasy, (2) Arthurian legend, and (3) heroic fantasy.

Light Fantasy

Light fantasy includes stories with elves and magic and fairy tales. As a rule, they are written for a younger age group than most other novels.[3,7-9]

J. R. R. Tolkien's *Hobbit* (1936) is set in a fantasy world called Middle Earth. There, small and timid Bilbo Baggins lives a pleasant but dull life in a luxurious hobbit hole under a hill. His life is completely turned upside down by the arrival of the wizard, Gandalf, and thirteen dwarves. The dwarves, led by the exiled king-in-waiting, Thorin Oakenshield, want to regain the Lonely Mountain from a dragon named Smaug, who drove out the dwarves long ago. Bilbo and the Dwarves battle goblins and spiders, are nearly eaten twice, and are captured. Bilbo is forced to riddle with the treacherous Gollum, and then ends up escaping with a magical Ring that makes the wearer invisible.[10]

Arthurian Legend

Arthurian legend involves the mythical 5th to 7th century Britain leader, Arthur, and the legends that grew up around him. Camelot was the most famous castle in the medieval legends of King Arthur, and where, according to legend, Arthur reigned over Britain before the Saxon conquest. At Camelot, Arthur established a brilliant court and seated the greatest and most chivalrous warriors in Europe—the Knights of the Round Table.[3,7-9]

In the movie *King Arthur* (2004), the Romans, impressed by the Sarmatian's weaponry and fighting skills, included them in their army as knights. Now, after 15 years, they are about to receive their freedom. The Romans are leaving Britain, but the Sarmatian Knights, lead by Arthur, must carry out one final order before they are free. A Roman priest and his family must be rescued from the invading Saxons. However there is another danger lurking on the road to freedom—the Woads—British rebels who hate the Romans.

Heroic Fantasy

Heroic fantasy, such as sword and sorcery, are stories in which muscular protagonists are in violent conflict with a variety of antagonists—wizards, witches, evil spirits, or other creatures—whose powers, unlike the protagonist's, are supernatural in origin.[3,7-9]

Robert E. Howard's stories about Conan the Barbarian are examples of sword and sorcery writing. *Conan the Barbarian* (1982), is a movie adapted from one of his stories. Conan (Arnold Schwarzenegger), trained in the arts of war, joins with thieves in a quest to find the sorcerer responsible for the genocide of his people. As a child, he saw his parents murdered and his village burned by a horde of savages lead by Thulsa Doom (James Earl Jones), who is now the head of a deadly snake cult. Sold into slavery and taken to the north, Conan grows up being trained by his master as a warrior to make money fighting other warriors. Eventually, the master gives Conan his freedom and the chance to take his revenge after so many years. But first, he must solve the riddle of steel.

GAY/LESBIAN

Gay and lesbian novels involve gay or lesbian main characters in what otherwise are usually mainstream plots, such as romances, mysteries, or any number of other genre. The main distinction is that the action is filtered through the perspective of a gay or lesbian character.[7]

Consider the following two examples of the gay/lesbian novel. The first is social science fiction; the second is a romance/western.

In *The Meadowlark Sings* (2006) by Helen Ruth Schwartz, a great earthquake hits California in the year 2008, creating a chasm that quickly fills with the raging waters from the Pacific. An island 40 miles off the coast is born. Within four years the religious right has affected an awful change in America's moral climate. Gay or lesbian adults are given a clear choice—conform to new, repressive sexuality laws or be exiled. Any child found to carry the newly discovered gay gene is put on a ship before reaching three years of age—banished forever from U.S. shores. On their island they build a new country and call it Cali. When it becomes known that citizens of Cali are living longer, healthier lives than citizens of most countries, the rest of the world wants to know why. For the first time, a delegate from Cali, Cara Romero, is invited to participate in an international conference on aging to be held in New York City.[11]

In a twist of the typical western plot, Annie Proulx's *Brokeback Mountain* (2005) tells the story of Ennis del Mar and Jack Twist, two ranch hands who are hired in the summer of 1963 to work together as sheepherders on a mountain range above the tree line in Wyoming. At first, sharing an isolated tent, the attraction is casual, but then, during a freezing cold night of too much whisky they fall into each other's arms and their relationship becomes something more. When the summer ends they return to their conventional lives. Both men work hard, marry, and have children because that's what cowboys do. But over the course of many years and frequent separations the relationship becomes the most important thing in their lives, and they do anything they can to preserve it.[12]

HISTORICAL

Historical novels involve stories set in the past. The author tries to portray that era realistically; that is, to accurately reconstruct characters, events, and ways of life of those days. The novels are set in well-defined periods and depend on the readers' enjoyment of vicariously experiencing another time and place.[3,7-9]

One of the most popular historical novels ever is *Gone with the Wind* (1936) by Margaret Mitchell. The story is set during the Civil War and the reconstruction period immediately after the war. It tells the story of Scarlett O'Hara, a Southern belle who lives on her family's plantation, Tara. Most of the novel concerns Scarlett's infatuation with her neighbor, Ashley Wilkes, and the pursuit of Scarlett by a charming and dashing man named Rhett Butler. Scarlett and Rhett eventually marry, but after the death of their daughter, Bonnie, in a horse-back riding accident, Rhett leaves her, uttering the now famous statement "Frankly, my dear, I don't give a damn." Grief-stricken and alone, Scarlett makes up her mind to go back to Tara to recover her strength in the comforting arms of her childhood nurse and slave, Mammy, and to think of a way to win Rhett back.[13]

HORROR

The defining characteristic of *horror* fiction is the frightening of readers by exploiting their fears of ghosts, vampires, werewolves, alien visitors, madness, death, dismemberment, being buried alive, possessed children, being captured by monsters, and other terrifying notions. Horror novels often deal with the occult, usually taking the form of a battle between the forces of good and the supernatural forces of evil. They are typically darker than fantasy novels and aimed more at adult readers.

Fans of horror fiction are quite accepting of revising the original premises. For instance, since Bram Stoker introduced the character of the vampire, Count Dracula of Transylvania, in 1897 there have been hundreds of vampire stories, many of which have altered one or more of the original rules. We've even seen the vampire as protagonist rather than his usual role as the antagonist. However, some guidelines do exist. You can't have your vampire immune to the normally feared daylight or your werewolf undeterred by the normally deadly silver bullet without logically explaining why.[2,3,7-9]

Steven King is the best-known horror writer today, having written among other things *Carrie* (1974), which is about Carrie White, a shy girl who is menaced by bullies at school and her religious nut of a mother at home. As the story unfolds, she discovers she has telekinetic powers—the ability to make things move by thinking about them. Her classmate, Sue Snell, feels sorry for her and asks her own boyfriend, Tommy Ross, to invite Carrie to the prom instead taking her. At the prom, when it comes time to pick the queen, Carrie's enemies rig the voting so that she wins. Then they humiliate her. In anger, Carrie uses her powers to lock the school doors and start a fire. Almost everyone is killed. Carrie then goes home where she makes the knives and forks on a wall rack fly across the room and into her mother's body. The house then bursts into flames, killing both Carrie and her mother.[14]

MYSTERY/DETECTIVE

Mysteries, also known as *whodunits,* focus on a crime, often a murder that has occurred prior to the start of action. Sherlock Holmes, in the series of novels by Sir Arthur Conan Doyle, is the classic mystery protagonist.

A basic rule in mysteries is, "Don't let the detective see clues the reader can't." The detective is not allowed to find a clue, cup it in his hand, and put it in his pocket. If he's going to find it, he has to share it.[2,3,7-9]

The basic forms of the mystery are (1) the amateur detective, (2) the cozy, (3) the police procedural, (4) the private detective, and (5) the puzzle.

The Amateur Detective

The antagonist of the *amateur detective* novel is usually, though not always, male. Amateur detective writers usually follow the model as first laid down by Edgar Allen Poe. As a rule, the protagonist has an independent income and tends to be eccentric in some way, such as Poe's C. Auguste Dupin, who disliked the light of day to the extent that he kept all the windows shuttered in his grotesque mansion.

Often the amateur detective has an encyclopedic mind. Sherlock Holmes, for instance, knew all the treads for different bicycle tires. The amateur detective usually has a partner or confidant, such as Holmes's Dr. Watson.

The Amateur detective pits his wits against the fiendish mind of the antagonist of the story, with the action tending to center on the attempts of the wily amateur detective to solve the crime. Throughout the story the reader remains as puzzled as the characters within the story. The climax usually occurs near the end in a leisurely setting where all the elements of the mystery are neatly assembled. The thrill for the readers of this genre is in the process of solving a crime. The identity of the antagonist usually is not known until the climax of the story.[15]

In J. G. Ballard's *Cocaine Nights* (1999), travel writer Charles Prentice arrives at Estrella de Mar, a wealthy British resort community near Gibraltar. There he discovers that his brother Frank, the manager of Club Nautico, has been jailed after confessing to an act of arson that left five people dead—a crime he didn't commit. Charles sets out to find the real culprit. The longer he stays the more confused he becomes by the residents' lack of concern about the constant background of vandalism, rape, prostitution, and drug dealing in the community. It's up to him to peel away the onion-like layers of denial and deceit that hide the rather ugly truth about this seaside town, its residents, and the horrific crime that brought him there.[16]

The Cozy

The *cozy* is the least realistic form of mystery/detective novels. Violence is generally minimal and offstage. The setting tends to be less urban than private detective and police procedural novels and the murders often taking place on country weekends at fine estates or in some such pleasant atmosphere; however; cozy novels can be set anywhere. Characters are often eccentric and the police usually are at loss for answers. The detective is a local citizen who is an amateur sleuth, such as Jessica Fletcher in the TV series *Murder She Wrote*. Jessica is a mystery writer who lives in Cabot Cove, Maine and solves murders on the side.[3]

In Tamar Meyers' *Statute of Limitations* (2004), petite but feisty Abigail (Abby) Timberlake is the owner of the Den of Antiquity antiques shop in Charleston, South Carolina. She and her best friend, Wynnell Crawford, take on a new venture—redecorating a very upscale bed-and-breakfast. They have a fall out over a tasteless three-foot high replica of Michelangelo's David that Wynnell has chosen for the garden's focal point. After exchanging heated words, the pair stops speaking to each other entirely—until Wynnell calls Abigail from jail where she's under arrest for fatally attacking the bread and breakfast owner with the tacky statue. To prove her friend's innocence, Abby turns her attention to the other suspects at the scene of the crime—like the not-so-grieving widower or the two strange guests at the bed-and-breakfast.[17]

The Police Procedural

The *police procedural* is the most realistic form of mystery/detective stories. While deduction and investigation play the same key roles as in the other forms, procedurals tend to have more characters because policemen are rarely loners. They have access to a wide range of investigatory help, have to deal with district attorneys and politicians, and come in contact with the general public on a regular basis.[3]

In Michael Connelly's *The Concrete Blonde* (1995), Los Angeles homicide detective Harry Bosch is charged with killing an allegedly innocent man. Bosch believes the man to have been a serial murderer named "The Dollmaker," who strangled his victims and made them up to look like dolls. The dead man's widow files a civil suit. The trial is excruciating, with the prosecuting attorney focusing on Bosch's violent past and portraying him as a vigilante murderer protected by his badge. Suddenly, a new murder occurs, with all the trappings of the Dollmaker's style. The body of a blonde woman is found beneath the concrete floor of a building that burned during the L.A. riots. Did Bosch actually kill the wrong man? Bosch believes the new murder to be the result of a copycat killer, and he sets out to prove it.[18]

The Private Detective

The *private detective* novel most often involves a private detective who is licensed by the state and who often does not carry a gun. Private detectives deal with street people, petty criminals, and the down and out on a regular basis. They also can be involved in cases dealing with industrial espionage, security matters, and the ugly side of family relationships. They tend to stumble onto murder only on the way to solving another case.[3]

In P. D. James's novel *An Unsuitable Job for a Woman* (2001), Cordelia Gray inherits full ownership of a detective agency on the brink of bankruptcy after her partner, Bernie Pryde, commits suicide. The agency's main assets are a gun and Cordelia's determination. She is soon called upon to solve a mystery connected with another apparent suicide, that of former Cambridge student, Mark Callender. He is found hanging by his neck, a lipstick stain on his mouth and a picture of a nude girl nearby. Although the official verdict is suicide, his wealthy father suspects murder and hires Cordelia to investigate. As she follows a twisting trail of guilty secrets and shameful sins, she soon reaches the conclusion that the nicest people can do the nastiest things.[19]

The Puzzle

The *puzzle* mystery novel is laid out to display the ingenuity of the gimmick used to commit the murder, which indisputably points to the antagonist's guilt.[15]

John Dickson Carr was famous for his "locked door" puzzle mysteries. *The Cavalier's Cup* (1953) features the irascible sleuth, Sir Henry Merrivale, in an ingenious and baffling locked-door mystery centering on a fabulously valuable goblet—the Cavalier's Cup. One night, in the Oak Room at Telford Old Hall, the goblet was removed from the locked safe and left standing on a table nearby. The room's windows had been firmly latched, the heavy doors double-bolted from the inside, and a live witness had spent the entire night there and seen nothing. It was up to Merrivale to unmask the guilty person before his actions materialized into a more murderous form of mischief.[20]

ROMANCE

Romance is a category aimed at entertaining women. It is intended to take readers away from their day-to-day routine lives. Romance stories have elements of fantasy, love, extravagance, and adventure. The heroic lover overcomes impossible odds to be with his true love. Marriage is almost without exception the desired goal of a romance plot.[8,9]

Probably the best known romance writer today is Danielle Steele, who has written such works as *Passion's Promise* (1997), *The Kiss* (2002), and *Sunset in St. Tropez* (2003). The titles say it all.[21]

Subgenres of romance novels are (1) contemporary, (2) gothic, and (3) regency.

Contemporary

The *contemporary* romance novel involves modern stories that are open and honest about sex. The setting is almost always somewhere exotic, the characters are usually wealthy, and the conflict often centers about control of a business. The male represents thrills and danger.[3,7-9,]

29

Fire in the Ice (2005) by Katlyn Stewart is a contemporary romance novel in which Deedra Marlan, hardened by her husband's death two years earlier, becomes known as "The Ice Princess" to her friends. She vows never to feel the pain of loss again. When Josh McKenzie enters her icy world, the handsome cattle rancher decides he must have this seemingly cold woman, and he is unwilling to take no for an answer. Feeling emotions she hasn't dared feel since the death of her husband, Deedra is brought almost to the point of fear of this hard-edged, strong, determined man. The journey moves through erotically charged passions and heart-wrenching ordeals as Josh struggles to unleash the fire in the ice of this beautiful woman.[22]

Gothic

The *gothic romance* novel adds a strong element of suspense to the story, and often a feeling of supernatural events. Usually a young woman governess, housekeeper, or relative arrives at a house for some reason. She immediately discovers that there are strange things going on. The handsome relative, employer, or owner seems to be at the bottom of it. The heroine is the target of whatever evil is afoot. She has to rescued by a valiant male.[3,7-9]

In *Beneath the Raven's Moon* (2003) by Emily LaForge, concert pianist Catherine Carmichael learns that she has been named as one of the heirs in her Uncle Malcolm Blount's estate. Catherine has not seen her deranged uncle since her mother fled their jointly shared upstate New York castle over two decades ago. She wants to learn about her father, who vanished just before her mother and she fled Ravenswood Castle. At the castle, Catherine meets three other beneficiaries—actor Everett Steele, an illegitimate cousin Billy Fortune, and her uncle's agent Madeline Treadwell. As Everett and Catherine fall in love, strange things happen as if the castle possesses an evil presence that no one can escape.[23]

Regency

Regency romance novels are noted for their wit, charm, and humor. They are usually set in England during the Regency period

(1811-1820). Mistaken identity is a favorite plot device. Research into this period is crucial. Readers know the period, the mores, and the language well; so must you if you choose to write in this subgenre.[3,7-9]

In April Kihlstrom's *An Honorable Rogue* (1997), Lady Barbara wagers that she can successfully masquerade for one night as a barmaid in London. In that single night she loses both her head and her heart to the notorious Lord Farrington, who plies her with liquor and seduces her into his bed. The next day he learns the truth of her identity and vows to rectify matters with marriage. But Lady Barbara, who wishes to marry for love, is less than willing and only extreme familial pressure persuades her to accept his offer. Everything turns out wonderfully when they fall head over heels in love with each other.[24]

Other Subgenres

In recent years, romance novels have branched out into *romantic mystery, time travel romance,* and *science fiction romance.* A subgenre that once was popular, *bodice ripper,* relied heavily on unrestrained passion (lots of sex). It has fallen into disfavor because of scenes in which the female character is sexually violated by force.[3,7-9]

SCIENCE FICTION

Science fiction deals with the influence of real or imagined science on a society or individuals. It involves plots which either extrapolate on existing scientific principles or involves some deviation from them. Common subjects include future societies, travel through space or time, life on other planets, crises created by technology or by alien creatures and environments, and the creation or destruction of worlds.[2,7,9]

There are a number of subgenres of science fiction, including (1) apocalyptic/post-apocalyptic, (2) cyberpunk, (3) first contact, (4) hard, (5) military, (6) soft/social, (7) space opera, and (8) time travel.

Apocalyptic/Post-apocalyptic

Apocalyptic science fiction focuses on the end of the world. *Post-apocalyptic* science fiction focuses on the world just after the end.[25]

In Stephen King's *The Stand* (1990), humanity must cope with the aftermath of a rapidly mutating superflu virus which has been released accidentally from a U.S. military facility. Wiping out almost all the world's population, the virus sets the stage for an apocalyptic confrontation between good and evil. In the bleak new world a handful of panicky survivors choose sides. It is a world in which good rides on the frail shoulders of 108-year-old Mother Abigail and the worst nightmares of evil are embodied in Randall Flagg, a man with a lethal smile and unspeakable powers.[26]

Cyberpunk

Cyberpunk science fiction is set in a high-tech, often bleak, mechanistic, and futuristic universe of computers, hackers, and computer/human hybrids.[25]

In the movie *The Matrix* (1999), computer hacker Neo (Keneau Reeves) lives a relatively ordinary life in what he believes to be the year 1999—until he is contacted by Morpheus (Laurence Fishburne) from whom he learns that incredibly it is 200 years later. Machines have created a false version of the 20th-century known as the Matrix. All life on Earth is nothing more than an elaborate facade created for the purpose of placating humans while their life essence is used to fuel the Matrix. Neo is hailed as "The One" who will lead the humans to overthrow the machines and reclaim Earth. He is joined by Morpheus and Trinity (Carrie Ann Moss) in a struggle to do so. They are pursued constantly by "Agents" who are computers who take on human form and infiltrate the Matrix.

First Contact

First contact science fiction explores the initial meeting between humans and aliens, ranging from tales of invasions to stories of benign visitors bearing the secrets of advanced technologies and world peace. H. G. Wells's *War of the Worlds* (1898), in which Martians reveal their true nature as 100-feet tall death machines rise up and begin laying waste to the surrounding land, helped define the alien invasion variant of this subgenre.[25,27]

In Arthur C. Clarke's *Rendezvous with Rama* (1972), it is the year 2130 and mankind has spread throughout the solar system. A mysterious object appears in space, hurtling through the solar system at inconceivable speed. Named Rama by astronomers, it is huge, weighing more than ten trillion tons. The citizens of the solar system send a ship to investigate the object and discover that it is not a natural object, but a cylindrical, interstellar spacecraft. Rama's secrets are clear evidence of an advanced civilization, but who are the Ramans? Their nature remains utterly shrouded in mystery. And what do they want with humans? Perhaps the answer lies with the busily working biots, the sealed-off buildings, or the inaccessible part of the enormous cylinder.[28]

Hard

With *hard* science fiction, plausible science and technology are central to the plot. Issues of technology are of greater concern than a character's personal life.[25]

In Wil McCarthy's *Bloom* (1999), nanotechnology in the year 2106 has gotten out of control. Fast-reproducing, fast-mutating, and endlessly voracious microscopic machine creatures have escaped their creators to populate the inner solar system, pushing the tattered remnants of humanity out into the cold and dark of the outer planets. Even while huddled beneath the ice of Jupiter's moons, protected by a defensive system known as the Immunity, survivors face the constant risk of mycospores finding their way to the warmth and brightness inside their habitat, resulting in a disaster.[29]

Military

Military science fiction focuses on combat in future locations (space, another planet) against a range of opponents (modified humans, aliens, machines) with futuristic, high-tech weaponry.[25]

In David Weber's *Ashes of Victory* (2000), Honor Harrington, a woman known as "The Salamander," escapes from the prison planet called Hell where she was thought to have been executed. Having lost an arm and an eye, she returns to the Manticoran Alliance at the head a fleet of almost a half a million liberated POWs. Honor's return comes at a critical time, providing a much-needed lift for the Allies' morale, for the war is rapidly entering a decisive phase. The Star Kingdom's superior technology and training increasingly give it the advantage, despite the People's Republic of Haven's efforts to catch up. The kingdom is approaching total victory, and the "Peeps" must purge the last ideologues on the Committee of Public Safety to maintain any hope of survival.[30]

Soft/Sociological

Soft or *sociological* science fiction is character-driven, with emphasis on social change, personal psychology, and interactions. While technology may play a role, the emphasis is not so much on how that technology works, but on how it affects individuals or social groups.[25]

Margaret Atwood's *A Handmaid's Tale* (1986) is set in the near future after the United States has undergone a nuclear war and the government has been destroyed. In place now is a strict and dangerous political scene where women are made secondhand citizens and are no longer able to hold jobs or read and write. The story is told through the eyes of Offred, who recalls the past and tells how the chilling society came to be. In this Republic of Gilead, Offred is a Handmaid (surrogate mother) for a top Commander in the new government. His wife, like most of the other women, is sterile. Offred's assignment, like other fertile women in the theocracy, is to get pregnant to help boost the population. However, the only legal way of getting pregnant is sexual intercourse, which causes jealousy and tension throughout the household. And with the rigorous government, Offred isn't allowed to complain or refuse, unless she wants to be shipped off to clean up toxic nuclear waste for the rest of her life.[31]

Space Opera

Space opera science fiction, like western "horse operas," often involves good guys "shooting it up" with bad guys (aliens, robots, or other humans) in the depths of space or on a distant planet.[25]

The 1977 *Star Wars* movie is an example of this subgenre of science fiction. A simple farm boy, Luke Skywalker (Mark Hammill), leaves his home planet and teams up with his newly met allies—Han Solo (Harrison Ford), Chewbacca (Peter Mayhew), Ben Kenobi (Alex Guiness), C-3PO (Anthony Daniels), R2-D2 (Kenny Baker)—and attempts to save Princess Leia (Carrie Fischer) and the galaxy from the evil clutches of Darth Vader (David Prowse) and the Empire. The movie concludes with the Rebels, including Skywalker, making an attack on the Empire's most powerful and ominous weapon, the Death Star, which is capable of destroying whole planets.

Time Travel

Time travel science fiction involves characters who travel to the past or future, or are visited by travelers from the past or future. This subgenre of science fiction was popularized by H. G. Wells in 1888 with *The Time Machine*.[32]

In Andre Norton's *Time Trader* (1958), intelligence agents have discovered that the USA's greatest adversary is sending its agents back through time, and someone or something unknown to history is giving them technologies and weapons far beyond our most advanced science. We have only one option—create time-travel technology ourselves. Then we have to find the opposition's ancient source and eliminate it. As part of Operation Retrograde, reluctant agents for the USA—a small-time criminal, Ross Murdock, and an Apache rancher named Travis Fox—are sent back in time to ancient Britain and prehistoric America in search of alien visitors to Earth's distant past.[33]

SPY/ESPIONAGE

Spy/Espionage novels usually follow the capers of a spy

working to defend his country's secrets or security against an enemy country.[25]

In Charles McCarry's *Tears of Autumn* (1974), Paul Christopher, at the height of career as a secret agent, believes he knows who arranged the assassination of President Kennedy and why. His theory is so dangerous to foreign policy that he is ordered to stop his investigation. But Christopher is a man who lives by and for the truth, so he resigns from the Agency and embarks on an investigation that takes him from Paris to Rome, Zurich, the Congo, and Saigon. Threatened by Kennedy's assassins and by his own government, he follows his suspicion—one step ahead of discovery and death.[34]

Some spy novels look at a darker side of life in espionage. For instance, in *The Secret Agent* (1907) by Joseph Conrad, Adolf Verloc is an eastern European secret agent posing as a London shop owner with anarchist leanings. He is pressured by his superiors into pulling off a shocking act of terrorism to prove his worth to his colleagues—the dynamiting of the Greenwich Observatory. The plot fails when Verloc's mentally retarded brother-in-law is accidentally killed by the explosives. Verloc's wife, Winnie, murders Verloc in a fit of rage. Then, after she is betrayed by Ossipon, who is one of her husband's anarchist associates, she commits suicide.[35]

THRILLER

Thriller novels are tense, exciting works with ingenious plotting, swift action, and continuous suspense. The genre is an offshoot of the mystery, but there are some differences. Unlike most mysteries, thriller novels offer multiple points of view, rather than just that of the detective. They tend to be longer books, with more involved story lines. They often have more characters and a wider scope, and present a greater threat to the protagonist. In the mystery, a crime has been committed and the criminal must be caught. In the thriller novel the fate of a city or the entire world often is the prize. Unlike mysteries, thrillers are dominated by action in which physical threat is a constant companion as a protagonist is pitted against an antagonist. Thriller novels are sometimes called *suspense* novels.[3,7,9]

Three major subgenres of thriller novels are (1) the medical thriller, (2) the legal thriller, and (3) the technothriller.

Medical Thriller

Medical thrillers involve a physician or other health professional as the protagonist who is trying to solve the underlying question in the novel.

Caduceus Awry (2000) is a medical thriller in which Dr. Mark Valentine, who has had his license revoked because of alcoholism, is forced to perform plastic surgery on an indicted mobster, Vito Maldini. Mark flees Atlanta when he discovers that Maldini has sent a vicious hit man, Jesus Dimaria, to kill him. He reverses the tables when Maldini kidnaps his daughter in an attempt to force him to show himself. Entwined in all this suspense is the fact that someone is murdering patients in an Atlanta charity hospital and Mark must solve that mystery and save the life of the hospital director if he has any hope at all of getting his medical license reinstated.[36]

Legal Thriller

Legal thrillers usually involve a lawyer as the main character. They often take place, to a large extent, in a courtroom setting.

In recent years, John Grisham has published a number of popular legal thrillers, including *The King of Torts* (2003) in which young litigator, Clay Carter, of the public defender's office reluctantly takes the case of a young man charged with a random street killing. He assumes it's just another of the many senseless murders that hit Washington D.C. every week. As he digs into the background of his client, Clay stumbles on a conspiracy that lands him in the middle of a complex case against one of the largest pharmaceutical companies in the world, looking at the kind of enormous settlement that would totally change his life, and that would make him, almost overnight, the legal profession's newest king of torts.[37]

Technothriller

Technothrillers are novels in which the plot turns on seemingly plausible technological wonders, such as in Tom Clancy's *The Hunt for Red October* (1997) in which a deadly game of hide-and-seek is played out over 18 days in 4000 miles of ocean. Red October is the Soviet Navy's newest and technologically-superior nuclear submarine. Men who hold Doomsday in their hands deal with high-tech anxiety and tension as Red October heads for the U.S. coast under the command of Captain Marko Ramius. The American government thinks Ramius is planning to attack. A lone CIA analyst has a different idea; he believes Ramius is planning to defect, but he has only a few hours to prove it because the entire Russian naval and air commands are also trying to find the submarine—to destroy it.[38]

WESTERN

Westerns are about life in America's post Civil War western frontier. They usually involve conflicts about land (cowboys versus Native Americans, cattle ranchers versus farmers, sheepherders versus ranchers), wealth (a gold mine, valuable land that the railroad is going to want), relationships (Easterners versus Westerners, cowboys versus outlaws), and revenge for past wrongs (murder of a brother, father, or wife). They feature cattle rustlers, Native-Americans, Mexicans, stage and train robbers, and gunfighters.[3,7,9]

The king of the westerns was Louis L'Amour, whose titles passed the 90 mark, with many becoming best sellers. Among his novels are *The Last Stand at Papago Wells* (1957), *The Broken Gun* (1966), and *Last of the Breed* (1986).[39]

Set in 1863, *Dances with Wolves* (1989) by Michael Blake features Lieutenant John Dunbar who is ordered to hold an abandoned army post where he finds himself alone, beyond the edge of civilization. Thievery and survival soon force him into a Comanche Indian camp. Though he does not speak their language, has no knowledge of their customs, and is considered a trespasser he finds himself intrigued by the exotic and alien culture of the buffalo-hunting people of the plains. Before he knows it he becomes one of them, loving an Indian woman and going by a new name, Dances with Wolves.[40]

YOUNG ADULT

Young adult novels generally have a main character in the 12 to 16 age range and speak to the interests of teenagers. J. K. Rowling's enormously popular Harry Potter stories (*Harry Potter and the Sorcerer's Stone* in 2001, *Harry Potter and the Chamber of Secrets* in 2002, *Harry Potter and the Prisoner of Azkaban* in 2004) fall into this category. Rowling's stories include fantasies laced with wizards, witches, warlocks, and flying soccer games. A seemingly normal Harry discovers that his parents, who have died, were witches and that he has inherited mysterious powers of his own, powers that he needs because of the dangers he faces.[7,9,41,42]

Cornelia Funke's *The Thief Lord* (2002) begins in a detective's office in Venice as a couple, the Hartliebs, request Victor Getz's services to search for two boys—Prosper and Bo—who are the sons of Esther Hartlieb's recently deceased sister. Twelve-year-old Prosper and 5-year-old Bo ran away when their aunt decided she wanted to adopt Bo, but not his brother. Refusing to split up, the boys escaped to Venice. Right away they hook up with a long-haired runaway named Hornet and various other ruffians. Their leader, a young boy named Scipio (Thief Lord), promptly steals jewels from fancy Venetian homes to pawn so he can buy his new friends the warm clothes they need. The plot thickens when the owner of the pawn shop asks the Thief Lord to carry out a special mission for a wealthy client—to steal a broken wooden wing that is the key to completing an age-old, magical merry-go-round.[43]

References

1. Silvester, Niko, Writing Fiction: A Beginners Guide, Creative Writing for Teens,
   http://teenwriting.about.com/library/weekly/aa111102a.htm.
2. Collier, Oscar and Frances Spatz Leighton, How to Write and Sell your First Novel, Writer's Digest Books, Cincinnati, 1990.
3. Seidman, Michael, Choosing your category, In The Writer's Digest Handbook of Novel Writing, Writer's Digest Books, Cincinnati,

1992, pp 204-216.
4. Cussler, Clive, The Golden Buddha, Berkley Trade; 1st edition, New York, 2003.
5. Harris, Robert, A Glossary of Literary terms, VirutalSalt, http://www.virtualsalt.com/litterms.htm, January 4, 2002.
6. Douglas, Lloyd C., The Robe, Houghton Mifflin, Boston, 1943.
7. Fiction Genre Definitions, Manus & Associates Literary Agency, http://www.manuslit.com/flash/index.html.
8. Novel, Microsoft Encarta Encyclopedia, 2003.
9. Zackheim, Sarah Parsons, and Adrian Zackheim, Getting Your Book Published For Dummies, John Wiley & Sons, New York, 2000.
10. Tolkien, J. R. R., The Hobbit, Harper Collins New Ed Edition, New York, 2001 (originally published in 1936).
11. Schwartz, Helen Ruth, The Meadowlark Sings, The Haworth Press, Binghampton, New York, 2006.
12. Proulx, Annie, Brokeback Mountain, Scribner, New York, 2005.
13. Mitchell, Margaret, Gone with the Wind, Warner Books, Reprint edition, 1993 (originally published in 1936).
14. King, Stephen, Carrie, Doubleday, New York, 1974.
15. Ocork, Shannon, How to Write Mysteries, Writer's Digest Books, Cincinnati, 1989.
16. Ballard, J. G., Cocaine Nights, Counterpoint Press, New York, 1999.
17. Meyers, Tamar, Statute of Limitations, HarperCollins, New York, 2004.
18. Connelly, Michael, The Concrete Blond, St. Martins Press, New York, 1995.
19. James, P.D., An unsuitable job for a Woman, Touchstone, New York, 2001.
20. Carr, John Dickson, The Cavalier's Cup, William Morrow, New York, 1953.
21. Danielle Steele: The official website, http://www.randomhouse.com-daniellesteele, 2005.
22. Stewart, Katyln, Fire in the Ice, PublishAmerica, Frederick, Maryland. 2005.
23. LaForge, Emily, Beneath the Raven's Moon, Pocket, New York, 2003.
24. Kihlstrom, April, An Honorable Rogue, Signet Regency, New York, 1977.
25. Glks, Marg and Moira Allen, The subgenres of science fiction, Writing-World.com, http://www.writing-world.com/sf/genres.shtml.
26. King, Stephen, The Stand, Doubleday, New York, 1990.
27. Wells, H. G., War of the Worlds, Bantam Classics, reissue edition, New York, 1988.
28. Clarke, Arthur C., Rendezvous with Rama, Harcourt Brace, New

York, 1973.

29. McCarthy, Wil, Bloom, Del Ray, New York, 1999.
30. Weber, David, Ashes of Victory, Baen, Riverdale, N. Y., 2000.
31. Atwood, Margaret, The Handmaid's Tale,1st Anchor Books ed edition, New York, 1998 (originally published in 1986).
32. Wells, H. G., The Time Machine, Bartleby.com, http://www.bartleby.com/1000/.
33. Norton, Andre, The Time Traders, Baen; Omnibus ed edition, Riverdale, N. Y., 2000 (originally published in 1958).
34. McCarry, Charles, Tears of Autumn, Overlook Hardcover, New York, 2005 (Originally published in 1974).
35. Conrad, Joseph, The Secret Agent, Dover Publications, Mineola, New York, 2001 (Originally published in 1907).
36. Milhorn, H. Thomas, Caduceus Awry, Writer's Showcase, San Jose, 2000.
37. Grisham, John, King of Torts, Doubleday, New York, 2003.
38. Clancy, Tom, The Hunt for Red October, Harper Collins, New York, 1998.
39. Louis L'Amour (1908-1988), http://www.kirjasto.sci.fi/lamour.htm, 2003.
40. Blake, Michael, Dances with Wolves, Facett Book Group, New York, 1989.
41. J.K. Rawling Official Site—Harry Potter and More, www.jkrowling.com, 2005.
42. The Magical World of Harry Potter, http://library.thinkquest.org/J001330/.
43. Funke, Cornelia, The Thief Lord, Scholastic, Inc, New York, 2002.

Chapter 3

Backstory to Description

There are a number of techniques you can use, or avoid using, to make your genre-fiction writing interesting and exciting to readers. This chapter discusses three of them: (1) backstory, (2) clichés, and (3) description. Other techniques are discussed in future chapters.

BACKSTORY

Backstory is the history existing before the start of the novel. It may include the history of characters, objects, countries, or other elements of the story. Backstory is usually woven into the fabric of the story as it unfolds, rather than being presented in one chunk. Above all, you should avoid the temptation to provide backstory by simply saying things like "Little did he know that Thelma had been a serial killer in her teens." Be more creative than that.[1-4]

You can reveal information about the past by using direct or indirect methods.

Direct Methods

Direct methods for revealing the past include (1) exposition,

(2) flashback, and (3) recollection.

Exposition

Exposition is explaining in the beginning of the novel that something happened in the past—information the reader needs to know to understand the story. Exposition, however, doesn't contribute to the forward momentum of the story, and it is telling rather than showing.

Some writers use the terms exposition and narrative synonymously; and in a way, exposition can be thought of as narrative that tells what happened in the past. Of all the methods of prose, exposition slows the story down most of all because the other methods, unlike exposition, do advance the story.

Exposition is used in some popular genre more than others. With science fiction a whole new universe may need to be accounted for, along with the language and customs of a different race. In addition, there may be a whole lot of hardware to explain. Westerns and historical fiction also are built on a lot of background historical information. Fantasy writers may have histories of imaginary empires and genealogical trees to deal with. And mystery writers may deal with lots of information, including lists of suspects, timetables, and maps with determinations of how long it would take to go from point A to point B by foot, bicycle, or car.

The basic rule is "no matter how much you know about the backgrounds of your characters and settings you are not obligated to share it all with the reader." In fact, tell only what the reader needs to know and no more.[5-9]

Exposition can be presented in a chunk of information or it can be woven into the story.

Chunk of Information. It is generally accepted that opening a story with a chunk of backstory tends to bore readers. However, it is sometimes done, and sometimes done successfully. For example, the movie *Indiana Jones and the Last Crusade* (1989) includes a scene at the beginning which is set during Indiana's childhood and explains where he acquired his hat, his whip, the scar on his chin, and his fear of snakes.[10]

Often, a writer uses the first paragraph or so of a novel to tell what has expired just prior to the beginning of the novel. For instance, in *Billy Straight* (1999), Jonathan Kellerman opens with:

- *In the park you see things. But not what I saw tonight. God, God ... I wanted to be dreaming but I was awake, smelling chili meat and onions and the pine trees. First the car drove up to the edge of the parking lot. They got out and talked and he grabbed her, like a hug. I thought maybe they were going to kiss and I'd watch that. Then all of a sudden she made a sound—surprised, squeaky, like a cat or dog that gets stepped on. He let go of her and she fell. Then he bent down next to her and his arm started moving up and down really fast. I thought he was punching her, and that was bad enough, and I kept thinking should I do something. But then I heard another sound, fast, wet, like the butcher at Stater Brothers back in Watson chopping meat—chuck chuck chuck.*[11]

Weaving Exposition. Weaving background information into the story is the most common way of using exposition. It generally involves the use of narrative and dialogue to bring the reader up to date on why the main character is in the state he is in when the novel begins. This may take place over several paragraphs, pages, or chapters.[3]

In *Seize the Night* (1999) by Dean Koontz, the story opens just after dark with 28-year-old Christopher Snow arriving on his bicycle at the scene of a recent kidnapping of a six-year-old boy. He is accompanied by his dog, Orson, who picks up the trail and pursues the kidnapper, with Chris following close behind on his bicycle. The chase ends on the sprawling grounds of Wyvern, a military base that had been shut down by the federal government two years earlier. During the chase and search of Wyvern, which takes place over several chapters, the reader learns a great deal about Chris's background, including the fact that he has a genetic disorder, Xeroderma Pigmentosa, which prevents him from being out in the daylight, and that he had a romantic relationship with the boy's mother prior to her marriage. The relationship dissolved because of Chris's disorder. We also learn that secret research had been carried out at the base by the Department of Defense. Retroviruses were used to alter the genetic makeup of a variety of animals. The retroviruses are now free and spreading among the residents of Moonlight Bay, producing uncontrolled genetic changes. We learn that the research was based on the work of Chris's mother, a Ph.D. biogeneticist, who was later murdered by the local officials to keep her quiet about the disastrous outcome of the work at Wyvern. In addition, we learn that Orson was one of the experimental animals which turned out right, having almost human intelligence. None of this background information we knew when the novel began.[12]

Flashback

Whereas exposition is telling, *flashback* is showing, but it is showing in the past. It is a device that allows the writer to directly present events that happened before the time of the current story or before the time of the current events in the story. Flashback techniques include memories, dreams, stories of the past told by characters, and authorial sovereignty; that is, the author might simply say, "But on grandmothers 20th birthday all hell broke loose" and go on from there to the scene in which it happened. Above all, a flashback should answer an important question the story has already raised.[5,13-15]

The use of an opening crisis followed by a medium-length flashback is the most traditional form of this technique. For instance, in Scott Turow's *Presumed Innocent* (1987), the novel opens at the funeral of murdered prosecuting attorney, Carolyn Polhemus. In the next scene, still in the present, the narrator, Rusty Sabich, examines criminal evidence, including some brutal pictures of Carolyn's body. A flashback chapter comes next in which the reader learns of Sabich's sexual involvement with the woman. The flashback adds tension (How will the affair affect the investigation?), emotional complication (Sabich is married.), and complexity (Sabich is not as hard and rational investigating the case as he would like to be.). Sabich makes little progress in finding the killer. When his boss loses his bid for re-election, Sabich incredibly finds himself on trial for Carolyn's murder.[16]

Sometimes backstory can be explored fully in a number of flashes back in time in which an element of the past provides the key to the mystery of the present. *Stir of Echoes* (1999) is a movie about a blue-collar man named Tom (Kevin Bacon) who laments his ordinary life, only to learn, when his sister-in-law Lisa (Ileanna Douglas) hypnotizes him, that he is a "receiver" capable of seeing spirits and split-second glimpses of past and future events. It's a torturous gift to have, since his friendly Chicago neighborhood possesses a dark secret. His new-found powers enable him to see a ghost in his house. We're then given back flashes to discover how a girl was killed there. The backstory is important to the present in the fact that her killer still lurks nearby, ready to kill to keep his secret.

Is it okay to use flashbacks in your novel? The opinion is divided. Some "experts" say "no," others say "hell no," but others say "yes, but keep them short." Now, having said that flashbacks should be kept short, there is an exception to every rule. David Morrell, in *The Fifth Profession* (1990), uses a long flashback quite well. Savage, a hired protector of rich clients, reluctantly takes on a new assignment—rescue a battered wife from her rich and powerful husband who is holding her against her will. The first 57 pages of the novel deal with this escapade. During this time we learn small details about the horrendous injuries Savage suffered in his last, and only, failed job. Then, having created sufficient curiosity about that job, Morrell launches into a 52 page flashback in which he details the prior assignment and how Savage came to be so seriously injured that it took six months for him to physically and emotionally recover. The flashback contributes so much to readers' understanding of the present story and Savage's emotional state that plays a role in the present story that they hardly notice the flashback has occurred.[17]

Like Morrell, if you decide to use a flashback of significant length in your story, be sure you have established your major characters and the current story line well before doing so. You must establish a strong enough reason for your readers to want to know what happened in the past so they can forgive you for delaying the forward motion of the present action.

Advantages and Disadvantages

Advantages. The advantages of flashbacks are that they can be used to explain motivations, character histories, background influences, or other information that cannot be told during the linear sequence of a story. For instance, if a character is an adult when the novel begins, a flashback can make plausible his motives by showing what events in his childhood compel him to act the way he does now. A flashback also can fill in events that show how the story situation reached its current state, and it can present crucial information that happened in the past in which there is simply no other way to include it. In some cases you simply want to slow down the action because it is moving too fast. A flashback can be an effective way of doing this.[14,15,18-20]

Disadvantages. Flashbacks do offer some pitfalls. Even the best-written flashback carries a built-in disadvantage—it is by definition already over. The scene you are detailing in your flashback happened sometime earlier, and so the reader is being given "old" information. As a result, the flashback lacks immediacy. Another problem with flashbacks is that readers already know that the character has lived past the point, so you can't create suspense about whether or not he is going to survive. Also, a flashback forces readers to look at a less-mature version of the character after they have already seen better. And as I have already stated, a flashback delays the forward motion of the story, raising the possibility of boring your readers.[14,15,18-20]

Start and End

Conventions have evolved about using verb tenses to signal both the start and the end of flashbacks. Most readers don't consciously notice these tense shifts; they register below the level of consciousness to signal "Now we've moved back in time" and "Now we've left the flashback to rejoin story time."

Story in Past Tense. If your story is being told in the past tense, write the first few verbs of the flashback in the past perfect and the rest of the verbs in simple past.

- *Past Tense (Present Time).* Jim *walked* through the woods.
- *Past Perfect (Beginning of Flashback).* Jim *had met* Alice at the ballpark.
- *Past Tense (Flashback Continues).* He *walked* up and introduced himself.

After that, continue the rest of the flashback in past tense. The reason for this is that an entire flashback in past perfect would be cumbersome, especially if it's very long.

When you're ready to end the flashback, revert to past perfect for the last few verbs, and then use past tense to resume story time.

- *Past Perfect Tense (End of Flashback).* He *had watched* her get in the car and drive out of his life.
- *Past Tense (Back to the Present).* Jim *glanced* through the tree tops and saw a soaring hawk.

Story in Present Tense. If your story is being told in present tense, the convention is even simpler. Put story-time action in present tense, and then put the entire flashback in past tense.

- *Present Tense (Present Time).* Jim *is walking* through the woods.
- *Past Tense (Beginning of Flashback).* He *met* Alice at the ballpark.

When you're ready to return to story time, simply resume present tense

- *Present Tense (Back to the Present).* Through the tree tops Jim *sees* a soaring hawk.[19]

Rules for Flashbacks

Jessica Morrell gives several rules that govern the use of flashbacks. If you use a flashback you should:

- Make certain that the plot, characters, and conflict are thoroughly established before introducing a flashback. This almost always means that the flashback should not be the first scene.
- Never insert a flashback in the middle of an emotional or eventful action.
- Never use flashbacks in climatic scenes.
- Be sure your flashback follows a strong scene.
- Orient the reader at the start of the flashback in time and space; that is, let the reader know you've moved back in time, how far, and to what place.
- As a general rule, be brief. Present the information, and then

quickly get back to the story.

- Make sure the flashback is vivid and interesting in itself. If not, it would be better as brief exposition.
- If your flashback runs through the entire novel, then treat it as a parallel plot or subplot, with one running in the present and one running in the past.[19] Parallel plots and subplots are discussed in Chapter 8.

Recollection

With *recollection*, a character simply remembers what happened in the past. Recollections should be very short, no more than a sentence or two.

- "If Mary hadn't had the affair with William, she wouldn't have been in the car the night he drove it head-on into the tree," Jack thought.

Maybe the reader hadn't been told that Mary had been having an affair with William, but only that Mary had died in a car wreck. The recollection, although brief, provides a vital piece of information.

Indirect Methods

Corbette Doyle gives three ways to reveal the past indirectly; that is, while still in the present: (1) Past as a present event, (2) implied past expectation, and (3) implied past network.[3]

Past as a Present Event

In *past as present event*, the writer has one character tell another character a story from the past in a manner that both reveals the past and adds to the present action. For example, one character may be explaining to another one why Sam broke out in a sweat and hesitated at the foot of the cliff as others began their journey upward. Turns out that Sam, as a small child, had fallen from a tall tree, resulting in serious injuries which caused him to spend several painful months in the hospital.

In the exposition to William Shakespeare's *Romeo and Juliet*, two servants of the house of Capulet discuss the feud between their master and the house of Montague, thereby letting the audience know that such a feud exists and that it will play an important role in influencing the plot.[2,3]

Implied Past Expectation

In *implied past expectation*, the writer has a character in the story imply something about his past. For example, if a woman cringes at an innocently raised hand, we assume instantly that she has been beaten in the past, and more than once.[2,3]

Implied Past Network

In *implied past network*, the writer reveals a character's past through the way others who know the character react to and treat him. For example, a man shopping in a store notices the way the people in the store are looking at the woman who is with him. He can't see anything obviously wrong with her. He doesn't catch on until he notices that the store detective is shadowing them. Apparently, the woman is well known there.[2,3]

Backstory Length

Backstory can vary in length from a sentence or two to a few paragraphs to a chapter or more to almost the entire book. A novel that consists almost entirely of backstory is called a *frame story,* and the writer avoids confusion because only the beginning and the end deal with the present. The advantage of a frame story is that it affords two points of view in one character; that is, the older protagonist can view the past through a different perspective than when he was younger.[3,14,20]

John Knowles's *A Separate Peace* (1959) is an example of a frame story. An adult man, Gene Forrester, revisits events that were important to him in his youth at Devon, a private boarding school in New Hampshire during World War II. The relationship between Gene and another boy, Finney, is explored. Gene is a brilliant student; Finney is a great athlete. Jealousy between them builds until Gene's internal battle for identity and security leads to a tragedy that changes both of their lives forever. The two boys plan to jump from a tree into the water at the same time—a very dangerous action because they must jump outward to land in the water or else they will hit the ground. During a jump, Gene jounces the limb and Finny reaches out to him for help; but Gene allows him to fall, causing him to break his leg—an event that ends his athletic career. The story opens and closes with Gene as an adult.[21]

Regardless of backstory length, at the end of the backstory the reader should be wiser, knowing something important that he did not know before.[3,14]

CLICHÉS

A *cliché* is a phrase that has been used so often it has become commonplace. By extension, the term cliché also applies to almost any character or situation that has similarly become overly familiar or commonplace. Clichés in general are to be avoided. The one exception might be when a character purposely speaks in clichés as part of his personality.

Cliché Phrases

Probably the best known *cliché phrase* is, "It was a dark and stormy night," thanks to the Peanuts character, Snoopy. Likewise, "and they all lived happily ever after," has been worn out. These phrases weren't always clichés. They, like other phrases that we now consider clichés, had an original beginning. They became clichés only after years of overuse. Other examples of cliché phrases are, "Every cloud has a silver lining" and "When at first you don't succeed, try try again." Clichés often take metaphorical forms, such as "white as a sheet" and "strong as an ox." Simply put, clichés are shortcuts to be avoided. So be aware that the more you avoid using clichés, the more interesting your writing will be.[22]

The following table is a list of some cliché phrases to avoid.

Acid test

Across the board

Add insult to Injury

After the rain comes a rainbow

All good things come to those who wait

All in a day's work

All is fair in love and war

Always look on the bright side

Back to square one

Better afraid than blind to my fear

Better safe than sorry

Blessing in disguise

Brink of disaster

Calm before the storm

Cheer up, it's not the end of the world

Cream of the crop

Cut and dried

Days are numbered

Die is cast

Doing stupid things is my way of making my life interesting

Don't rock the boat

Don't worry, be happy

Down and out

Down in the dumps

Drop in the bucket

Easier said than done

Every cloud has a silver lining

Every rose has its thorn

Everything is relative

Face the music

Feast or famine

Food for thought

From A to Z

Get your act together

Goodbye is not an easy word to say

Half the battle

Handwriting on the wall

Have an ax to grind

High and dry

Hit pay dirt

Hook, line, and sinker

I did it my way

If all else fails, manipulate the data

If at first you don't succeed, redefine success

If at first you don't succeed, destroy all evidence that suggests you tried

It's always darkest before the dawn

If you can't beat them, join them

I have to face my fear

Indecision is the key to flexibility

It has to get worse before it gets better

It is better to have loved and lost than to never have loved at all

It seemed like a good idea at the time

Keeps me off the streets

Keep your fingers crossed

Last-ditch effort

Laughter is the best medicine

Life is a bitch

Life is not hard, it only needs some positive thinking

Life is what happens while you're busy making other plans

Life's not so bad, when you

If nothing else, I can always serve as a bad example

Life's not bad when you consider the alternative

Life sucks, and then you die

the sea

Live and let live

Making a bad decision is better than making no decision at all

Moment of truth

Muddy the waters

No guts, no glory

Never forget that you are unique, just like everybody else

Nip in the bud

No news is good news

Off the deep end

Of course life is hard, that's why they pay you the big bucks
Once in a blue moon
One day I will wake up, and it will all fit together
One step at a time
Pain in the neck
Parting is such sweet sorrow
Play it by ear
Rack my brain
Rome was not built in one day
Run of the mill
Safe and sound
Seat of the pants
Shot in the arm
Sink or swim Sitting pretty
Skating on thin ice
Some day my ship will come in
Sour grapes
Stretch the truth
The devil made me do it
The meek shall inherit the earth
The more things change, the more they stay the same
The one who makes no mistakes does none of the work
There are lies, damned lies, and statistics
There are plenty more fish in
There is a light at the end of the tunnel
There is nothing to fear but fear itself

The road to success is always unpaved
This too shall pass
Time will tell
Tip of the iceberg
Today is the first day of the rest of your life
Too many irons in the fire
Truth is nothing but a feeling that something is true
Turn over a new leaf
Under a dark cloud
Uphill battle
Vicious circle
Water over the dam
Water under the bridge
Wet behind the ears
Wild-goose chase
Win hands down
Wit's end
Word to the wise
Worth its weight in gold
What goes around comes around
When at first you don't succeed, try try again
When in doubt, consult your inner child
When it rains, it pours
When the going gets tough, the tough get going
When the pony dies, the ride is over
Winning is about power, not about the quality of your weapons[23,24]

Cliché Characters

Cliché characters are characters we all are familiar with—too familiar. An example is the pirate with an eye-patch, a hook for a hand, a peg-leg, and a parrot on his shoulder. Similarly, the vampire cliché consists of a mysterious man with a long black cape, slick black hair, and an Eastern European accent.[25]

A *Mary Sue* is a fanfiction (fanfic) writer's term for a cliché character who is an alter-ego for the author. Fanfic is fiction written by fans as an extension of an admired work or series of works, especially a television show such as Star Trek. Fanfic is often posted on the Internet or published in fanzines (amateur-produced magazines written for a subculture of enthusiasts devoted to a particular interest). The term, Mary Sue, can be a put-down or just a convenient label, depending on how it's used, but usually a Mary Sue is a little too perfect, a little too central, and sleeps with one or more gorgeous characters before she either (1) saves the day and lives happily ever after or (2) dies and is mourned by everyone. The term has been extended to male counterparts—Marty *Stus, Murray Stus, Harry Stus, Gary Stus*, and so forth. You have to be careful that you don't write a Mary Sue type character into your novel.[26]

Cliché Situations

Overused *situations*, such as the cavalry arriving just in the nick of time to save the day, also are to be avoided. One of the most well known situation clichés occurs in horror movies when a woman who is being chased by a killer always runs up the stairs to be trapped instead of out the door to safety, or the woman who is locked securely in her house, hears a strange noise outside, and goes outside into the darkness to investigate its source. Another example, used to increase the suspense, is when someone falls to the ground while being chased by a bad guy, even when running over level, unobstructed terrain. When a man and woman are being chased, usually the woman falls and then the man pauses to help her up, thus letting the bad guy get closer in the chase.

A cliché situation sometimes used by novice writers is to open their story with the protagonist waking up, getting dressed, and traveling to some site where the action begins. Along the way, backstory is filled in. By the time he finally gets to his objective the reader has lost interest and picked up another book. Begin your story when he gets there and the action has started. Fill in the backstory later.

Another cliché situation often employed by new writers is to have a character stare into a mirror. The writer then describes the image the character sees in the mirror.

Still another cliché situation is the *overheard conversation,* whose use at one time was popular among writers but has now fallen from favor. Two or more people just happen to be in the right place at the right time—one talking to someone and the other accidentally hearing the conversation.[22,27]

DESCRIPTION

Writing *description* is often described as painting a picture with words. Without description, people move through vague buildings or fuzzy landscapes, and the time and place may be unclear. At the same time, some writers err in the other direction—including too much description. You don't want the descriptive passages in your story to be so long they put your readers to sleep; however, you do want to add enough description to give vivid pictures of the setting and characters, while avoiding huge chunks of it.[28,29]

Blending Description

Use description to set the scene, move the plot, set the mood, foreshadow events, give a sense of character, or whatever it has to do to keep the story moving, but blend the description into the story. By using description in combination with action and dialogue you can cut the description down into palatable chunks. For instance, instead of stopping a story to describe trees, flowers, and a waterfall in a plush lobby of a hotel, come up with a reason for this description to be in the story; that is, a reason for the characters to be interacting with that setting. If your protagonist has been in the lobby of that hotel dozens of times, he will only give it a passing glance, unless something has changed or something usual is going on. For example, he normally might not take much notice of the details of fountain in the center of the lobby, but he would notice it if his girlfriend were passionately kissing the hotel manager, standing up to their knees in the water.[29]

As an example of blending description with action and dialogue, consider the following:

- As Beth turned the corner into the parking lot she spotted John sitting on the hood of an aging, blue Ford—a car she hadn't seen before. The paint was chipped on the front fender and a nasty crack ran across the windshield. The Ford and John made a strange picture together. She was use to seeing him driving around town, showing off his ten-year-old, white Beemer.

  Seeing Beth, John threw up his arm and waved—a vigorous wave. His ill-fitting, black leather jacket crept up his skinny arm, showing a fake-gem studded bracelet. "Where the hell have you been" he growled. He hopped off the car onto the asphalt, stumbling slightly as one of his imitation patent-leather shoes caught in a rough place on the pavement.

  "What have I done now?" Beth muttered to herself. Apparently John wasn't as happy to see her as she thought. She stopped 20 feet from the car and ran a nervous hand through her cropped, bottle-blond hair. She had painted her fingernails a light blue—John's favorite color.

  John righted himself and took a step toward her. A broad smile crossed his narrow face, showing the perfect white teeth she had worked nights to pay for. She ran to his open arms.

Brand Names

While using brand names is acceptable, using too many is annoying. So don't waste valuable narrative telling the reader all about the protagonist's designer clothes or the antagonist's expensive car. However, don't avoid brand names altogether. If your protagonist drives a brand-new Jaguar as opposed to an old, rusty Volkswagen bus, the reader learns quiet a bit about him without a lot of description.[29]

The Words to Use

Use strong, active, concrete words when writing description; the stronger the writing, the better the description. In general, mainly use nouns and verbs while using adjectives and adverbs sparingly. However, keep in mind that sometimes people do speak "softly" or walk "slowly" or move "quickly."

In writing description, many novice writers tend to concentrate only on sight and sound. This is natural as those are the main ways in which we observe the world. However, you can better bring a scene to life by including the other senses, such as the senses of smell and touch. Taste is harder to include because humans don't tend to go around tasting things, unless they're eating.

If you're writing an action-oriented story, too much description will get in the way of the pace. A star NFL halfback isn't going to be describing his girlfriend who is sitting in the stands as he darts between 300 pound defensive linemen. On the other hand, description is a more important part of many slower-paced stories.[28,29]

Description uses all parts of speech, although each writer favors a different selection of words, depending on his style. Schnelbach and Wyatt describe three forms of description: (1) noun-based, (2) verb-based, and (3) adjective-based.[28]

Noun-based Description

If a writer primarily favors facts, then he prefers *noun-based description*. Noun-based description is cold, fact-based, and unbiased. It uses nouns and nouns as adjectives to present information. Consider the following example from Schnelbach and Wyatt:

- *A **white convertible Mustang**, driven by a 50-year-old man in an **ill-fitting charcoal department store suit**, pulled up to the light. **Distorted classic rock music** blared from the speakers, the vibrations moving the **two dozen strands of died brown hair** he still possessed.*[27]

Notice the use of nouns and noun forms within the passage. The car is a specific model and color, the driver is an exact age, the narrator knows the suit is from a department store, and the number of hairs moved is very specific. As you read the passage, the image presented is precise. Mystery and suspense writers tend to use noun-based descriptions.[28]

Verb-based Description

Some writers favor *verb-based description*. In verb-based descriptive passages, everything seems active. Western and horror writers like this type of description because it maintains a sense that the action never stops. The reader moves from action to action without pause, often using personification (giving human qualities to animals, objects, or ideas). Again, an example from Schnelbach and Wyatt:

- *The wind **howled** as she **ran** across the dusty plains. **Scorching** the earth mercilessly, the sun **sought** any plants not yet destroyed. Together, this couple set forth to **ruin** us all.*[28]

We know the wind does not howl and certainly is not a "she" running across the land, and the sun is not a seeker of plants. The passage uses personification and verbs to create a sense of intentional action.[28]

Adjective-based Description

Writing that consists of flowery passages seeded with figurative language is *adjective-based description*. It relies on adjectives, adverbs, similes, and metaphors to create images. Another example from Schnelbach and Wyatt:

- *Maybe mansions are meant to be **cold and musty**. I was **uncomfortable** standing alone in the anteroom, as **isolated** and **outside** as I could be. Today might be special for the lady of the house, but for me it was **horrible**.*[28]

Adjectives lack the precision of nouns. The description relies upon the point of view of the narrator.[28]

References

1. Back-story, free-definition, http://www.free-definition.com/Back-story.html.
2. Card, Orson Scott, Creating Characters that Readers Care About, In

The Writer's Digest Handbook of Novel Writing, Ed. By Clark, Tom, William Brohaugh, Bruce Woods, Bill Strickland, and Peter Blocksom, Cincinnati, 1992.
3. Doyle, Corbette, Washington Romance Writers, Backstory without Boredom, http://www.wrwdc.com/Backstory.htm, January 2002.
4. Spencer, Wen, Writing back-story, http://www.wenspencer.com/blog/archives/000025.html, November 8, 2003.
5. Dibell, Ansen, Plot, Writer's Digest Books, Cincinnati, 1999.
6. Bickham, Jack M., The 38 Most Common Fiction Writing Mistakes, Writer's Digest Books, Cincinnati, 1992.
7. Bokesch, Laura, Literary terms, Literary elements, Academy of the Arts, http://www.orangeusd.k12.ca.us/yorba/literary_elements.htm.
8. Hinze, Vickey, Exposition vs. Narrative, http://www.fictionfactor.com/guests/exposition.html.
9. Swain, Dwight V., Techniques of the Selling Writer, University of Oklahoma Press, Norman, 1974.
10. Back-story, Encyclopedia.com, http://www.reference.com/browse/wiki/Back-story.
11. Kellerman, Jonathan, Billy Straight, Ballantine Books, New York, 1999.
12. Koontz, Dean, Seize the Night, Bantam Books, New York, 1999.
13. Collier, Oscar, How to Write & Sell Your First Novel, Writer's Digest Books, Cincinnati,
14. Kress, Nancy, Using the Flashback, In The Writer's Digest Handbook of Novel Writing, Ed. By Clark, Tom, William Brohaugh, Bruce Woods, Bill Strickland, and Peter Blocksom, Cincinnati, 1992.
15. Kress, Nancy, 3 tips for writing successful flashback, Writer'sDigest.com, http://www.writersdigest.com/articles/column/kress/flashbacks.asp.
16. Turrow, Scott, Presumed Innocent, Farrar Straus & Giroux, New York, 1987.
17. Morrell, David, The Fifth Profession, Warner Books, New York, 1990.
18. Harper, Tara K., Should you use flashbacks?, Writer's Workshop, http://tarakharper.com/k_flshbk.htm#use.
19. Morrell, Jessica Page, Flashback, The Writing Life, http://www.writing-life.com/fiction/flashbacks.html.
20. Noble, William, Conflict, Action & Suspense, Writer's Digest Books, Cincinnati, 1999.
21. Knowles, John, A Separate Peace, Bantam; Reissue edition, New York, 1985 (Originally published in 1959).
22. Ashley (Finn21), How to avoid clichés. What is a cliché?

http://writers.crashintoyou.com/clicheessay.html.
23. Morrell, Jesica Page, Modifiers and clichés to avoid, http://pages.ivillage.com/bcjessica/basics.html.
24. The Book of Clichés, http://utopia.knoware.nl/~sybev/cliche/index.shtml, August 27, 2000.
25. Clichés, Wikipedia, http://en.wikipedia.org/wiki/Cliche. 1999.
26. Mary Sue Merchandise, Sci-Fi/Fantasy, About.com, http://scifi.about.com/library/weekly/aa031498.htm?once=true&iam=dpile&terms=fanfiction+writers,
27. Csernica, Lillian, Horrible clichés to avoid, http://www.speculations.com/cliches.htm.
28. Schnelbach, S. and C. S. Wyatt, Tameri Guide for Writers, http://www.tameri.coml, March 14, 2005.
29. Marble, Anne M., Romancing the keyboard, Writing-World.com, http://www.writing-world.com/columns/romance/marble17.shtml, 2004.

Chapter 4

Figurative Language to Introspection, Insight, & Perception

Continuing with writing techniques, this chapter discusses (1) figurative language; (2) foreshadowing and flash forward; (3) form and structure; (4) imagery; (5) information; (6) interlocking episode; and (7) introspection, insight, and perception.

FIGURATIVE LANGUAGE

Figurative language is language that compares something to something else or language that goes beyond the literal meaning of words to furnish new effects or fresh insights. Figurative language may be used for (1) painting mental pictures, (2) substituting words for sounds, or (3) other functions.

Painting Mental Pictures

Common types of figurative language include (1) analogy, (2) hyperbole, (3) metaphor, (4) periphrasis, (5) personification, (6) simile, and (7) synecdoche.[1,2]

Analogy. An *analogy* compares two different things by

identifying points of similarity. It is created for the purpose of conceptual clarity. An example is comparing the physical details and functioning of the human heart to a mechanical pump.[2,3]

Hyperbole. *Hyperbole* is an exaggerated statement used to heighten effect. It is not used to mislead the reader, but to emphasize a point. Examples are "She's said so a million times," "I'm so hungry I could eat a horse," "My birthday cake was as high as a mountain," or "But dad, everybody's doing it."[1,4]

Metaphor. A *Metaphor* is a figure of speech that involves an implied comparison between two relatively unlike things. The comparison is not announced by "like" or "as." For example, "The road was a ribbon of moonlight," "the ship ploughs the sea," "Julie is a gem," or "Rain falls in teardrops from the sky."[1,5]

Periphrasis. *Periphrasis* is substituting a descriptive phrase made up of a concrete adjective and abstract noun for a precise word, such as "fringed curtains of thine eye" for eyelashes.[3]

Personification. *Personification* is a figure of speech that gives the qualities of a person to an animal, an object, or an idea. For example, "This coffee is strong enough to get up and walk away," in which coffee is given the human quality of walking.[1,3,5]

Simile. *Simile* is a figure of speech that involves a direct comparison between two unlike things, usually with the words "like" or "as." Examples are "She's *as* happy as the day is long," "He smelled *like* a wet dog," "Her lips are *like* red roses," or "Her coat looked *like* a wet paper bag that had been trampled on."[1,3,5,6]

Synecdoche. *Synecdoche* is substituting a part for a whole or a whole for a part, such as "fifty sails" for "fifty ships" or "the smiling year" for the "spring."[3]

Substituting Words for Sounds

Figurative language that depends on sound includes onomatopoeia and puns.

Onomatopoeia. *Onomatopoeia* is the use of words that appeal to our sense of hearing by mimicking sounds; that is, using syllables the author has made up to represent a sound. For example, the use of the word "crack" for a gunshot, "pop" for a balloon bursting, or "clang" for the sound a bell makes when it is struck.[1]

Pun. A *pun* is the deliberate confusion of words based on similarity of sound (waist and waste, pin and pen) or words that are spelled alike but mean different things, depending on how they are used (It's a muggy day in New York today.). The word "muggy" that is normally used to describe an aspect of weather is used here to refer to New York's high crime rate (mugging).

Wordplay is a serious pun, as when a dying man says "Tomorrow you shall find me a grave man."[3]

Other Functions

Other types of figurative language include apostrophe, irony, metonymy, oxymoron, and paradox.

Apostrophe. *Apostrophe* is an address to a person (corpse, mummy) or thing (tree, wall) not literally listening. For instance, "Western wind where art thou?" Clearly, the wind can't hear when spoken to.[4]

Irony. *Irony* involves making a statement that means the opposite of what it states literally. Suppose you've just found out your teenaged daughter is pregnant, your house has been robbed, and your wife has just wrecked the family car. You cry in exasperation: "Well that's just great!" Clearly you don't mean that you're happy about this sequence of events. You have just made an ironic statement.

Sarcasm is cutting, sneering, or taunting irony. It is a form of wit marked by the use of sarcastic language intended to make its victim the butt of contempt or ridicule. "He's handsome, if you like rodents."[4,7]

Metonymy. *Metonymy* is substituting the name of something for its attribute or whatever it is associated with. For instance, "Arnold must wait on word from the Crown." Crown here means King (or Queen).[3]

Oxymoron. An *oxymoron* is the deliberate combination of seemingly contradictory words, such as "helpful bureaucrat" or "bitter sweet."[3]

Paradox. A *paradox* is something that at first seems to contradict itself, such as "A little learning is a dangerous thing," "less is more," and "Some people are more equal than others."[4]

FORESHADOWING AND FLASH FORWARD

In fiction, two mechanisms that exist for looking into the future are foreshadowing and flash forward. Each has its own way of being written and its own purpose.

Foreshadowing

Foreshadowing is a narrative device that takes place in the present and hints at coming events. Because foreshadowing is used to create suspense, if it is too obvious it can spoil the surprise. Frequently, future events are merely hinted at through dialogue, description, or the attitudes and reactions of the characters.

In addition to building suspense, foreshadowing raises questions that encourage the reader to read on in hopes of finding out more about the event that is being foreshadowed. Foreshadowing is also a means of making a story more believable by partially preparing the reader for events that are to follow. For instance, consider the situation in which a man has a history of epileptic seizures. In the story he is forced to descend a high mountain peak with a number of vertical walls. Will he have a seizure on the way down? If he does, it will seem like a natural occurrence rather than something just out of the blue if it's been foreshadowed.[1,6,8]

Character dialogue can plant future story in the present action. For example, in the movie *Gremlins* (1984), Rand Peltzer (Hoyt Axton) is trying to find a gift for his son, Billy (Zach Galligan), before returning home from a New York trip. He settles on a unique pet in a Chinatown curio shop—a cute, furry, little creature known as a Mogwai. Before he leaves, the shop's owner warns him that three rules must be obeyed by a Mogwai owner:

- *"Keep it away from bright light, don't get any water on it, and never, never ever feed it after midnight."*

Is there any doubt at this point that the warning is going to play an important role in future developments in the story?

That something unusual is going to happen in the movie *The Caine Mutiny* (1956) is foreshadowed by a scene in which a U.S.

Naval Captain, Francis Queeg (Humphrey Bogart), nervously rolls three metal balls in his hand during a tense moment between him and his crew.

In *Caduceus Awry* (2000), Mark Valentine mysteriously finds a gun on his car seat after an alcoholic blackout and places it in the drawer of his bedside table. This sets the stage for his use of the gun in a later chapter. You just know it's going to happen, but you don't know when and how.[9]

Foreshadowing can be used as an omen without directly referring to the factor in the upcoming event. For instance, in Daphne du Maurier's short story *The Birds* (1963), the weather is the omen (foreshadow) of something bad that's going to occur.

- *The cold comes in too quickly, too early for the season, and settles in and stays.*[10]

Foreshadowing has a linkage effect in establishing continuity throughout the story because one scene suggests the later appearance of another scene and the later scene causes a recollection of the earlier one.

Foreshadowing should not occur after the three-quarter point in the novel. The remainder of the novel should move in a linear fashion toward its conclusion. Foreshadowing is unnecessary beyond this point because whatever happens after that point should have already been prepared for. From this point forward the reader should be kept busy with on-going events.[1,6,8]

Flash Forward

A *flash forward* is a narrative device in which the scene changes to a later time. It can provide information that the reader needs to know to understand the plot, or it can contribute to the suspense. A common mechanism for instituting a flash forward is for a character to imagine a scene that is apt to happen or that he fears will happen. Flash forwards tend to be very brief, often only a single sentence, although they can be longer.

- *Brief Flash Forward.* John looked at Mary lying beside him on the grass. God, he loved her. Little did he know that in a year she would pregnant by another man.

- ***Longer Flash Forward.*** The longer flash forward usually occurs in phases, such as the following: **Phase 1.** Sam knows or fears something bad will happen at a future time (say he expects to be fired), **Phase 2.** Then he imagines the confrontational scene in which the dreaded action takes place (he's fired), and **Phase 3.** The story moves back to the present in which the bad event has happened. (Sam is venting his feelings about being fired.).

You also can start your novel with a flash forward, taken from near a highpoint of action in the middle of the book. The flash forward grabs the reader's attention, after which the entire story can be told in chronological order more or less. Since the flash forward tells the reader the essential nature of your story right away, it can serve as a hook.[6,11]

FORM AND STRUCTURE

Form and structure give a fictional work its shape. The two are different, but interrelated, so it is difficult to talk about one without the other. Structure is more like the 2x4s, braces, and other materials inside a house. Form is what's been done with the structure—whether the house is colonial or contemporary, large or small, or one story or two.[12]

Form

The *form* of a piece of writing indicates whether it is a poem, a work of prose, a play, or something else. Form can also be used in a more specific sense to talk about the way a fictional work is written. For instance, a piece of fiction may be in the form of a letter, a journal, a diary, or a series of e-mails between characters. You can combine several forms in one piece of fiction. A good example of this is the novel *Dracula* (1897) by Bram Stoker, which uses diaries, telegrams, and letters as part of the story.[8,13]

Structure

Structure is the arrangement of the pieces; that is, the order in which your scenes (peaks of action) and sequels (valleys of contemplation) appear in relation to one another. The structure may involve a single incident or many incidents, there may be a few setbacks for the characters or there may be many, the climax may be reached early on or later in the novel, there may be a lengthy final part after the conflict has been resolved or there may be no final part at all. The work could be a single, long, third-person narrative, a series of short first-person passages from the point of view of different characters, or many other possibilities.[8,12]

IMAGERY

Imagery is the use of vivid language to represent objects, actions, or ideas. It uses language that appeals to the senses; that is, descriptions stated in terms of the five senses—seeing, hearing, smelling, tasting, and touching. It also makes use of figurative language; that is, metaphors, similes, personification, and so forth, which produce mental images for the reader. Imagery is used to replace a set of dull, mechanical details because it brings a scene alive for the reader.[1,8,14]

An example of imagery is the manner in which Nathaniel Hawthorne uses the letter "A" in his story, *The Scarlet Letter* (1850). A young woman, Hester Prynne, is led from the town prison with her infant daughter, Pearl, in her arms and the scarlet letter "A" tattooed on her breast. Hester is being punished for adultery. Her husband, who was to follow her to Boston, had sent her ahead. She will not reveal her lover's identity, and the scarlet letter, along with her public shaming, is her punishment for her sin and her secrecy. The letter serves a purpose for the Puritans. It reminds the other men and women of the crime of adultery and the punishment of committing such a crime. It symbolizes how the Puritans are unrelenting and unforgiving.[15]

In his novel *Seize the Night* (1999), Dean Koontz describes, with a bit of humor, a huge man's beard as "so lush and wavy that he couldn't possibly shave it off with anything less than a lawnmower" and the man's general appearance as having "the presence of a guy who might be called down to Hell by Satan to unclog a furnace chimney choked with the gnarled and half-burnt contentious souls of ten serial killers."[16]

Moderation is necessary with imagery. You don't want to overload readers. You can avoid this overload in several ways. First of all, consider what it is you are describing. If it is something that is not really central to the story, you can mention only a few details, or only a single, unique detail. If, on the other hand, you are talking about a vital scene or a central character, more detail is necessary.[1,6,8,14]

Levels of Imagery

There are two general levels of imagery: The *physical character image* and the *overall tone-setting image* as shown in the following examples from Bishop:

- **Physical Character Image.** *He leaped from the bed like a suddenly uncoiled spring.*[8]

The simile replaces the details of arms, legs, and torso. The image defines the general mood of the character. He leaves the bed quickly.

- **Overall Tone-Setting Image.** *Jeff felt naked and trapped in a celebration of lunatics. The masquerade party was a blast of noise, a blare of color. He had forgotten which costume Laurie said she would wear. A clown leaped before him and shrieked some giggles. He squinted at the garish cosmetics to know if it was Laurie. Feathers scraped his face.*[8]

The images in this example set the tone and type of party and the attitude of the participants. Not every costume and action need be detailed.[8]

Suggestions for Using Imagery

William Noble gives three suggestions for using imagery: (1) Be specific, (2) use animal-like words, and (3) use charged images.[18]

Be Specific. Instead of saying something "smelled bad," tell us what the smell was like (It smelled like rotten meat.). Instead of "storm" say "raging hurricane." Instead of "bad criminal" say "seven-foot-tall, blood-thirsty criminal."[17,18]

Use Animal-like Words. Instead of "said angrily" you might use "growled." Instead of "he waved his hand" you might use "he pawed at the air." And instead of "he yelled" you might use "he bellowed."[18]

Use Charged Images. Charged images produce feelings in readers and get them involved in the story. Think excitement and bursting emotion—"the engine roared," "the woman radiated," "the ship bucked and wallowed."[18]

INFORMATION

As a writer of fiction, don't give a tutorial; that is, don't try to over-educate the reader about a topic by presenting an excessive amount of information. Give only as much information about the topic as necessary to allow the reader to make sense of the story. If you need to present a significant amount of information, break it up into palatable chunks by using dialogue and narrative so you don't appear to be giving a lecture. One way to do this is by letting one character question another and the other respond to him. Another way is to interrupt a character's dialogue with description or activity. Remember, if your readers wanted to learn about Egyptology or meteorology in detail, they would have taken Egyptology 101 or Meteorology 101, respectively, at their local college, not read a novel. A novel is no place to get on your soapbox.[8]

INTERLOCKING EPISODES

Interlocking episodes are connected to each other by how the closing of one episode contains the beginning of the episode that follows. An interlocking episode allows the writer to get right into the next scene. Consider the following example from Bishop:

- **End of current scene.** *Eddie is almost broke. He doesn't have all the money he needs to pay off the loan-shark to whom he owes money. He's scared the loan-shark will come after him. He decides to pack a suitcase and get out of town.*
- **Beginning of next scene.** *The contents of Eddie's suitcase are scattered on the bed. Eddie is lying on the floor in a pool of blood. A loan-shark thug is standing over him, taking what money Eddie has from his billfold.*[8]

The two scenes are interlocked because before the first scene ended, a connecting factor, the suitcase, was provided to lead into the next scene.[8]

INTROSPECTION, INSIGHT, AND PERCEPTION

Although introspection, insight, and perception are related because they all three take place inside a character's head, there are marked differences.

Introspection

Introspection is *internal dialogue*; that is, a thought in a character's mind that occurs in response to some event.[8] The following is an example of introspection:

- The President of the United States pointed at Senator Archibald and denounced him as disloyal.

  General Archibald tensed. "Oh my God, he's learned of my arrangement with the opposition," he thought. He forced himself to relax. "There's no way he could have found out."

Introspection lets the reader know the exact reaction of a character's response to a circumstance. It should be kept brief so the flow of the dramatic moment is not hindered.[8,19]

Insight

An *insight* is the act of grasping the true or hidden nature of something (human behavior, a relationship, an event, a conflict) that happens after the fact. Insight may be immediate or delayed. *Immediate insight* occurs right after the fact. With *delayed insight*, a character receives knowledge at one point in the story, but only understands it fully at a later point in the story.

An insight usually is a sudden occurrence, although it may develop slowly during which time the reader follows the character's logic as he assembles it into the insight. The information on which it is based may come from one or a number of sources.[8,19] The following is an example of delayed insight:

- Samuel stands in the woods with his rifle at his side. Suddenly a shot rings out and he feels a sharp pain in his shoulder. His hunting partner rushes up to him and apologizes profusely. "My finger slipped on the trigger," he says. He rushes Samuel to the hospital where his wound is treated.

  A week later Samuel awakens, shouting, "My God, he shot me on purpose."

The value of delaying the knowledge contained in an insight is in returning a past scene into the present.[8,19]

Perception

A *perception* is a character's sudden emotionally-charged realization of the true significance of the event that is occurring before his eyes; for example, consider the following scene from Bishop:

- *Peggy heard her small son laughing. She snuck to his room. She gasped at how he methodically stabbed a raggedy-Ann doll. "My God, how he hates his sister."*[8]

Perceptions are always related to on-scene actions and characters. They should be short and succinct.[8,19]

References

1. Bokesch, Laura, Literary terms, Literary elements, Literary Terms, Academy of the Arts, http://www.orangeusd.k12.ca.us/yorba/literary_elements.htm.
2. Novel, Microsoft Encarta Encyclopedia, 2003.
3. Schwartz, Debora B., Figurative language and rhetorical devices, English Department, California Polytechnic State University, http://cla.calpoly.edu/~dschwart/engl331/figurative.html.
4. Figurative language, http://literacyproject.org/Charboneau/tunits/CurriculumBackground/Writing/FigurativeOrnamentalLanguage/FigurativeLanguage.htm.
5. Baltz, Spry, Bart Critser, Jay Adams, and Will Boynton, Figurative language, http://www.baylorschool.org/academics/english/studentwork/stover/toolbox/figlang.html.
6. Silvester, Niko, Creative writing for Teens, http://teenwriting.about.com./library/weekly/aa111102a.htm.
7. Irony, The Writing Center, Delmar College, http://www.delmar.edu/engl/wrtctr/handouts/irony.htm.
8. Bishop, Leonard, Dare to be a Great Writer, Writer's Digest Books, Cincinnati, 1992.
9. Milhorn, H. Thomas, Caduceus Awry, Writer's Showcase, New York, 2000.
10. Du Maurier, Daphne, The Birds, In The Birds and Other Stories, Penguin Books, New York, 1963.
11. Collier, Oscar and Frances Spatz Leighton, How to Write and Sell Your first Novel, Writer's Digest Books, Cincinnati, 1990.
12. Bickham, Jack M., Scene & Structure, Writer's Digest Books, Cincinnati, 1993.
13. Stoker, Bram, Signet Classics; 100th Anniversary edition, 1997 (Originally published in 1897).
14. A Pattern of Imagery In The Scarlet Letter And The Tempest, NovelGuide, http://www.studyworld.com/newsite/ReportEssay/literature/Novel%5CA_Pattern_Of_Imagery_In_The_Scarlet_Letter_And_The-81350.htm.
15. Hawthorne, Nathaniel, The Scarlet Letter, SparkNotes, http://www.sparknotes.com/lit/scarlet/.
16. Koontz, Dean, Steal the Night, Bantam Books, New York, 1999.

17. Delton, Judy, The 29 Most Common Writing Mistakes and How to Correct Them, Writer's Digest Books, Cincinnati, 1990.
18. Noble, William, Conflict, Action & Suspense, Writer's Digest Books, Cincinnati, 1994.
19. American Heritage Dictionary, Houghton Mifflin Company, Boston, 2000.

Chapter 5

Linking Episode to Series Novels

Continuing with techniques for writing genre fiction, this chapter discusses (1) linking episodes, (2) modifiers, (3) narrative, (4) point of view, (5) sentences, and (6) series novels.

LINKING EPISODE

Linking episode means to begin a new episode before the previous episode has been completely resolved. For example, consider a portion of P. D. James's *Death in Holy Orders* (2001):

- *He* (Commander Dalgliesh) *was turning to go back inside the house when he caught sight of the sidelights of a car. It had just turned from the approach road and was coming fast along the path. Within seconds he had identified Piers Tarrant's Alfa Romeo. The first two members of his team had arrived.*

The story then jumps back in time a few hours.

- *He* (Detective Piers Tarrant) *collected his Alfa Romeo from the garage space which was his by courtesy of the City of London Police, slung his murder bag in the back and set off eastward on the same route along which Dalgliesh had traveled two days before.*[1]

MODIFIERS

Modifiers are words or phrases that affect the meaning of another word or phrase, usually describing it or restricting its meaning. In general, modifiers are adjectives and adverbs.[2]

Adjectives

An *adjective* is any word that modifies a *noun* and generally answers the question "what kind of" or "which one?" For example, in the sentence "I saw a *spotted* dog," spotted is an adjective because it modifies the noun "dog," thus answering the question of "what kind of dog?"[3,4]

Nonspecific Adjectives

Nonspecific adjectives are vague references to people, circumstances, or objects. They require the reader to fill in the details or images. "Beautiful," "handsome," "lovely," "charming," "sophisticated," "pretty," and so forth are imprecise generalities that should be used only in dialogue and in introspection. Examples:

- Jake is a *handsome* man.
- Alice has *beautiful* hair and *pretty* teeth.
- Jack and Jill make a *darling* couple.
- I had a *good* meal.
- Bill is a *nice* man.

All of the adjectival details in these sentences (handsome, beautiful, pretty, darling, good, nice) are non-specific. In writing fiction, you must be specific. A scene, a character, a situation is founded on precise details. Describe the features that make Jake a handsome man instead of just saying he's handsome. Similarly, describe Alice's hair and teeth. What makes her hair beautiful and her teeth pretty? What makes Jack and Jill a darling couple, it a good meal, and Bill a nice man? Use adjectives sparingly. These words tend to weaken your writing.[3,4]

Adverbs

An *adverb* is any word that modifies a *verb*, an *adjective*, or even another *adverb*, and generally answers the questions "why," "when," "how," or "how much." For example, in the sentence "I walked along the shore *slowly*," the word "slowly" is an adverb because it answers the question of "how was I walking?"

Adverbs should not be used when precise descriptions are possible, since accurate and concise descriptions are more effective. For instance, if you say "he ran quickly," then just how fast did he run? Other adverbs, such as "very" can be replaced or omitted in most sentences. Consider the following examples:

- ***Bad.*** He was *very tall*.
- ***Better.*** He was *tall*.
- ***Even Better.*** He was *the tallest man I've ever seen*.
- ***Still Better.*** He was *an inch or two above six feet*.
- ***Still Better.*** He was *so tall he made Shaquille O'Neal look like a normal-sized man*.

A few adverbs are precise and possess the strength of adjectives. The adverb "weakly," for instance, indicates a degree of precision that adverbs often lack (*Weakly*, he rose from the bed).[5]

Nonspecific Adverbs

Nonspecific adverbs, like non-specific adjectives, require the reader to fill in the details or images. "Angrily," "wearily," "deeply," "slowly," and so forth are adverbs that are imprecise generalities. Adverbs should be used sparingly, and when they are used they should be placed at the beginning or the end of sentences.

- *Angrily*, she turned and left the room.

- *Wearily*, he slumped in the chair.
- His feelings were hurt *deeply*.
- He walked along the beach *slowly*.

Rather than nonspecific adverbs, when possible, substitute action, thereby going from the nonspecific to the specific. For example, instead of using the adverb "angrily" substitute something like "Her face stiffened and her hands clenched to small, white-knuckled fists."[3,4,6]

Overuse of Adverbs

If an adverb does not enhance the meaning of a verb, do not use it. To do so is overuse. Examples:

- He clenched his fist *tightly*.
- *Swiftly*, he raced across the street.

When someone clenches his fist, the word "clench" implies tightness. There's no such thing as a loosely clenched fist. And anyone who races across the street must do so "swiftly." There's no such thing as racing across the street slowly.

If verbs like "clenched" and "raced" are used effectively, there's no need to add emphasis. If an adverb does not enhance the meaning of a verb, don't use it. Unnecessary adverbs provide clutter.[3,4]

Valueless Modifiers

Valueless modifiers are words, including many adverbs, which make statements vague. "She was *rather* beautiful." "Rather beautiful" is vague. It means "almost beautiful" or "not quite beautiful." She is either beautiful or she isn't. The same is true for "He is *perhaps* a bit too vain." Either he is vain or he isn't. In general, avoid the following qualifiers and intensifiers: "quite," "rather, "really," "very," "kind of," "actually," "basically," "perhaps," "practically," and "virtually."[3]

NARRATIVE

Narrative, in contrast to action and dialogue, is essentially stagnant blocks of information inserted into scenes. It is "telling" as opposed to "showing" (see Chapter 7). Regardless of how engaging and well written narrative is, it won't hold a reader's attention for long because nothing is actively happening in the story. There's no action.

With narrative, the character is "on stage" telling what is happening. It is in the present and is useful when the acting out of the story (by dialogue and action) would do nothing more to further the reader's understanding of the characters or plot. However, it is information the reader needs to know to understand what is happening now or information used to foreshadow a coming major event. Because narrative is summarizing, it lacks the excitement of dramatization. Therefore you want to be certain your narrative doesn't drag down the novel's pacing.[7-10]

Consider the following example of a narrative in which a character witnesses a robbery:

- Jack entered the liquor store around 7:00 o'clock in the evening. As he was paying for a bottle of Jack Daniels at the counter he noticed a short Spanish-looking man with a beard come through the door and head toward the wine section at the back of the store. Jack left the store to get into his car. As he crossed the parking lot, he heard a loud gunshot behind him. He turned and saw the Spanish-looking man running from the store, carrying a pistol in one hand and a wad of money in the other. The man ran to the passenger side of a blue sedan parked by the curb in front of the store and got in. Then the blue sedan screeched away from the curb and sped down Oak Street. Jack went back to the store and saw the clerk sprawled out on the floor in a pool of blood. Immediately, he called 911, and then waited outside by the door for the paramedics to arrive.

The paragraph advances the story without acting it out. Jack simply tells about the robbery as it occurs. Not very exciting is it?

Narrative of dramatic situations, such as a car chase or a fight, is known a *dramatic summary.* With this, material that might take several pages of action and dialogue might take only a few paragraphs of narrative.[7]

POINT OF VIEW

The *point of view* of a literary work is the perspective from which the reader views the action and the characters. There are a number of points of view for a writer to choose from, and each has its advantages and disadvantages. Different writers have categorized them in different ways, but the system used in this book is the most common. Whatever point of view you chose to write from, choose it before you start writing. Changing your mind well into the manuscript or even after completing it can lead to a frustrating task.

The points of view most often used in fiction are *first person* (*I* pulled the trigger) and *third person* (*He* pulled the trigger.).[6,10,11,12]

First-Person Point of View

With *first-person point of view* a single character narrates the story from his point of view. You must be very careful to stay in that character's head. The reader knows exactly what the character is thinking and what he believes. However, one of the disadvantages of this point of view is that it limits the writer. The reader doesn't know anything that the character doesn't know. If a character is standing in one room, he doesn't have a clue what is happening anywhere else, and he is not allowed to know what other people are thinking, unless they tell him of course.

- I looked up at my mother. I wanted some candy, but I didn't think she would buy it for me. She looked sterner than usual today.

The child wanting the candy thinks his mother won't buy candy for him, but he doesn't know that for sure. Furthermore, he assumes that she is in a bad mood because he perceives her as appearing sterner than usual, but he really doesn't know for a fact what her mood is because he doesn't have access to what she's thinking.

Beginning writers particularly like first-person viewpoint because it's so similar to how we think as individuals, and it has the advantage of being very personal. It's easier to capture one character's thoughts and dialogue than with the other points of view.

A story written in the first person can be told by the main character, a less important character witnessing events, or a person retelling a story he was told by someone else. Whoever the viewpoint character is he can't lie about his inner feelings. The reader is inside his head, so whatever the character feels or thinks, the reader knows about it. A con man who is the viewpoint character, for instance, can con other characters, but he's not allowed to con the reader.

First-person point of view is used most often by writers of mystery novels and short stories.[10,11-13]

Third-Person Point of View

Third-person point of view is the one most commonly used for writing genre fiction. It consists of four main types: (1) Third person objective, (2) third person omniscient, (3) third person limited, and (4) third-person variable.

Third-person-objective Point of View

With the *third-person objective point of view* (also know as the *camera eye point of view*), the narrator knows only what can be heard and seen from outside the characters, much like watching a play. The thoughts and emotions of the characters are unavailable, so the story must speak for itself.

- John stood next to his mother. He scratched his head and looked up at her. Mrs. Wilson looked down at her son and moved a strand of hair from her face.

The main disadvantage of this point of view is that the lack of emotion can make the story feel cold and uninvolved.[11,12]

Third-Person-Omniscient Point of View

In a novel written from the *third-person-omniscient point of view*, the narrator, who is not one of the characters, knows everything, including what every character does and thinks. Besides knowing what's in the minds of different characters, the narrator can allow the reader to see into the future or see things that none of the characters can see. This point of view is not used as much now as it once was.[11,12]

- John stood next to his mother. He wanted to ask her to buy him some candy. Mrs. Wilson looked down at her son and moved a strand of hair from her face. She was determined not to buy him anything today, even if he did cry and carry on.

In this example, the reader sees inside John's mind. He wants his mother to buy him some candy. Also, the reader sees inside his mother's mind. She is determined not to buy it for him.

The third-person-omniscient point of view has advantages and disadvantages. Using an omniscient narrator allows a writer to be extremely clear about plot developments. This point of view also exposes the reader to the actions and thoughts of many characters and deepens the reader's understanding of the various aspects of the story. However, using an omniscient narrator can make a novel seem too artificial, because in their own lives readers don't have this all-knowing power.[11,12]

Third-Person-Limited Point of View

With *third-person-limited point of view*, as with first-person point of view, the narrator knows everything about one character, including his thoughts and feelings, but knows the other characters only through that one person. Thus, the third-person-limited narrator can only relay one character's perspective to the reader.

- John knew he shouldn't ask his mother for candy. She looked like she was in a bad mood. Maybe if he threw a tantrum she would give in.

Here we are allowed only inside John's mind, not his mother's. One problem with this point of view is the character cannot describe himself physically, unless he is describing his image in a mirror, but this has been used so much that it's gotten to be a cliché.[11,12]

Third-Person-Variable Point of View

A variant of third-person-limited point of view used by most modern-day writers of genre fiction is to allow this point of view for a single character, but allow that character to be different from scene to scene or chapter to chapter. For instance, in one scene the point of view might be that of the protagonist; in the next scene the point of view might be that of the antagonist; in a third scene it might be that of a foil character. A change in point of view is usually indicated in a published novel by skipped lines between scenes or by chapter breaks. In this way confusion is minimized. It should be noted that two or more scenes in a row can have the same viewpoint character.[11,12,14]

As an example of third-person-variable point of view, consider the first four scenes from Michael Palmer's *Silent Treatment* (1995). The point of view in the first scene is that of DEA agent Ray Santana. In the second and third scenes it is that of murder victim Ron Farrell. In the fourth scene it is that of the novel's protagonist, Dr. Harry Corbett.

- *Scene 1.* Drug Enforcement Association agent Ray Santana is gagged and lashed to a high back chair. The adhesive tape blindfold had been ripped of 10 hours earlier. Soon he was about to meet The Doctor, and soon—very soon—he believes he will be dead.
- *Scene 2 and 3.* Six years later, Ron Farrell is eating dinner in the Jade Dragon restaurant with his wife, Susan, and another couple. Suddenly, severe cramps begin knotting in his gut, accompanied almost immediately by a wave of nausea. He is transported by ambulance to the hospital were a "doctor" injects a clear liquid into the intravenous line. Ron dies.
- *Scene 4.* A year later, family practitioner Harry Corbett has chest pain while running around an indoor track. He blames it

on indigestion. Returning to the hospital he saves a patient's life in the Emergency Room. A conflict between Corbett and chief cardiologist, Casper Sardonis, becomes evident.[14]

Multiple Points of View

With multiple points of view we can only see, hear, feel, think, and know what each character sees, hears, feels, thinks, and knows at a given time. Writing from more than one point of view in the same scene means doing something like writing from Nell's view, then switching to Bill's view, then back to Nell's view, and then switching to Susan's view, and so forth.

- Nell looked at Bill. "Are you going to the party tonight?" she asked, feeling ill.

    "Not unless Susan is going." Bill responded, hoping Susan would say she wasn't going.

    "Well Susan, are you going to go?" Nell asked.

    "I'm confused," Susan said as her head started to spin.

Obviously, writing from more than one point of view in the same scene can be distracting to the reader.[11,12]

Second-Person Point of View

Second-person point of view is rarely used (*You* pulled the trigger). This point of view is extremely difficult to pull off. The reader may find it difficult to accept that he is actually doing the things the narrator says he is doing. If used, second-person point of view must be done very carefully. [6,11,15,16]

Jay McInerney successfully uses second-person point of view in his novel *Bright Lights Big City* (1984). It opens in a Manhattan night spot with the line: *You are not the kind of guy who would be at a place like this at this time of the morning.* The nameless protagonist of the novel hops from night club to night club looking for cocaine and women, with no goal higher than pursuit of pleasure.[16]

SENTENCES

Sentence Fragments

A *sentence fragment* is a dependent clause or phrase used by a writer as a complete sentence. Sentence fragments are common in writing, possibly because the writer has made a mental connection between two ideas, but has not made the connection in the writing. For instance:

- *Incorrect.* Dr. Walenburg's book is difficult. Being that it uses a lot of complex equations.
- *Correct.* Dr. Walenburg's book is difficult because it uses a lot of complex equations.
- *Incorrect.* Ed is muscular. Because he works out with weights a lot.
- *Correct.* Ed is muscular because he works out with weights a lot.

Unlike non-fiction, sentence fragments are accepted and used frequently in fiction. The best rule for fiction writers is to see if the fragment sounds right in a given text. If it does, use it.[5,17]

- *Rachael listened for the sound of footsteps. Nothing. In fact, there were none of the normal sounds of night. Absolute silence.*[5]

Sentence Variety

Since too many successive sentences of the same length can sound singsong, effective prose varies sentence length. A short sentence following a series of long ones has punch and drama. A long sentence following a series of short ones requires heightened attention from the reader.[17]

Steven Popkes' *The Egg* (1989) is the story of a boy and his alien friend who find a strange egg while exploring the wreck of the Hesparus. The opening paragraph of this work illustrates the use of sentence variety. It includes sentence fragments and simple, compound, and complex sentences of different lengths:

- *The rusty, pitted steel was soft but sharp as a knife. It was thirty or forty feet back to the beach. I didn't really want to climb back down; I didn't even have to look to convince myself. I knew how far it was. I tried rehearsing things I could say to my Aunt Sara: "Once I got that high, I had to keep going. It was too far to get back down;" or "I was just trying to go up a little ways, but I got stuck." I shook my head. Didn't wash. She'd never told me not to come here.*[18]

SERIES NOVELS

There are a number of successful *series novel* writers, including Jonathan Kellerman, who features psychologist Alex Delaware. Delaware serves as a police consultant when the demand arises for his special talents. In Patricia Cornwell's series, Virginia's Chief Medical Examiner, Kay Scarpetta, gets involved in solving one case after another. And L.A.P.D. Detective Harry Bosch is the protagonist in Michael Connelly's series.

The attractions of writing series novels include the development of characters, the ability to have their relationships change and grow slowly, and to be able to explore a set of issues from the same perspective. Also you can bring back minor characters from earlier stories and see what has happened to them, sometimes elevating them to major characters.

If you decide that you are going to write series novels, you will have to leave the plot situation in each sufficiently unresolved to spawn new novels. And if your characters are to be able to support additional stories about them, they will have to be complex.

Perhaps the major problem with a series character is the need for continuity, but with enough change to keep the reader interested. A single book in a series must stand on its own as a satisfying experience to the reader. It must also leave the door open for the next book. The reader who has read all the books in a series has to learn something new, while the reader who is seeing your characters for the first time must understand them pretty completely. This means that things can't be completely wrapped up in the resolution. If the protagonist is dead, the lovers married, or the world destroyed, that pretty well ends your idea of a series.

Other problems with series novels are that you can never have a grand finale (tying up all the loose ends) and you can eventually get tired of your character. Even Sir Conan Doyle got tired of Sherlock Holmes and tried to kill him off. Because Doyle was not able to gain success with his more serious novels and because the public outcry was so great, he had to bring Holmes back.[19-22]

Henry Kemelman found a way around the boredom problem. His series involving Rabbi David Small began with *Friday the Rabbi Slept Late*. It was followed by all the other days of the week: *Saturday, the Rabbi Went Hungry*, *Sunday, the Rabbi Stayed Home*, *Monday, the Rabbi Took Off*, *Tuesday, the Rabbi saw Red*, *Wednesday, the Rabbi Got Wet*, and *Thursday, the Rabbi Walked Out*. After all the days of the week had been written in as many novels, his series was completed.[23]

Of course, before you become a successful writer of a novel series you have to write your first novel and get it published. Keep reading.

References

1. James, P.D., Death in Holy Orders, Alford A. Knopf, New York, 2001.
2. Bishop, Leonard, Dare to be a Great Writer, Writer's Digest Books, Cincinnati, 1992.
3. American Heritage Dictionary, Houghton Mifflin Company, Boston, 2000.
4. Snyder, Hollie, Adverbs and Adjectives, Colorado Fiction Writer's Group, http://www.csfwg.org/resources/editing/adjectives.htm.
5. Schnelbach, Susan D., and Christopher Scott Wyatt, Tameri Guide for Writers, http://www.tameri.com/edit/gramerrors.html, June 15, 2005.
6. Swain, Dwight V., Techniques of the Selling Writer, University of Oklahoma Press, Norman, 1974.
7. Bickham, Jack M., Scene & Structure, Writer's Digest Books, Cincinnati, 1993.
8. Bokesch, Laura, Literary terms, Literary elements, Literary Terms, Academy of the Arts, http://www.orangeusd.k12.ca.us/yorba/literary_elements.htm.
9. Hinze, Vicki, Exposition vs. narrative, Fiction Factor: The Online

Magazine for Fiction Writers,
http://www.fictionfactor.com/guests/exposition.html.
10. Silvester, Niko, Creative writing for Teens,
http://teenwriting.about.com/library/weekly/aa111102a.htm.
11. Colburn, Jeff, Stop Teasing (Show Don't Tell), FictionAddiction.net,
http://fictionaddiction.net/articles/contributed/colburnshow.html.
12. Novel, Microsoft Encarta Encyclopedia, 2003.
13. Tritt, Sandy, Tell, Don't Show, Elements of Craft,
http://tritt.wirefire.com/tip10.html.
14. Rosenberg, Joes, Choosing your storyteller, In The Writer's Digest
Handbook of Novel Writing, Ed. By Clark, Tom, William Brohaugh,
Bruce Woods, Bill Strickland, and Peter Blocksom, Writer's Digest
Press, Cincinnati, 1992.
15. Palmer, Michael, Silent Treatment, Bantam, New York, 1995.
16. McInerney, Jay, Bright Lights Big City, Vintage, New York, 1984.
17. Grammar, Illinois Wesleyan University,
http://www.iwu.edu/~mcriley/papers/grammar.html.
18. Popkes, Steven, The Egg, Isaac Asimov's Science Fiction Magazine,
Ed. by Gardner R. Dozois, v13 # 1 January 1989.
19. Douglas, Carole Nelson, Interview of Ann Perry, At Home Online,
Mystery Readers International,
http://www.mysteryreaders.org/athome.html.
20. Kress, Nancy, Beginnings, Middles & Ends, Writer's Digest Books,
Cincinnati, 1999.
21. Ocork, Shannon, How to Write Mysteries, Writer's Digest Books,
Cincinnati, 1989.
22. Paretsky Sara, Writing a Series Character, In Writing Mysteries, Ed.
By Sue Grafton, Writer's Digest Books, Cincinnati, 1992.
23. Kemelman, Harry, Friday the Rabbi Slept Late, New Ed Books,
2002 (Originally published in 1964).

Chapter 6

Setting to Special scenes

Continuing with writing techniques, this chapter discusses (1) setting, (2) simultaneity, and (3) special scenes.

SETTING

Setting is the background of your novel on which you build your plot and characters. It involves the entire environment—time, place, experience, and mood. Although details are important, you don't want to dump all the information about your setting on your readers all at once. Let your description unfold as a character moves through the scene, rather than presenting paragraph after paragraph of narrative description. The reader most likely will skip this to get on with the action. In addition to narration, setting can be revealed through dialogue and illustrated by the characters' actions, thoughts, and speech patterns.

Consider which details your character would notice immediately and which might register more slowly. Let your character encounter those details interactively. You can describe the fragrance of flowers in a vase as the character enters the room, how a plush carpet feels under his feet as he walks across the floor, and how soft the sofa is when he sits on it. Let your character walk around a heavy marble table or blink at the bright light from a crystal chandelier. Letting your character "walk" through a description breaks the details into bite-sized pieces, and scatters those pieces throughout the scene so that the reader never feels overwhelmed or bored.[1,2,3]

Time

The *time* is important to your story. Is it just after the Civil War, during the great depression, or 50 years in the future? Different time periods have different looks and atmospheres. New York City, for instance, is a much different place today than it was in 1880. Not only has the landscape changed, but so has the feeling of being in that city.

The year in which your story takes place is not the only temporal aspect of setting to consider. How might the time of year change the physical setting—winter (snow, ice, and leafless trees), spring (bright sun-shiny days, flowers in full bloom and birds chirping), fall (cool nights, warm days, and multi-colored trees)? In general, the winter is a more gloomy time than spring, summer, or fall, but not always. Children laughing and frolicking in the snow certainly makes a happy scene.

The time period will dictate many other aspects of your story. For instance, if your plot involves tattooed characters with body piercing, then the Victorian era is a bad choice. On the other hand, if their only means of communication is through letters, they might be out of place in the world of telephones and e-mails. So research the time period you have chosen and use the most interesting things you've learned in your story.[1,3-5]

Place

Place includes the bigger picture (city, county, state, country) and the smaller picture (local businesses, characters' places of residence, streets, avenues, and other local details). The place in which your story takes place may be real or fictitious.

Real Place

The Bigger Picture. Once you have the setting in mind,

gather as much information about it as possible, whether through firsthand experience or research. Do this, even though you will not use all of the information in your story. The newspaper of the locale you chose can be a valuable resource, as well as the telephone directory. What is the history of the area? If your city has no past beyond the beginning of the story, it will seem contrived. The Internet has become a valuable resource for searching out needed details for a novel. Use it often. If you don't know how to use the Internet, take a computer course and learn how. It's too valuable a resource to miss out on.

If you decide on a place that's unfamiliar to you, visit it if possible. Drive around, learn the layout, and get a feel for the people who live there. Even if you are using a place you know, it is still a good idea to do some research. Obtain a map. It will help you keep everything in its correct location and give you a visual reference as your characters move from place to place.

What size city or town is it? What are the seasonal weather patterns of your setting? What kinds of restaurants are available? What is the crime rate, and in what part of town is the crime rate the worst? Are the streets clean and well maintained or are they full of potholes? Does the city have a popular sports team with long-standing rivalries with neighboring cities? What colleges or universities are in the town? What's the name of city bus transportation and the names of the various taxi services? And what's the primary industry? Is the city hugely dependent on this industry?

What is the make up of the population, including attitudes, mores, education levels, and ethnic and cultural backgrounds? How are outsiders and strangers treated? Are they welcomed, distrusted, or totally ignored? Are there only a few churches in the community or do church steeples dominate the landscape? What denominations are present in the town—Catholic, Lutheran, Baptist, Church of Christ? Which one dominates? Are there mosques or synagogues? What types of cars, trucks, and vans are parked in the mall parking lot?[1,3-6]

The Smaller Picture. Once you've selected the bigger setting, done your research, and organized your information you need to focus on the smaller locations within your bigger setting; that is, public buildings (city hall, police station, court house), the arts (Art Museum, Symphony House, Little Theatre), streets (Elm

Street, 43rd Avenue, Martin Luther King Drive), and detailed aspects of the location of your character's places of residence and work and the residences and places of work of the other main characters in the story.

Is the main character's place of residence a house or an apartment? What kind of trees, shrubbery, and flower beds surround it? If it's a house, how big of a house is it (tract house or mansion)? How many rooms does it have? What style is it (Georgian, Victorian, Creole plantation, colonial, tutor)? Is it packed to the rafters with furniture or sparsely furnished? What style is the furniture—early American, Queen Ann, Chippendale, Victorian? Is the residence furnished with expensive antiques or furniture bought at Sears? Is the house new or so old that generations of inhabitants have lived there? Does it creak and groan every time the wind blows?

What about the inside of the house, say a particular room? Is it spacious or small? What is the dominant color of the walls and carpet? What are the windows and curtains like? What kind of pictures are on the wall? Is the room excruciatingly tidy or appallingly messy? Sometimes you aren't so much interested in the room as a whole, but a particular object (caked blood covering a brass door handle, overturned chair)."

The details of setting can be used to create expectation. For instance, if violence is going to happen, you can use the symbols associated with violence (gun on the table, a large knife on a butcher block, a chain saw hidden behind a sofa)

If you are using a real locale, get it right. Nothing stops a story colder than putting the high school where city hall is, or having a character drive the wrong way on a one-way street, unless it's part of the story.[1,3,4,7-9]

Fictitious Place

Fictitious places are more difficult to use because the details needed to describe them aren't readily available; you have to make them all up. Is your would-be setting near water, in a desert, in the city, or way out in the country? What sort of people and animals might your characters encounter? What is the social and political environment? Does your story take place in New England, the Deep South, way out West, London, Paris, or Kabul?

Whether your novel is set in a real place or a fictitious one it is important that you make it believable and resonate through details. But above all, don't make the reader feel he is being given a geography lesson. [1,3,4,6-8]

Single versus Multiple Locations

In some stories, the setting seemingly varies all over the place. In *Caduceus Awry* (2000), action takes place from Atlanta to Valdosta to Columbus, Georgia as Dr. Mark Valentine and his companion, a mobster's ex-girlfriend, are pursued relentlessly by vicious hit man, Jesus Dimaria. The story ends up in New Orleans after Mark decides to reverse the role of hunted and hunter.[10] In other stories, the setting is confined to a single place. In *Murder on the Orient Express* (1934) by Agatha Christie, the characters are confined to a train that is stuck in a snow bank. Detective Hercule Poirot discovers that a man named Ratchett has been murdered and the murderer is still aboard the train. Poirot slowly pieces together the pieces of the mystery. At the end, he gathers all of the passengers into the dining car to expose the murderer.[11]

Experience

Be aware of whose eyes the setting is "seen" through. Your character's *experience* will directly influence what he sees. Different characters will perceive the same surroundings in very different ways, based on their familiarity with the setting. A man who was born and lived all his life in Brooklyn might describe the city differently than someone from a small town in the Mississippi Delta who is seeing it for the first time. [1,3]

Mood

The *mood* or *atmosphere* of a story is the impression it creates and the emotions it arouses in the reader through the author's choice of setting, specific details, images, and choices of words and phrases. Filtering a scene through a character's feelings can profoundly influence what the reader experiences. The same setting may portray more than one mood, depending on how the writer approaches it. For instance, it can convey the moods of contentment or gloom—or as Moira Allen puts it "blossoms or thorns."[1] The first example below illustrates contentment. The second illustrates gloom.

- Strolling through the field, Greta breathed the pleasant scents of grass and clover. Warmed by the sun, she looked up and watched clouds drifting overhead like fuzzy sheep herded by a gentle wind. An eagle glided gracefully overhead.

- In the meadow, sparse clumps of grass and clover struggled for survival among the tangle of weeds. Sweating from the intense heat, Greta glanced at the dark clouds that cast an eerie pall over the landscape. An eagle screeching loudly overhead reminded her of how hopeless she felt.

The choice of words is extremely important in setting the mood. Consider the following paragraph from Bram Stoker's famous vampire novel *Dracula* (1897) as illustrated by Moira Allen. The words and descriptive phrases (in bold) were carefully selected by Stoker to add to the feeling of apprehension and fear as the character, Jonathan Harker, gets closer and closer to Dracula's castle.[1]

- *At last there came a time when the driver went further afield than he had yet done, and during his absence the **horses began to tremble** worse than ever and to **snort and scream with fright**. I could not see any cause for it, for the **howling of the wolves** had ceased altogether; but just then the moon, sailing through the **black clouds**, appeared behind the **jagged crest of a beetling, pine-clad rock**, and by its light I saw around us a ring of wolves, with **white teeth and lolling red tongues**, with **long, sinewy limbs and shaggy hair**. They were a hundred times more **terrible in the grim silence** which held them than even when they howled. For myself, I felt a sort of **paralysis of fear**. It is only when a man feels himself face to face with such **horrors** that he can understand their true* *import.*[6,12]

The Five Senses

One way of making the setting come to life is to employ the five senses—seeing, hearing, smelling, touching, and tasting. A ribbon of light across the desk, classical music in the background, the scent of air freshener, the taste of the flat Coke, the feel of the soft carpet under bare feet all help the reader "see" the setting vividly.[1]

Seeing. Sight is used in fiction in two main ways. The first is when the author describes the way something or someone looks, and the second is when the writer describes something as seen through the eyes of a character. Your character can notice the color of the sky and the formation of the clouds, the architecture of a building, the ugliness of a bloody murder scene, the colorful array of leaves on the trees in the fall, or another character's red hair and freckled face—or the writer can describe the same.[1,13]

Hearing. We hear dogs bark, birds sing, the wind howl, crickets chirp, leaves crunch under foot, twigs crack, murder victims scream, people sing, and an almost endless array of sounds. If someone keys a car, it sounds like fingernails going down a chalkboard. We're all familiar with that sound.[1,13]

Smelling. Your character may notice the fragrance of the grass, the delicate scent of perfume, the acrid smell of newly-poured asphalt, the nauseating smell of body odor, the smell of new-car leather, the odor of a wet dog, or the putrid smell of a decaying body. We often smell something that reminds us of a familiar place or even another person. For instance, fresh bread may remind a character of the pleasant summer he spent with his grandmother.[1,13]

Touching. Touch evokes a sensory response—the roughness of a brick wall, the warmth of dad's wool sweater, the smoothness of a baby's skin, the pain from thorns, or the icy chill of a cold wind.[1,14]

Tasting. The sense of taste is the most difficult to incorporate into a setting. An example of the use of taste is *His kiss tasted like stale cigarettes.* Often the sense of taste simply doesn't belong in the scene. For the record, the four taste sensations are sweet, sour, bitter, and salty. Use them when appropriate.[1,13]

The Weather

In the real world, w*eather* happens twenty-four hours a day and seven days a week, and so it should in the world of fiction. Depending on the season, you may have rain, thunder and lightening, hail, wind, snow, freezing cold, or blistering heat. Weather is a powerful and useful tool no matter what genre you choose to write. When you neglect to insert it into your writing, you miss an opportunity to better express the prevailing mood.

Used properly and creatively, weather can have a tremendous impact on your story—a dreamy summer day with a woman you love, a raging hurricane at sea in a small ship, or all alone in a strange house in the middle of the night in a violent thunderstorm.[1,14]

With weather you can also evoke the senses, at least four of them. We see, hear, smell, and feel aspects of the weather. Consider the following attributes of weather from Keith Heidorn (The Weather Doctor):

We See

- *The ever changing vista of sky and cloud*
- *The fiery yellow, reds, and oranges of sunrise and sunset*
- *The flashes of lightning*
- *The dance of snowflakes in the wind*
- *The shapes of clouds*
- *The beauty of the rainbow*

We Smell

- *The morning after a cleansing rain*
- *The sea drifting inland on the wind*
- *The local source of pollution or a foul odor*
- *The airs of spring and fall*

We Hear

- *The wail of the wind*
- *The crack and rumble of thunder*
- *The patter of rain*
- *The rattle of hail*
- *The rustle of leaves in autumn*

We Feel

- *The bite of winter cold*
- *The heat and humidity of tropical summer*
- *The touch of the wind*
- *The coolness of rain*
- *The warmth of the sun*
- *The electricity in the air before a thunderstorm*
- *The relief of rain during a drought*[15]

Now consider the following examples from the literature of

the use of weather to set the mood:

- *Hurricane season comes when the year is exhausted. In the damp, choking heat of August and September, the days go on forever to no purpose. Hurricanes linger in the back of the mind as a threat and a promise.*[16]
- *Outside, the sun shines brightly in the cloudless azure sky, birds chirp and flit through trees, and children laugh as they play in the park.*[14]
- *There was a desert wind blowing that night. It was one of those hot, dry Santa Anas that come down through the mountain passes and curl your hair and make your nerves jump and your skin itch. On nights like that every booze party ends up in a fight.*[16]
- *Twenty miles outside Atlanta the sky darkened and the wind picked up. Only a sliver of blue sky was left in the east, and it was fading fast.*[10]

Dean Koontz uses weather exceptionally well to establish mood. In *Mr. Murder* (1993), for instance, a rain storm begins as Paige Stillwater is driving her two young children home, signifying that, unknown to her, something bad is happening at their house. As the story comes closer and closer to its climax, the weather becomes worse and worse, culminating in a heavy snowstorm in the mountains.[17]

If you do use weather in your story, make sure you use it correctly. Raindrops aren't tear-shaped, cumulus clouds aren't wispy and feathery looking, and snow isn't just frozen water.

SIMULTANEITY

Generally, you should avoid having a character do two or more things at the same time. To do so is usually impossible. For instance:

- *Incorrect.* Jack stood up and left the room.

How can Jack stand and leave the room simultaneously? Clearly he can't.

- **Correct.** Jack stood, and then left the room.

Now, having said that, there are some things a character can do simultaneously.

- Frowning, he twisted in his chair.
- Taking a puff on his cigarette, he eyed Priscilla's hourglass figure.

So the rule is: Think about what you are doing. If it is possible for a character to do two things simultaneously, it's okay to have him do them. If it's not possible, obviously you shouldn't have him do them.[18]

SPECIAL SCENES

There are many kinds of scenes in fiction. Four deserve special attention: (1) Action Scenes, (2) crowd/battle scenes, (3) death scenes, and (4) love scenes.

Action Scenes

By definition, all scenes are action scenes; however, some scenes involve more action than others, such as a car chase, a fist or gun fight, a heated argument, or an escape from a burning building. General principles of writing action scenes include those dealing with (1) surroundings, (2) introspection, (3) dialogue, (4) sounds and sight, (5) physical limitation, and (6) the unexpected.

Surroundings

Where are the characters standing in regard to each other? What are their surroundings? What might serve as cover in case it's needed? What's the lighting like—bright sunshine or morning haze? Who's observing the action—bystanders observing a fight or people in helicopters observing a car chase?

If you're going to write a chase scene, describe the landscape before the scene starts. Give the reader some idea what kind of terrain the characters will be covering. If you wait to do this until the chase is underway, you may find yourself putting the characters and the reader on hold. In other words, once the action starts try not to interrupt it. The same goes for a fight scene or any other action scene. Describe whatever part of the surroundings you wish, but do it before the actual conflict.[19]

Introspection

Action implies movement; that is, people in motion, doing something, expending energy—physical energy rather than mental or emotional energy. When your characters are in the middle of the action, they don't have time to do much thinking about what's happening. If you interrupt the action with too much introspection, you can slow the pace to a crawl or bring it to a dead stop. Action scenes aren't the place for your characters to examine their relationship or their feelings. This also means that an action scene is not a good place to bring in internal conflict. The conflict in action scenes should be external. Issues that involve introspection should be dealt with either before the action scene or afterward.

And don't forget that in action scenes you should use active-voice, grammatical constructions; that is, crisp, sharp verbs; limited use of adjectives and adverbs; no wasted words; short sentences, sentence fragments, and short paragraphs. And in general, don't use any excessive verbage.[20] For instance, you wouldn't say

- Arnold throws a punch at Wilbur. Wilbur sees Arnold's fist coming towards his nose and thinks "He's going to hit me. I should duck."

Instead, you tell it straight and to the point.

- Arnold throws a punch at Wilbur. Wilbur ducks.

Dialogue

Dialogue in action scenes usually should be short and to the point. People in the middle of a fight or chase have neither the time nor the breath to waste on snappy commentary. The exception to this rule is when two opponents are circling each other in some form of hand to hand combat looking for weaknesses.[19]

Sounds and Sights

In an action scene, what do your characters hear—the thup of a bowstring, the chatter of automatic gunfire, the swish of a knife blade? And what do they see—the steely look in his opponent's eyes, the cavalry charging over the hill?   Are combatants surrounded by noise, or is it so quiet that all they can hear is their breathing and hearts beating?[19]

Physical Limitation

Your characters, like real people, have physical limitations. People do get tired during a fight—so should your characters. Not only may they become fatigued if the fight continues very long, they may become short of breath as well. Is your character in good or poor physical condition? The better shape he's in the longer he can go without getting fatigued or short of breath. Also, a punch hurts. Characters should respond in some manner to the pain of a solid blow. Blood getting in a character's eyes is going to partially blind him. This will affect how he functions in the fight until he gets the blood cleared. Adrenaline may help to diminish the effects of pain and fatigue during the fight, but when the end of the fight comes, so will the pain and the fatigue.[19]

The Unexpected

Action allows you to show the unexpected resolve of characters who might normally be more intellectually than physically inclined. What hidden weakness does your big, strong, physical character have that might come out in an action sequence? What inner strength does your protagonist have? [19]

Crowd/Battle scenes

Any scene that has scope and involves multiple characters,

including major and secondary characters, should be structured though the cinematic film technique of *four lenses*: (1) A *panoramic view* of the battle scene, (2) a *pocket view* (closer view of a *pocket* of the battle), (3) a *close-up view* of the viewpoint and/or secondary characters' parts in the battle, and finally (4) an *interior view* (interior dialogue) of the major character. This approach can be used for any crowd scene. A battle is a type of crowd scene in which the action is much greater than in most crowd scenes, although crowds can be pretty rowdy, and fights can break out in crowds.[7]

The following is adapted from an article by David G. Woolley in which he uses a Book of Mormon battle scene to illustrate the four lenses technique:

Panoramic View. First show the sweeping *panoramic view* of the battle field. Include the strategic positioning of armies and geographic descriptions that may impact the course and outcome of the battle. Describe what the foot soldiers, archers, swordsmen, horsemen, lama riders, sling shooters, battering rammers, oil fire throwers, ladder carries, tower watchers, city gate keepers, and generals are doing. Hold your writing at this level long enough to establish the reality of the battle and the strategies involved.

Pocket View. When you move to the *pocket view*, focus on some secondary characters familiar to the reader. You may want to include a bit of dialogue from these characters; or better yet, narrate the dialogue that the viewpoint character can hear amidst the sounds and cries of war. When you narrate the dialogue you are free to interpret the character's words, describe the quality of the character's cry for help, or give meaning to the directions to push back the ladders on the south wall.

Close-up View. At this point in the battle consider showing a *close up view* of the protagonist in a sharply detailed struggle. Hold on to his physical actions long enough to fix his situation in the reader's mind.

Interior View. Once you've achieved the reality of your protagonist's situation you can very subtly, and for very brief snippets of writing, move to the *interior view*. Don't slow the action down by offering extended introspection, and don't encumber the character's thoughts by using speech tags like "he thought" or "he wondered." Simply mix the action with the thoughts. If your character is wondering something, then turn it into a question as indicated by italics in the following:

- Moroni raced across the clearing and jumped behind a sandstone outcrop. *Did he lose them on the last cliff?*[21]

If your character is simply thinking something, but not wondering it, then simply place it into their consciousness like this:

- Moroni raced across the clearing and jumped behind a sandstone outcrop. *There was time to dress his wound. Lamanite bows didn't have the strength to reach this far up the summit.*[21]

At this point in your battle scene you can reveal the protagonist's thoughts, feelings, strategy for winning, or his hopelessness at the possibility of losing the battle or his life. You can reveal his courage in the face of insurmountable odds or his cowardice in hiding from the ugliness of genocide of the Nephite nation. You can also reveal his mission or purpose in the battle.

You should consider carefully planting interior dialogue amidst the viewpoint character's actions in battle, essentially mixing the close-up view and the inner view into a seamless, tight-fitting whole. But don't spend to long on the interior view. To do so would slow down the drama of the battle. Here is an example of the close-up view with an interior view carefully placed within it:

- Setti raced across the open field between the tree lines. He jumped the corpse of a fallen comrade and kept driving his legs faster. Two arrows snapped dirt at his feet. He gripped the mail pouch at his waist and kept running. *He couldn't die, not until he delivered the message from their spies to general Moroni.* The soldiers behind him shouted encouragement. His breath burst from his lungs. Another arrow cut the air near his head. Pain slashed across his neck. *Cursed stone. Why did he let the sling shooters get a bead on his path?* He cut to the side and veered back again, running toward the general's outpost.[21]

Now return to the pocket lens involving familiar secondary characters, even dropping the inner lens into them to reveal bits of information for future scenes. Then use any of the four lenses you feel suitable for keeping the battle ongoing.[21]

Death Scenes

From time to time deaths occur in fiction, more often in some genres than others. There are two types of death scenes as described by Leonard Bishop: (1) Off-scene deaths and (2) on-scene deaths.

Off-Scene Deaths

The *off-scene death* stresses the significance and effects of the death on family members, lovers, and friends. The characters in the story are viewed after the brunt of the effects of the death has already been experienced. The characters may still be reacting with grief, but not at their original intensity. They recount their experiences with the death, have individual thoughts (good or bad) about the deceased, and share memories. The character who died is not present.[7]

On-Scene Deaths

The *on-scene death* takes place with the character who is to do the dying present and suffering. Love, hate, fear, greed, lust, cunning, and revenge all can occur in a prolonged death scene. A scene in which someone is dying is in the here and now always carries more impact than passive off-scene deaths.

In novels in which characters dominate the plot, rather than the other way round, the death scene of a major character should become a dramatic scene, with much heart rendering and soul purging and the exchange of important, even astonishing, information.[7]

Love Scenes

According to Deirdre Savoy, the three basic elements of a love scene are (1) place (What is the couple's location?), (2) emotion (Where are they in their relationship to one another?), and (3) action (How do they kiss, caress, and respond to each other sexually?). You should blend these elements into a cohesive scene that builds on the plot you have already established. Of these elements, emotion is the most important. It is the glue that bonds the love scene together.[23]

Love can take a lot of forms (burning love, lost love, memories of a lover who is deceased, a woman or man with an insatiable sexual appetite, a female gigolo or dominatrix, male or female love with a much older or younger person, sexually wicked male or female, forbidden love, homosexual or lesbian love, men as sex objects, teenaged love, geriatric love, and so forth).

How do the characters feel about coming together in the scene? Are they shy, insecure, brazen, driven primarily by lust, or culminating a love they already acknowledge? The sexual tension is more important than sex itself; that is, the buildup, the desire, and the longing are the elements that build up to the actual scene so that when the love scene finally does take place it's more meaningful and exciting.

So, how many love scenes should you have in your novel and how steamy should they be? The answer is as many as you need and as steamy as they need to be to advance your plot or provide new and interesting information about your characters. However, there are some tendencies that depend on the genre. In the past, a happy ending for a cowboy was to ride off into the sunset, leaving the woman behind. Mysteries were built on reason and intellect, and since love is only an emotion the two didn't co-exist. Things have changed. Nowadays it is fashionable to have a little interest in love and sex even in westerns and mysteries. It makes characters more contemporary and realistic. Steamy love scenes would, of course, be out of place in novels for teenagers and in Christian novels.

In general, westerns and mysteries still tend to have the least sex, and romance novels have the most (the hotter and steamier the better). In a spy thriller, a lot of sex helps. James Bond without women would be like Detective Colombo without his wrinkled raincoat.[7,22,23]

Effective Love Scene

For a love scene to be effective it must have a number of

characteristics as suggested by David Groff: (1) It must be central to the story and advance the plot, (2) it must be shaped to maintain the novel's conflict and suspense, (3) it must be consistent with the story characters, and (4) its language must be consistent with that of the novel.[24]

Central to the Story and Advance the Plot. You should never write a love scene just for the sake of sex thrilling the reader or to provide a break in the action. The purpose of a love scene is to change lives and relationships, to cause or resolve conflicts, and to reveal depths in characters that cannot be revealed in any other way. It is a situation of physical, emotional, and intellectual pressure. As a result of these changes, opportunities are opened for changes in the story. If you can eliminate the love scene and not change the story, then you don't need the love scene.[23,24]

Shaped to Maintain the Novel's Conflict and Suspense. A love scene, like any other scene, has a rising action, a complication, a climax, and a final resolution. Therefore, it is shaped to maintain the novel's conflict and suspense.[24]

Consistent with the Story Characters. The scene should be consistent with the characters' personalities. The characters should act in ways consistent with the attitudes and emotions you've given them prior to the love scene. A character, male or female, who is lively and interesting with clothes on shouldn't automatically become cruel and unbelievable in bed. And don't forget that this is the age of AIDS and safe sex. There is something unrealistic about two characters who have just met jumping in bed without any concern for safety and birth control.[24]

Language Consistent with the Novel. More than any other type of scene, you must be careful to create strong, precise, and vivid phrases when writing about love. The language should neither be overly pornographic nor overly modest.

There are many ways to write metaphorically about love and sex, but be careful not to make them sound too corny, and use them sparingly. Remember, when it comes to sex, the reader's imagination should be allowed to do a great deal of the work. Gypsy Rose Lee is reported to have said that "A glimpse of black net stocking is sexier than a bare leg could ever be." When dealing with a love scene, you are better off referring to the entire body rather than the specific parts in use.[24]

Ineffective Love Scene

Groff also discusses five things that make a love scene ineffectual: (1) being over clichéd, (2) being too clinical, (3) being too physical, (4) having too many points of view, and (5) failure to use dialogue.[24]

Over Clichéd. Groff intentionally shows us how a love scene should not be written:

- *Dirk clasped Amber's hair in one broad fist and felt her bosom heave beneath him, his manhood readying itself for the awesome challenge. Her lips parted, dewily, and she whispered breathlessly to him, "I love you, come to me." Her arms locked across his slick back, she squirmed beneath him, gasping. Later, once the stars had exploded and sky had gone black and then all bright, she lay exhausted against his torso, wishing this moment could last forever.*[24]

Bosoms should not heave; men do have manhoods, but not in love scenes; lips shouldn't part; people shouldn't be breathless and announce their love for each other; stars shouldn't explode; and the sky shouldn't perform tricks. Also, stay away from crashing waves, lightning, dynamite, and runaway railroad trains, and don't use words or phrases like "his manhood bobbed up and down like a flagpole" or "their love exploded into infinity." I think you get the idea.[24,25]

Too Clinical. A love scene is not a collection of gyrating body parts. It shouldn't be a play by play account of every physical action. Clinical love scenes in which the reader is privy to all the body parts (breasts, nipples, clitoris, vagina, penis, testicles, anus) fail when they violate the overall tone of the novel in an attempt to give the reader a thrill for no dramatic purpose.

The opposite of the clinical love scene is what Groff calls *the kiss-to-cigarette approach*. After the first kiss there's a skipped line (scene break) and suddenly both individuals are smoking cigarettes. The implication is that sex did occur. The emotional exchanges that took place between the characters is given as passive information after the fact, so the impact of the emotion is lost. Before you use the kiss-to-cigarette approach ask yourself if this best serves your work. If not, dig in and write a really good love scene.[7,24]

Too Physical. A love scene in which a woman is taken by force by her male partner is an outdated social and sexual attitude that good fiction writers nowadays avoid. Romance novels known as *bodice rippers* once used this technique. Rape, of course, does occur in novels. The act is best done as an off-scene presentation.[24]

Too Many Points of View. How many points of view should you have in a love scene? Hopefully, you only have an option of one or two, but these days who knows. I recommend one. First, you'll confuse and possibly annoy readers if you use more than that because it will be difficult for them to keep up with who is speaking. Second, it's not realistic to give both characters' reactions to every single thing. If you write with one point of view, after the love scene you can give the pertinent reactions of the other character.[25]

Failure to Use Dialogue. Using dialogue within a love scene can heighten the erotic edge and contribute to the advancement of the plot or to character development. On the other hand, you may consider certain words too crude, rude, or shocking to use in a novel. But what if those words fit the character's personality? What if it's something you know he would say? If so, do use words that would be appropriate for the character, even if it makes you a little uncomfortable. Don't worry about what your mother will think.[25]

References

1. Allen, Moira, Four ways to bring setting to life, Writing-World.com, http://www.writing-world.com/fiction/settings.shtml, 1999.
2. Elements of fiction, VirtuaLit : Interactive Fiction Tutorial, http://bcs.bedfordstmartins.com/virtualit/fiction/elements.asp.
3. Kay, Kim, It's your world: Setting your novel: It's Your Novel, Suite101.com, http://www.suite101.com/article.cfm/novel_writing/13665/1, December 15, 1998.
4. Kelman, Judith, How to write and publish a novel, http://www.jkelman.com/fiction/index.html.
5. Morrell, Jessica Page, The power of place, http://www.writing-life.com/fiction/place.html.
6. Silvester, Niko, Glossary, Creative Writing for Teens, http://teenwriting.about.com/library/glossary/blglossary.htm.

7. Bishop, Leonard, Dare to be a Great Writer, Writer's Digest Press, Cincinnati, 1992.
8. Hart, Geoff, Houses are people too: The structure of a literary device, Writing-World.com, http://www.writing-world.com/fiction/house.shtml, 2002.
9. Noble, William, Conflict, Action & Suspense, Writer's Digest Books, Cincinnati, 1994.
10. Milhorn, H. Thomas, Caduceus Awry, Writer's Showcase, San Jose, 2000.
11. Christie, Agatha, Murder on the Orient Express, Berkley; Reissue edition, 2000 (Originally published in 1934).
12. Stoker, Dram, Dover Publications, Mineola, N.Y., 2000 (Originally published in 1897).
13. Duncan, Apryl, Heighten your senses in writing, FictionAddiction.net, http://fictionaddiction.net/articles/senses.html.
14. Estell, Larissa, Partly Cloudy, Scattered Showers: Setting the Scene with Weather, http://www.writing-world.com/fiction/weather.shtml.
15. Heidern, Keith, Sensing the Weather, The joys of weather watching, http://www.islandnet.com/~see/weather/eyes/sense.htm, January 1, 2000.
16. Smith, Julie, Background, Location, and Setting, In Writing Mysteries (Ed. By Sue Grafton), Writer's Digest Books, Cincinnati, 1992.
17. Koontz, Dean, Mr. Murder, Penguin Group, New York, 1994.
18. Swain, Dwight V., Techniques of the Selling Writer, University of Oklahoma Press, Norman, 1974.
19. Action Scenes, Sqidge.org, http://www.squidge.org/mice/action.txt
20. Watson, Mary, Writing action scenes, http://members.aol.com/lynnturner/action.htm, 1995.
21. Woolley, David G., Book of Mormon Battle Scenes, LatterDayAuthors.com, http://www.latterdayauthors.com/fiction/dgw+battles.htm, March 1, 2005.
22. Ocork, Shannon, How to Write Mysteries, Writer's Digest Books, Cincinnati, 1989.
23. Savoy, Deirdre, Writing love scenes that sizzle, http://www.dsavoy.com/text/scenes_that_sizzle.htm, October 25, 2005.
24. Groff, David, How to write believable love scenes, In The Writer's Digest of Handbook of Novel Writing, Ed. By Tom Clark, William Brohaugh, Bruce Woods, Bill Strickland, and Peter Blocksom, Writer's Digest Books, Cincinnati, 1992, Pp 164-170.
25. Flynn, Connie, Creating sensual tension, The Romance Club, http://www.theromanceclub.com/writers/articles/art0023.htm, 1997.

Chapter 7

Style and Tone to Verb Strength

Continuing with writing techniques, this chapter discusses (1) style and tone, (2) symbolism and allegory, (3) telling versus showing, (4) time, (5) transitions, and (6) verb strength.

STYLE AND TONE

Style

Style in fiction refers to the writer's choice of words and phrases he uses in sentences and paragraphs, along with dialogue and pacing, to construct the story. One writer may use simple sentences and straightforward vocabulary, while another may use difficult vocabulary and elaborate sentence structures. Thus a story's style could be described as having simple sentence structures and a low range of vocabulary or being richly detailed and flowing.

Style can be broken down into three types: (1) Simple, (2) complex, and (3) mid-style.

Simple style uses common words and simple sentences, even if the situation described is complex. The effect of simple style is to present facts to the reader without appealing to the reader's emotions directly. Instead, the writer relies on the facts themselves to affect the reader.

Complex style uses long, complex sentences that contain many ideas and descriptions. The writer uses lyrical passages to create the desired mood, whether it is one of joy, sadness, confusion, or any other emotion.

Mid-style is a combination of the simple and complex styles. It can give a neutral tone to the work, or it can provide two different effects by contrast.

Sometimes writers carry a single style throughout an entire work. Other times, the style may vary within a work.[1,2,3]

Tone

Tone is the author's attitude, stated or implied, toward the subject of a novel. An author's tone can be revealed through a choice of words and details. Some possible attitudes are pessimism, optimism, earnest, serious, bitter, humorous, contempt, affection, and joyful.[1,2]

SYMBOLISM AND ALLEGORY

Symbolism

Symbolism involves a person, place, or object which has a meaning in itself, but suggests other meanings as well. Travel, for instance, can represent life, black can represent death, an American flag can represent patriotism, motherhood and apple pie can represent goodness, and a lion can symbolize courage. For Captain Ahab in Herman Melville's *Moby Dick* (1851), the white whale symbolizes evil.[1,4]

Allegory

Allegory is a story in which characters and events form a system of symbolic meanings. It is the presentation of a subject disguised as something else. A common kind of allegory is a narrative in which abstractions, such as love, hate, or fear, are made concrete, perhaps embodied in characters such as *Mr. Hate* or *Ms. Spendthrift* or landscape features such as the *Valley of Fear*.

Allegory can generally be read on two levels—that of the surface narrative and that of the deeper level, which is often moralistic. George Orwell's *Animal Farm* (1946) is a story in which each animal stands for a specific individual from the Russian Bolshevik revolution.[1,5,6]

TELLING VERSUS SHOWING

The first rule of writing is said to be "show, don't tell." But if you showed everything, your novel would run thousands of pages and readers would become bored and stop reading; that is if you could get it published, which is highly unlikely. So what do you do? There are times when action that could be shown would be more interesting if told. At other times, the content of what is being told would be more dramatic if shown. You must decide what information the reader needs and in what form (telling or showing). In general, sequels (valleys of contemplation) are places to tell and scenes (mountains of action) are places to show.[7,8]

Telling

The following statement is one of telling:

- Jimmy was nervous as he approached Susan's house. Her father answered the door. As Jimmy stepped into the house her father blocked his path.

Clearly, the statement conveys information, but it's not very exciting. Vicki Hinze gives five reasons to tell: (1) to convey necessary information; (2) to create emotional distance; (3) to cue the reader; (4) to establish setting, tone, and emotional impact; and (5) to smoothly transition.[9]

Convey Necessary Information. There are times when background information is essential for the reader to grasp the significance of something currently occurring in the story. When this situation arises, narrative can be the best means of effectively conveying that information in a minimum of space, thereby negating a long disruption in the forward momentum of the plot.[9]

Create Emotional Distance. Sometimes telling information about an event is necessary for the reader to understand conflict that the writer does not want the reader to experience firsthand, such as a rape. Narrative allows you to convey the event and yet maintain emotional distance between the event and the reader.[9]

Cue the Reader. Frequently, characters say one thing when they mean something else, or the character's perception of something is different from the facts. In these situations, narrative can be effective for cueing the reader in to the actual intent versus the perception of the event.[9]

Establish Tone and Emotional Impact. Narrative is vital to creating the details the writer selects to interest the reader in the scene. In doing so, it can assist in conveying tone and emotional impact. For example, if a man has just lost his wife and he's mourning, he isn't apt to notice bright, sunny, or airy objects. He's far more apt to notice those aligning with his current emotional mood, which is depressed, dark, and gloomy. Narrative allows the writer to use details of setting which convey those emotions. In doing so, the writer sets the appropriate tone and the emotional mood of the character.[9]

Smoothly Transition. At times, the writer skips ahead in time or flashes back to previous times. The writer also takes the reader from one setting to another. The most common means of accomplishing these changes is by incorporating narrative transitions. A transition is simply a bridge that fills the gap between two scenes, and is discussed later in this chapter.[9]

Showing

To make the previous "telling" example more interesting you might consider "showing" the situation.

- As Jimmy approached Susan's house the tightening knot in his stomach felt as big as a basketball.

  Her father answered the doorbell. "Oh, it's you," he said.

  Jimmy stepped inside the door and stopped abruptly. Her father stood in the foyer blocking his path—his dark eyes staring straight at Jimmy. Sweat soaked the armpits of Jimmy's shirt and trickled down the sides of his chest. He was glad to have on his leather jacket to hide it. The man cleared his throat.

"Here it comes," Jimmy thought. "He's going to tell me I can't see Susan anymore." His mouth went so dry it felt like he had just swallowed a wad of cotton. His stomach began to cramp. He said a silent prayer, hoping he wouldn't need to make a mad dash to the bathroom.

In the "telling" example, the reader is expected to do all the work, while in the "showing" example the work has been done by the writer.[8,10]

TIME

There are two kinds of time—chronological and emotional. One you measure with a clock; the other with the limbic system of the brain. Chronological time is objective. There are 60 seconds in every minute and 60 minutes in every hour. Emotional time, on the other hand, is subjective. In no two of us is it the same. In pleasant situations, such as talking with a pretty girl, emotional time moves quickly. In unpleasant situations, such as being forced to sit on a tack, emotional time passes very slowly. What causes this wide variation in emotional time you might ask? The answer is tension—fear that something will happen or won't happen, anxiety over two extremely important choices, physical pain, or deep depression over a love gone wrong. All of these slow emotional time to a crawl. The more tense the situation, the longer the emotional time and the more words you give it—words that express the tension.[11] Character emotions are discussed in Chapter 13.

TRANSITIONS

Transitions are bridge passages between scenes in a story. Without transitions, *bumps* seem to appear between scenes. For a transition to be effective, it should be short, logical, and unobtrusive. The purpose is to carry the reader smoothly from one scene to the next without confusion. The new scene needs to establish as quickly as possible (1) when it is occurring, (2) where it takes place, (3) who the viewpoint character is, (4) and how he got there. Chapter breaks usually involve bigger changes in the plot than a simple transition.[12]

Simple Transitions

The most famous simple transition of them all is "Meanwhile back on the farm." Simple transitions can be made a number of ways, including: (1) activity, (2) appearance, (3) emotion, (4) foreshadowing, (5) location, (6) objects, (7) seasons, (8) sound, (9) telephones, (10) time, and (11) weather.

Activity. *Swinging his tennis racket in anticipation, Frank loped down to the court where Ruth waited for him, her brief white dress gleaming in the sun. Three sets later, they were warm and pleasantly exhausted, ready for a shower and a leisurely dinner.*[13]

Appearance. Jeremy saw his father off at the airport 20 years ago. Now his father returns. *Jeremy remembered his father as he looked the day he waved goodbye to him at the airport—a tall, slim, dark-haired man, the light of adventure in his eyes. Surely it could not be his father coming toward him now. Even twenty years could not have changed him into this white-haired, stooped old man with faded eyes. Jeremy felt a little sick as he walked toward him and said, "Hello, father."*[13]

Emotion. William knew he would never get over Elizabeth's death. Gradually his sadness dissipated; new hope and a growing sense of purpose stirred within him. Then one morning he woke up happy.

Foreshadowing. *His orders were to meet his contact and make the transfer on the Orient Express. At the train station, he spotted his contact.*[12]

Location. Jan placed Ted's picture upside down on the table and began to cry. Meanwhile, in Atlanta Ted kissed Edna passionately.

Objects. If it's an object that changes with time (a snow bank, a flower, a burning candle) it can be used to show elapsed time. If the objects themselves do not undergo a change, they can still be used to show the passing of time.

Charles would surely return in a few minutes, Mr. Thompson assured himself. He picked up the book, intending to read only a few pages, but he became so engrossed he was half way through the volume when he became aware of the chiming hall clock. Midnight, and Charles still hadn't come back.[13]

Seasons. The icy wind whipped around outside. Icicles hung form the huge limbs of the sycamore tree in the front yard. God, he hated winter. Spring came at last and he saw the first robin.

Sound. Shortly after the party started next door, Edna had to close her window so she could hear her TV. By bed time, no volume setting was high enough to hear the TV over the roar of the crowd.

Telephones. Barbara paced the floor, trying to make a decision. "Stan," she thought. "Stan could tell her what to do." She reached for the telephone. In an apartment across town, Stan put his drink down and reached for the phone. "Don't stay on the phone too long," Anna cooed, stroking Stan's hair.

Time. Walter kissed her and knew in his heart that she was the woman for him. Three years later he couldn't stand her guts.

Weather. That morning John planned an entire day of working in the garden. Why not? It was a beautiful day. By noon, the sun had vanished and a cold rain fell.

Jump-Cut Transitions

The most common way to transition from one scene to the next in a modern-day genre novel is to use a *jump-cut transition*. These are big changes in scenes. In published novels, they are indicated by a blank line or symbol, such as * * *, between the two scenes. Jump-cut transitions are most often used to switch to a parallel plot or subplot and back.

Common practice is to change the point of view following a transition between scenes, but this is not a hard and fast rule. These scene jumps are often places where readers stop or pause in their reading of a novel.[15] Consider the following action sequence:

- Down six points with 30 seconds left on the clock, Jack broke through the line at mid-field with the football tucked under his left arm. He cut to the right, stiff-armed a linebacker, and then headed up field. One player to beat—the other team's All America safety who had put him in the hospital the last time the teams met. "We're going to win. We're going to win," Jack's mother yelled, waving her arms wildly. Jack's father didn't answer. His fists were clenched and his head was bowed in silent prayer.

Notice that there are parts of two separate scenes—one from Jack's viewpoint and another from his mother's viewpoint. Bunched into one paragraph they are confusing and the impact from either one is blunted. Now, consider the same two partial scenes separated by a line break:

- Down six points with 30 seconds left on the clock, Jack broke through the line at mid-field with the football tucked under his left arm. He cut to the right, stiff-armed a linebacker, and then headed up field. One player to beat—the other team's All America safety who had put him in the hospital the last time the teams met.

  "We're going to win. We're going to win," Jack's mother yelled, waving her arms wildly. Jack's father didn't answer. His fists were clenched and his head was bowed in silent prayer.

Jump-cut transitions can be used in combination with other techniques to move from one scene to another. For instance, in *Isle of Dogs* (2001), Patricia Cornwell uses jump-cut transitions in combination with ending one scene with a statement and then beginning the next scene with a statement that contains the same or similar thought. One of many examples from her novel is:

- *"Find out where the state police airport is," Smoke ordered his road dogs. "Look it up on the GPS."*

  Unique didn't need a GPS to find her way around, nor did she have one. Smoke did not supply her with special weapons and equipment, although she could get anything she wanted from him.[14]

Chapter Breaks

Chapters usually consist of three, four, or more scenes, so where should you break for a chapter? The answer is simple. Always end your chapters at a point where the reader will have trouble putting the book down, and that's also the best place to change viewpoint—at the moment of a disaster-ending scene. The reader will eagerly turn the page to see what happens in the next chapter.

The next best place to end a chapter probably is right in the middle of the conflict. The goal is set, the fight starts, the reader is excited about the action—and then you break the chapter.

Other good places to end a chapter are with your character in the dilemma stage thinking "There's no way out." Similarly you can end a chapter just as the decision is about to be made or at the beginning of the new action, before conflict starts again.[12,15,16]

VERB STRENGTH

Active versus Passive Voice

Verbs can be *active* or *passive*, thus giving rise to active and passive tenses.

- **Active Verb.** He *tested* the *water* by sticking his big toe into it.
- **Passive Verb.** The water *was tested* by sticking his big toe into it.

In much academic writing, the passive voice is preferred to the active one because it depersonalizes the writing. It removes "I" and "we" and focuses the reader's attention on the information rather than on the person carrying out the action. In fiction, however, the active form is much preferred over the passive one. In fact, in fiction you should use the passive form only if it more precisely states what you want to say or avoids verbosity. For instance, in the following example from Niko Silvester, passive voice is preferred because it places the emphasis is on the lion, not on the pepper spray.

- *Active. The pepper spray **repelled** the lion.*
- *Passive. The lion **was repelled** by the pepper spray.*[17]

Strong Verbs versus Weak Verbs

Verbs vary in strength for strong verbs to weak ones, generally classified as (1) strongest, (2) next to strongest, (3) intermediate, (4) next to weakest, and (5) weakest. Verbs are strongest when they are precise and concrete. *Concrete* is the quality of expressing real movement; in other words, strong verbs tell us exactly what is done in real action. They should be used as much as possible when writing fiction.

The weaker verbs express less real-world action. At the bottom are the being verbs which express no action, and should be used least often when writing fiction.[22] Lars Eighner gives an excellent description of the various levels of verb strength.[18]

Doing Verbs (Strongest). Doing verbs include verbs like "shot," "walked," "detonated," "grinned," "strangled," "sang," and so forth. Obviously, some of them are more exciting than others. Strengthening your story is a matter of learning to express what happens with strong, active verbs.

- Bill *vomited* on the floor.

Saying Verbs (Next to Strongest). *Saying verbs* are "said" and "asked." These are perfectly good for most dialogue, and you generally do not improve on them by making them "shouted," "whispered," or "inquired" just for the sake of variation. You strengthen dialogue by promoting much of it to actions; that is, when possible you show the reader the action rather than letting the characters talk about it.

- "I *feel* sick," Bill said.

Thinking and Feeling Verbs (Intermediate). *Thinking and feeling verbs* are much like saying verbs, but a little weaker because they don't happen in the real world; they happen only in a character's head.

120

- Bill *felt* sick.

Like saying verbs, feeling and thinking are best when they express the action, rather than reflecting or commenting upon it. "Suspected" is a good thinking or feeling verb because it is an action that occurs in the mind. "Recalled" and "reflected upon" are not as good because they are employed merely to convey some bit of information about the past.

Being-done-to Verbs (Next to Weakest). *Being-done-to verbs* are verbs in the passive voice. They still express a bit of action, although in a backhanded way. In addition, the passive voice tends to create a fatalistic tone because the world is always doing things to characters. In other words, if people take advantage of kind-hearted Mary that is fine, but avoid having Mary being taken advantage of.

- Bill *was made sick* by the tuna salad.

Being Verbs (Weakest). *Being verbs* are the weakest. Ideally, you should show Bill doing something instead of telling us he is in a state of some sort.[18]

- Bill *was* sick.

References

1. Bokesch, Laura, Literary terms, Literary elements, Literary Terms, Academy of the Arts,
   http://www.orangeusd.k12.ca.us/yorba/literary_elements.htm.
2. Elements of fiction, VirtuaLit : Interactive Fiction Tutorial,
   http://bcs.bedfordstmartins.com/virtualit/fiction/elements.asp.
3. Novel, Microsoft Encarta Encyclopedia, 2003.
4. Baltz, Spry, Bart Critser, Jay Adams, and Will Boynton, Figurative language,
   http://www.baylorschool.org/academics/english/studentwork/stover/toolbox/figlang.html.
5. Bliss, Curtis Nehring, Elements of fiction, Introduction to Literature,
   http://www.hcc.cc.il.us/online/engl111/fiction.htm, August 3, 1998.
6. Orwell, George, Animal Farm, SparkNotes,
   http://www.sparknotes.com/lit/animalfarm/summary.html.

7. Bishop, Leonard, Dare to be a Great Writer, Writer's Digest Press, Cincinnati, 1992.
8. Tritt, Sandy, Tell, Don't Show, Elements of Craft, http://tritt.wirefire.com/tip10.html
9. Hinze, Vicki, Exposition vs. narrative, Fiction Factor: The Online Magazine for Fiction Writers, http://www.fictionfactor.com/guests/exposition.html.
10. Colburn, Jeff, StopTeasing (Show Don't Tell), FictionAddiction.net, http://fictionaddiction.net/articles/contributed/colburnshow.html.
11. Swain, Dwight V., Techniques of the Selling Writer, University of Oklahoma Press, Norman, 1974.
12. Hamper, Rich, Transitions, The Dimension, http://home.comcast.net/~rthamper/html/body_transitions-rth.html, September 3, 2003.
13. Kent, Janet, Transitions, Romance Writing Tips, http://groups.msn.com/RomanceWritingTips/elements1.msnw?action=get_message&mview=0&ID_Message=64&LastModified=4675408830566568349.
14. Cornwell, Patricia, Isle of Dogs, G. P. Putnam's Sons, New York, 2001.
15. Bickham, Jack M., Scene & Structure, Writer's Digest Books, Cincinnati, 1003.
16. Noble, William, Conflict, Action & Suspense, Writer's Digest Books, Cincinnati, 1994.
17. Silvester, Niko, Creative Writing for Teens, http://teenwriting.about.com/library/weekly/aa111102a.htm.
18. Eighner, Lars, Online writing course, How can I identify weak verbs, Writing Course, http://www.io.com/~eighner/writing_course/oldquestions/qa050152.html.

Chapter 8

Plot

*P*_{lot} is the sequence of events in a work of fiction as the author chooses to arrange them. *Story,* on the other hand, is the sequence of events in the order they occur. Therefore, the events as laid out in the plot may not be in the same order that they happen in the story. This is because writers use devices like flashbacks and flash forwards so that the plot, unlike the story, does not proceed in a chronological order.

A story concerns someone's reactions to what happens, his emotions, his ambitions, his drives, his inner conflicts and the force that opposes him and attempts to prevent him from achieving his goal.[1,2]

PLOT STRUCTURE

The *plot* of a story is a chain of events, each event the result of some prior events and the cause of some subsequent events. Each character has a personal agenda, modified by conflict or the agendas of others. The protagonist doesn't get everything his way any more than the antagonist does; each keeps thwarting the other, who must then improvise under pressure. This continues until finally one gains the upper hand. Plot gets the reader involved by revealing events, developments, connections, and hints that create tension and a need to know what happens next.

Plot brings the reader into the story at the moment the status quo is threatened. The closer the opening scene is to the precipitating event, the more force and emergency it will have. The reader should find characters in difficulty within the first chapter, the first page, and ideally the first paragraph.

After the opening, every attempt to solve a problem should make the problem worse or create a new, more tenacious problem. Even if the protagonist's situation improves, the forces arrayed against him should grow comparably in magnitude.

If the plot is organized around a single central problem, it usually ends when that problem is resolved. If the plot deals with a series of problems, it ends when the last problem is dealt with.

Whatever happens to the protagonist, at some point he must take charge of events and step up and refuse to be pushed around any longer. In the end, he should be the one who solves the mystery, discovers the secret, or arrives just in time to save the day.

The resolution of your story should be the logical coming together of the facts and events known to the reader. It can be thought of as the ultimate surprise, the revealing of the answer to the central mystery. It is the moment that relieves all the tension that has built up through the middle of the story.

The events should cause a change in the protagonist's inner life; that is, he might trade his original goal for a more worthy one, face a personal issue he has ignored before, or resolve a longstanding internal conflict.[2-5]

Most plots of genre novels can be summarized as follows:

- *The Backstory.* What is really important that happened before your novel begins (murder of a child, a rape, a kidnapping, a cowardly act)?
- *Inciting Incident.* What event sets the plot into motion (the discovery of a murder, a plane crash, an escape from a prison)?
- *The Prize.* What is it your character wants (possession of something, prevention of something, relief from something, revenge for something)?
- *The Strategy.* What does your protagonist decide to do in order to get what he wants, and how does he set about doing

it?

- **The Conflict.** Who are some of the people or forces that are working against your protagonist (the antagonist and his cronies, a storm, an earthquake, a killer lion).
- **The Stakes.** What will be the consequence if the protagonist's plan doesn't work (loss of life, loss of the one he loves, loss of his fortune)?
- **The Bleakest Moment.** What happens to make things look hopeless?
- **The Conflict.** What is the big event that brings the story to its conclusion?
- **The Lesson.** What does your character learn about himself, others, or life in general?
- **The Decision.** What does your character do because of what he has learned?[2-5]

PARALLEL PLOTS AND SUBPLOTS

You may choose to tell two or more stories at once, making use of parallel plots or subplots. The main plot and a *parallel plot* generally tell two stories of about equal importance, usually moving from one to the other and back again. A *subplot* tends to be secondary—a story within the story. Both of these strategies are common with novels, but are less often encountered in short stories. Subplots can support and flesh out the main story. Parallel plots and subplots both make the story more complex, and certainly make it more interesting.[6,7]

Parallel Plots

Parallel plots are of about equal importance. Two choices for approaching parallel plots are available. In the first, the characters are initially established together, the story splits into two plots, which then converge toward the end of the story. In the second, the characters and plots start out separately, but come together toward the end. These two plots obviously have to have some strong connection, even though the reader may not be aware of it for a substantial part of the story.[7]

An example of a parallel plot takes place in Robin Cook's

Chromosome 6 (1998). A group in the medical examiner's office in New York City, including two pathologists, tries to figure out why a murdered mobster's body was taken from the morgue and mutilated in an attempt to hide the fact that he had gone through a very unusual liver transplant. While they follow clue after clue, sometimes in fear for their lives, a genetic scientists, a nurse, and a reproductive technician in Equatorial Guinea on the west coast of Africa try to figure out why smoke is sometimes seen rising from the island where genetically altered bonobos (an ape related to chimpanzees) are kept isolated. The story goes back and forth between the two groups until approximately 85 percent of the way through the novel the two groups meet in Equatorial Guinea where the story comes to a climax and the crisis is resolved.[8]

Subplots

Subplots may run for a while before coming to resolution, or continue almost throughout the entire novel, being resolved just before the novel's end. Sometimes subplots center on the protagonist and sometimes on one of the subordinate characters or even the antagonist.

Once you've got your main plot up and going, with the major characters established and facing some problem the reader can tell isn't going to go away, you can bring in a subplot, which you make clear and leave unresolved so the reader knows there are more developments to come. It is helpful to build in connections between the main plot and the subplot from time to time.

You should show events in the main plot affecting what's happening in the subplot, and the other way round. You may want to have characters overlap, figuring in both main plot and subplot, although more important in one than the other. And remember, like main plots, subplots need developments, crises, big scenes, and resolution. You may want to let the main plot and subplot converge to a simultaneous ending or resolve the subplot prior to the resolution of the main plot, but never after it.[9]

A subplot in *Caduceus Awry* (2000) is the fact that patients are dying in Atlanta's Charity Hospital, apparently as the result of murder, despite the fact that they are alone in their rooms at the times of their deaths. Hospital administration is trying to figure out what is going on. In the main plot, Dr. Mark Valentine and a mobster's ex-girlfriend stay just one step ahead of the hit man the mobster has sent after them. The main plot and the subplot converge about two-thirds of the way through the novel where the subplot is resolved.[10]

CRISIS AND CHALLENGE

A story is about a person with a problem—your protagonist. Your story will be more powerful if it is about the biggest problem he has ever faced. The plot should force the protagonist to make choices and take actions, and the course of plot events should change in response to those choices and actions. You may choose to have him lose the battle or achieve it and realize he doesn't really want it.

There are two kinds of problems you can have your characters face—crisis and challenge. Since plot often arises from characters dealing with problems, the distinction between the two types of problems can be useful to consider.[1]

Crisis

A *crisis* is a situation that a character finds himself in, but did not choose it. The crisis demands action. It has to be dealt with immediately, meaning there is a deadline involved. The deadline gives the crisis a built-in means for increasing tension in a story.[1]

Challenge

A *challenge* is a problem that a character decides to take on himself because he finds the problem exciting, interesting, or necessary. A challenge usually has a character attempting to find, discover, or create something, and is a way of expressing what is meaningful to him.

A crisis and a challenge can be combined; for example a general situation could arise, such as a threat to society (crisis) that the character chooses to take on, even if he isn't required to (challenge).[1]

CONFLICT AND SUSPENSE

Stories are about desire versus danger. This leads to a *conflict*, which is a struggle—a give and take—between opposing forces as each attempts to achieve his goal. The issue behind the story is "Will the protagonist overcome danger, defeat his opponent, and achieve his goal?"

Conflict is the driving force behind all good genre fiction. Without it there is no story. Conflict leads to *suspense* (Who is going to win the battle and how are they going to do it?).[2,11]

Conflict

There are two main kinds of conflict in stories—external and internal. Often, through plot and subplots, more than one kind of conflict takes place in the same story. In every case, however, the existence of conflict enhances the reader's understanding of a character and creates the suspense and interest that makes the reader want to continue reading.[12]

External Conflict

A struggle between a character and an outside force is an *external conflict*. The outside force may be (1) the environment, (2) a machine, (3) another person, (4) a force of nature, (5) society, or (6) a supernatural force.

Man versus Environment. A *Man versus environment* conflict is a struggle between man and the environment—a storm, an earthquake, a tornado, a hurricane, a flood, a tsunami, terrible heat, or freezing cold.[13,14]

In *The Perfect Storm* (1998) by Sebastian Junger, Billy Tyne is the captain of a sword-fishing boat, the Andrea Gail, in the North Atlantic. Highly competitive and stung by a string of poor outings, his crew is hardly back in port when Tyne tells them he's going out again, even though it's October and the weather can turn ugly. Five men join him. They catch little, so they sail east, with Tyne ignoring storm warnings behind him. Finally, the fish bite, but the ice machine fails. Things turn from bad to worse when a confluence of weather conditions combine to catch them in the middle of a killer storm.[15]

Man versus Machine. In recent years, *man versus machine* has become a popular source of conflict, such as in the movie *The Terminator* (1984) in which a cyborg (robot with the form of a man) has been sent from the year 2029 to present-day Los Angeles. Representing a world that has become dominated by machines, the robot (Arnold Schwarzenegger) has been programmed to seek out and kill a young waitress named Sarah Connor (Linda Hamilton) before she can conceive the son who will lead the future-era humans to victory over their mechanical enemies.

And in the movie *The Matrix* (1999), a computer hacker named Neo (Keanu Reeves) discovers that all life on Earth may be nothing more than an elaborate facade created by a cyber-intelligence. The life essence of all humans is being used as fuel for the Matrix's campaign of domination in the real world. Neo joins like-minded Rebel warriors Morpheus (Laurence Fishbure) and Trinity (Carrie-Anne Moss) in a struggle to overthrow the Matrix.[11,16]

Man versus Man. Conflict that pits one person against another is *man versus man*. It can involve a physical fight or a battle of wits. Two characters want the same thing—love, money, fame, a woman, to stay alive—but only one of them can succeed.[10,11,13,16,17]

Fourth Estate (1997) by Jeffrey Archer is the story of two men who, though they come from totally different backgrounds, stand face-to-face, prepared to risk everything to beat each other and control the biggest media empire in the world. One man, Lubji Hoch, comes from humble beginnings as the son of an illiterate Jewish peasant. He changes his name to Richard Armstrong and becomes a decorated officer in the British army. He ultimately finds himself in Berlin, where his sharp mind and killer instincts win him the opportunity to head up a floundering newspaper. As rival papers in the city fail in the wake of his ruthlessness, he is poised to move on to even greater things. On the other side of the world in Australia, Keith Townsend, son of a millionaire newspaper owner, is being groomed to follow in his father's footsteps. Private schools, an Oxford degree, and a position at a London newspaper lead him up to the time of his father's death when he takes over the family business. His energy and brilliant strategic thinking quickly make him the leading newspaper publisher in Australia. Yet he too longs to move on to the world stage.[18]

Man versus Nature. Examples of *man versus nature* include an individual or group trying to survive in a jungle, a group of scientists trying to overcome a plague, or a man trying to survive against a pack of wild dogs in the Australian Outback. Daniel Dofoe's *Robinson Crusoe* (1719) and Herman Melville's *Moby Dick* (1851) are two well-known man versus nature stories.[11,13,16,19]

In the movie *Jaws* (1975), Martin Brody (Roy Scheider), the new police chief of Amity, an island resort town somewhere in New England, is called to the beach where the mangled body of a female vacationer has washed ashore. The medical examiner tells Brody that it could have been a shark that killed her. Mayor Larry Vaughn (Murray Hamilton), who is desperate to not lose the money which will be brought in by 4th of July tourists, wants Brody to say the woman's death was caused by a motorboat propeller. Shark expert, Matt Hooper (Richard Dreyfuss), confirms that she was killed by a very large shark. After several more shark attacks, Vaughn finally agrees to hire a shark hunter named Quint (Robert Shaw) to find and kill the shark. Brody, Hooper, and Quint venture out to sea in a small boat to find and to do bloody battle with the huge shark.

Man versus Society. In *man versus society* conflicts, man battles the forces of society. Society could be the government or any other organized group of people. The values and customs by which everyone else lives are challenged. The protagonist may come to an untimely end as a result of his convictions. On the other hand, he may bring others around to a sympathetic point of view, or it may be decided that society was right after all. In science fiction, the society could be the inhabitants of a foreign world or a parallel universe.

An example of man versus society would be a poor, uneducated black man trying to make his way in a higher level of white society. The problem lies between his abilities and beliefs and those of the society he is entering.[13,14,19]

In *One Day in the Life of Ivan Denisovich* (1962) by Aleksandr Solzhenitsyn, Ivan represents the common man; the immediate society he lives in is a Soviet prison. Every day, in a labor camp in Siberia, he struggles to survive physically and psychologically. He schemes for an extra ration of bread, he survives an inspection, and he grasps the crumbs of existence that literally are the difference between life and death.[20]

Man versus the Supernatural. In *man versus the supernatural*, the protagonist must battle some force that is not human or not part of the natural world. The supernatural force could be God, a ghost, fate, a witch, a werewolf, a vampire, or any number of such foes.[10,13,14,19]

In Washington Irving's short story *The Legend of Sleepy Hollow* (1917), Sleepy Hollow was an enchanted region where you could hear astonishing tales of ghosts and goblins; of haunted fields, brooks, and bridges; and in particular of a terrible headless horseman who raced along dark roads in the dead of night. It tells the story of schoolmaster, Ichabod Crane, a Connecticut native who comes to teach in a one-room schoolhouse. He competes with Brom Bones for the affections of Katrina. One afternoon, after being rebuffed by Katrina, Ichabod briskly rides off on his landlord's horse, sees an apparition of a headless horseman, and is never seen again. The townspeople have a myriad of theories concerning his disappearance.[21]

Internal Conflict

A struggle that takes place in a character's mind is called *internal conflict*. It may involve such things such as a struggle with belief in God or trying to overcome self-doubts, anxieties, indecision, a physical handicap, or alcoholism.[10]

Man versus Self. A *man versus self* conflict is a good test of a character's values. Does he give in to temptation or rise above it? Does he demand the most from himself or settle for something less? Does he even bother to struggle? A character may have to decide between right and wrong or between two seemingly equal solutions to a problem. Sometimes, a character must deal with his own mixed feelings or emotions (an ethical dilemma, a choice between two terrible options, or the choice of loyalties). Internal conflicts are usually subplots.[10,16]

In a parallel plot of *Caduceus Awry* (2000), Dr. Mark Valentine struggles to overcome alcoholism so he can get his medical license reinstated. His struggle is complicated by his denial of his need to attend Caduceus meetings with other physicians to help him get a grip on his problem.[10]

Suspense

Suspense arises out of conflict. It is the quality of the story that makes the reader worry what will happen next—the thing that keeps him turning pages long after he should have turned out the light and gone to sleep. Suspense makes the reader fear for the fate of one of the characters. Complications and twists and turns in the plot create tension and further conflict, and hence more suspense.

The first basis of suspense is the foreknowledge that something bad may happen. The reader has to anticipate an event for there to be suspense associated with that event. A surprise bombing creates no suspense, but leads to suspense if it creates an expectation of future bombings. Often, in stories relying heavily on suspense, the reader will be given information that the characters don't have. The reader will be told that a character's car is wired to explode, and then will be given time to think about that fact as the character walks through the parking garage unaware of the danger.

Suspense can be defused completely if the reader is convinced that the writer is going to figure some way out for the character in trouble. So, if you wish the reader to feel real suspense, you have to convince the reader that you will occasionally let bad things happen to good characters. For instance, if you let the car explode at least once you let the reader know you could do it again, but this time maybe your character will be in it.

The minimum ground laying for an upcoming event would be simply to name the event so the reader knows something is coming. The best way, however, is to use one or more small preview scenes that hint of a larger upcoming scene so when it arrives the reader will be prepared for it. For example, If you are going to have a big scene in which an over-stressed office worker blows everyone away with a couple of assault rifles, you need to show him reacting to stress in less lethal ways prior to the big scene. Perhaps he has a fall out with a fellow worker the day before and storms out of the office. The point is, you need to build up to the big scene. If you do, then when the big scene occurs, the reader won't be overly surprised and will buy into it.[8,12,16,22]

Creating Suspense

Consider the following example of a way to build suspense:

- *Adam is flying his twin engine plan.* So what? People fly every day and it's no big deal. Let's give him an objective.
- *Adam is flying his twin-engine plane to Miami.* Okay, still no big deal. People fly to Miami every day. Let's raise the stakes.
- *A mobster has kidnapped his teenaged daughter and threatened to hill her if Adam doesn't come to Miami and save her. It's Adam he really wants.* It's getting better. Let's add a complication.
- *Adam has the flu—high fever, cough, muscle aches—and is feeling pretty bad. Will he be able to face the mobster successfully in his weakened condition?* Better, but I'm starting to get sleepy. Something exciting had better happen soon.
- *The plane is being bounced all over the place by a major storm. Thunder and lightening are all around. A lightening bolt barely misses the wing tip.* Now you're talking. I've fluffed up my pillows and slid up in the bed. Let's start a clock ticking during Adam's journey.
- *Adam has one more hour to get there if he is to meet the deadline set by the mobster. He constantly glances at his watch. Time is passing too quickly. Will he make it on time or will his daughter die.* Now I'm wide awake. Let's add an element of the unknown.
- *One of the engines starts to sputter and choke. Will it quit altogether?* Okay. I'm going to have to go to work tomorrow short on sleep. Let's add a little dramatic irony.
- *The reader is given the information that the mobster has had a change of heart and released Adam's daughter. Will Adam end up dying unnecessarily in a plane crash because he recklessly continues his flight in a storm with one engine that's threatening to quit, or will he land safely at the nearest airport, or against all odds will he make it to Miami?* Now we have suspense. I'm turning another page, and then another, and then another. Maybe I'll call in sick to work in the morning.[8,12,23,24]

Mechanisms for Creating Suspense

Use every mechanism available to you to create suspense: (1) Character thoughts, (2) character emotions, (3) settings and situations, (4) narration, and (5) dialogue.

- ***Character's Thoughts.*** "What was that noise?"
- ***Character Emotions.*** Character jumps at every little sound
- ***Settings and Situations.*** The crackling of leaves and snapping of branches in the woods at night
- ***Narration.*** Woodhaven was a strange town. A series of bloody murders had taken place there in recent years, but nobody seemed to give a damn.
- ***Dialogue.*** "I don't know why I let you talk me into taking a shortcut through the cemetery this late at night. You know there's been something strange going on here."[25]

COINCIDENCE

Coincidence is a shift of events independent from the action of the main character. Coincidence should not make things easier. To do so kills plausibility. That said, sometimes you can get away with using an accidental coincidence of events in a story, such as having otherwise unrelated characters be at the same place at the same time. You can do this in two cases. The first is when the coincidence is one of the initiating forces of the story. The second is when the coincidence makes things worse for the protagonist. Coincidences seem contrived and false when they're used to help a character.

If the main character is allowed to win the battle by a stroke of good luck, readers will become cynical and quickly lose interest in your story. If the coincidence goes against the main character, it is an unanticipated but believable misfortune. It's one more obstacle for him to overcome, leading to an increase in suspense.

One form of coincidence is the *overheard conversation,* whose use at one time was popular among writers, but now has fallen from favor. Two people just happen to be in the right place at the right time—one talking to someone and the other accidentally hearing the conversation. This device usually takes the form of the person doing the hearing being just out of sight of the person doing the talking, say just around the corner or in another room of the house listening on an extension phone. However, these days the talker could be speaking on a cell phone or accidentally send an e-mail to the wrong person. Most often this type of coincidence has been used when one spouse is having an affair and the other spouse accidentally overhears the conversation with the spouse's lover. This cliché type of scene device always furthers the plot line and changes character relationships quickly, but it does so way too easily. Think of a better way.[12,26]

WITHHOLDING INFORMATION

Never withhold information the reader should know. For instance, let's assume that your detective discovers a clue under the bed of the murder victim. He reaches under the bed, picks up the clue, closes his hand around it, and then slips it into his pocket. The reader is kept in the dark about what the clue is. Fair? Not at all. It's cheating. All such clues should be shared with the reader. Holding back information does not create surprise, mystery, or suspense; it creates confusion and annoyance on the part of the reader.[26]

STORY FOCUS

All stories have plots, ideas, and characters, but some stories focus more strongly on one of these aspects than the others. In some stories the characters are much more important than the plot, and in other stories an idea may be central. Still in other stories, the plot is of prime importance. Whether a story is focused on plot or idea or character will influence how you write it. Thus, it is important to know something about the differences between the types of stories and the demands each type makes on you as a writer.[1,27]

Plot-Driven Story

A *plot-driven story* is one in which the intricacies of the plot are the most important aspects of the story. The focus is on the developing events, uncovering of information, and how each of these draws the reader deeper into the story. Readers get caught up in the action that's unfolding. They expect escalating action that leads to the climax and resolution of the story, with some twists and turns along the way.

Plot-driven stories have characters and ideas of course, but these are secondary to the functioning of the story. The characters act in accordance with the plot, and never for any other reason. Readers keep reading, not because they are fascinated by the characters, who may seem flat, but because they want to find out what happens next.

The most well-known plot-driven stories are murder mysteries; the plot creates the mystery, so it is the focus of the story. As a rule, plot-driven stories must be outlined carefully before the writing begins so that you don't lose track of where the story is and where it needs to go.[1,27]

Idea-Driven Story

An *idea-driven story is* about the process of discovering information. It is much like the plot-driven story, since the plot becomes the means of discovery. However, with an idea-driven story the central idea structures the plot, and the characters and events are arranged so as to express the idea. The main idea of a story could be something like "Drilling for oil in Alaska is wrong," so the whole story aims to illustrate why drilling for oil in Alaska is wrong.

The idea is central, so all other aspects of the story must focus on it. It affects the plot (which must be constructed so that the idea is expressed) and it affects the characters (everything they do and say must contribute to the expression of the idea). Science fiction novels are often written as idea-driven stories.[1,27]

Character-Driven Story

In a *character-driven story*, the characters and their development tend to propel the story forward. The events in the story arise from the characters, and each new scene is the result of the reactions and interactions of the characters. As a result, this kind of story, more than any other, requires deep development of characterization. The interest for the reader is in following the actions and interactions of a character with whom they identify with or sympathize with. They expect characters who seem real, with strengths and weaknesses, issues they have to overcome, oddities, and all sorts of other things that make them interesting and complex.

Throughout the story, readers want to see the characters confront some of their fears, prejudices, and beliefs; challenge them; learn from their experiences; and continue forward with their newfound knowledge.[1,27]

TWENTY BASIC PLOTS

People often say that there are only a certain number of basic plots in all of literature, and that any story is really just a variation on these plots. Depending on how detailed writers make a plot, different writers have offered a variety of answers, ranging from one to 37. My favorite is the 20 basic plots in *20 Master Plots and How to Build Them* (1993) by Ronald Tobias, who states that *these are not the only plots in the world, just the most basic ones.* [17] I highly recommend Tobias's book to anyone wishing to write genre fiction.

1. Quest. This plot involves the protagonist's search for a person, place or thing—tangible or intangible. It may be the Holy Grail, Atlantis, the Middle Kingdom, or almost anything of major significance. The main character is looking for something that will significantly change his life.

A hallmark of the quest plot is that the site of action moves around a lot, visiting many people and places. Therefore, the protagonist and his traveling companion, usually a woman, are always on the move. The protagonist must ask questions, find clues, and solve problems.

A major part of the quest is the search itself and the wisdom the protagonist picks up along the way. The protagonist is shaped by his quest and his success or failure in finding the object of the quest. Many times what the character discovers is different from what he originally set out to find.[17]

In Dan Brown's *Da Vinci Code* (2003), the murder of the elderly curator of the Louvre museum reveals a sinister plot to uncover a secret that has been protected by a clandestine society, the Priory of Sion, since the days of Christ. The victim is a high-ranking agent of this society whose members included Sir Isaac Newton, Botticelli, Victor Hugo, and Leonardo Da Vinci. Famed Harvard symbologist, Robert Langdon, joins forces with gifted French cryptologist, Sophie Neveu, and learns the late curator, her grandfather, sacrificed his life to protect the Priory's most sacred trust—the location of a vastly important religious relic hidden for centuries. A quest for the Holy Grail takes them through England and France. The story ends with a surprising twist.[28]

2. Adventure. Whereas the focus of the quest plot is on the character, the focus of the adventure plot is on the action. The protagonist travels to new and strange places in search of his fortune. Because the focus is on the action, it's not important that the hero change in any appreciable way. The protagonist may prevail through skill and daring, but in adventure plots the events are always bigger than the character. The *Indiana Jones* stories are examples of adventure plots.[17]

In the movie *Raiders of the Lost Ark* (1981), the year is 1936. Renowned University of Chicago archeology professor, Indiana Jones (Harrison Ford), is hired by the U.S. Government to find the Ark of the Covenant, which is believed to still hold the Ten Commandments and to carry an incredibly powerful energy that must not fall into Nazi hands. Unfortunately, Hitler's agents are also after the Ark. The quest takes Indiana and ex-girlfriend Marion Ravenwood (Karen Allen) from Nepal to Cairo. Along the way they do battle with their rival, Dr. Rene Belloq (Paul Freeman) and face dangers in the form of Nazi thugs, spiders, and poisonous snakes.

3. Pursuit. The basic premise of the pursuit plot is that one person chases another. The good guy doesn't always chase the bad guy; often it's the other way around, as in the TV series *The Fugitive,* in which Dr. Richard Kimble (David Janssen) is wrongfully accused of murdering his wife. He is pursued relentlessly by Lieutenant Gerard (Barry Morse). The stakes of the chase are death or imprisonment. The chase is more important than the people who take part in it, and the story relies heavily on action and a variety of twists and complications.[17]

In the 1971 TV movie *Duel*, mild-mannered traveling salesman David Mann (Dennis Weaver) unintentionally angers the driver of a Goliath-like truck. Suddenly, the truck is not only riding the tail of his red Valiant but trying to run him off the road along a deserted stretch of California highway. No matter what Mann does (pulling over, stopping at a diner, calling the police) he can't get rid of the truck. Each time he thinks he's finally in the clear, the truck returns to terrify him more. Finally, the horrific conflict builds to a point where Mann realizes that running won't save him, and that he must take a stand and fight back against the insane trucker. Because the face of the truck driver is never shown, the truck itself takes on an air of satanic menace as it seems to hunt its human prey.

4. Rescue. This plot depends on the dynamic among three characters—a protagonist, an antagonist, and a victim. The conflict is the result of the search and the protagonist's attempts to gain back someone he considers rightfully his. In this plot, the protagonist is always right and the antagonist is always wrong. The protagonist usually must contend with the antagonist on the antagonist's turf.[17]

In the movie *Proof of Life* (2000), drug-dealing rebels in the fictitious Latin American country of Tecala kidnap Peter Bowman (David Morse) who is a U.S. engineer working for an oil company's subsidiary which is building a corporate-funded dam there. The company calls in a negotiator, Terry Thorne (Russell Crowe), who is an Aussie ex-soldier turned kidnap and ransom negotiator for a global firm that collects a commission for rescued hostages. When the subsidiary goes bankrupt, the oil company washes its hands of the matter and pulls Thorne. Bowman's wife Alice (Meg Ryan) begs him to stay. She and Peter's sister manage to gather enough money to interest him, Thorne talks ransom terms with the cash-strapped rebels, while Peter, chained high in the mountains, is sustained by a photo of Alice.

5. Escape. In this plot, the protagonist is confined and wants to escape. Sometimes the essence of the escape plot is nothing more than a test of wills between two strong personalities—the jailer and the jailed.[17]

In the movie *Papillon* (1973), a petty criminal, Henri "Papillon" Charriere (Steve McQueen), is sentenced to life in a penal colony in French Guiana for a murder he didn't commit.

There he becomes friends with another convict, a counterfeiter named Louis Dega (Dustin Hoffman). The two men struggle to survive amidst the horrible conditions in the prison. The only thing that keeps Papillon alive is the thought of escape and freedom. Attempt after attempt result in eventual recapture and harsh treatment.

6. Revenge. The dominant motive for the revenge plot is retaliation for a real or imagined injury. Almost always the retaliation is outside the law. The authorities can't or won't do what the protagonist, who is a good person, considers to be the right thing, so he takes the law in his own hands. It is a plot of vigilante justice. The more heinous the crime (rape, murder), the more the protagonist is justified in seeking justice. The revenge must always equal the crime; thus, the concept of getting even.[17]

In the movie *The Outlaw Josey Wales* (1976) starring Clint Eastwood, Josey is beat up and thrown to the ground were he witnesses his wife's rape and murder, his son's killing, and the burning of his home. He is left for dead. All that's known to him is that the killers are a group of Union soldiers led by "Red Legs" Terrill (Bill McKinney). Picked up by a band of Missouri bushwhackers, Josey joins their cause of killing union soldiers to even the score, and eventually tracks down Terrill and kills him.

7. The riddle. This plot offers a puzzle for the reader to solve. The plot focuses on events that must be evaluated and interpreted. Things are not what they seem on the surface. The answer is not obvious, but it is there in plain view, cleverly hidden. The challenge to the reader is to solve it before the protagonist does.[17]

In Edger Allan Poe's short story, *The Purloined Letter* (1917), the prefect of the Parisian police bursts into Detective Auguste Dupin's apartment to tell him that a certain minister of the court has stolen a compromising letter from the Queen. Dupin asks some questions about the appearance of the letter and the police prefect's method of searching the minister's apartment. A month later, the letter still missing, the Queen offers to pay 50,000 francs for return of the letter. Dupin instantly produces the letter. Based on the clues given, how did Dupin know where to look? Dupin, of course, explains all.[29]

8. Rivalry. This plot deals with two people competing for a common goal. The two adversaries should have equal strengths, although they can have different weaknesses. Most rivalries are struggles between good and evil, but some are struggles between opponents, both of whom deserve to win. In the end, however, one must win and the other must lose.[17]

The movie *Mutiny on the Bounty* (1962) illustrates the rivalry plot. Sailing from Portsmouth in 1787 under the tyrannical rule of Captain William Bligh (Trevor Howard), the H.M.S. Bounty begins a voyage around Cape Horn in search of the South Pacific plant, the breadfruit. As the months wear on, Bligh's backbreaking discipline, including flogging and keelhauling, as punishment for minor offenses starts to create a powerful sense of ill-will among the crew. Eventually, even 1st Lt. Fletcher Christian (Marlon Brando) begins to sympathize with the crew's suffering. Despite the brutal winter storms that threaten to tear the ship apart, the Bounty and its battered crew manage to reach Tahiti where they enjoy the warm sun and friendly native women while waiting for the plants to be harvested. When Bligh orders the ship home and subsequently cuts off the crew's water ration to save the plants, Christian rebels and leads the men in a mutiny, with tragic results.

9. Underdog. This plot is a form of rivalry plot. However, in the rivalry plot the protagonist and antagonist are equally matched; in the underdog plot they are not. The protagonist is at a disadvantage and is faced with what appear to be overwhelming odds. Because the protagonist is the underdog, the reader roots for him. The underdog plot represents the weak versus the powerful, one versus many, and the small versus the large.[17]

In the movie *One Flew over the Cuckoo's Nest* (1975), a loveable rebel, Randle Patrick McMurphy (Jack Nicholson), in an Oregon psychiatric hospital, rallies the patients together to take on the oppressive Nurse Mildred Ratched (Louise Fletcher). Ratched is a woman who is the embodiment of everything inhumane and unfeeling—more a dictator than a nurse. McMurphy is a small-time criminal serving a jail sentence for statutory rape of 15-year old girl. He is faking being crazy to avoid doing hard time on a work farm. He quickly begins schemes of his own, determined to have his way in the hospital and drive nurse Ratched crazy. Along the way, he befriends the other patients and helps them slowly to rid themselves of their frustrations and fears and begin standing up to Ratched, who responds with measures of her own—measures that lead to a final showdown with tragic consequences. The reader recognizes "the system" in Nurse Ratched and roots for

McMurphy because he is an underdog dedicated to overthrowing a system that squelches individuality and creativity.

10. Temptation. This plot is a character plot. It examines the motives, needs, and impulses of human character. By the end of the story, the protagonist should have moved from a lower moral plane in which he gives in to temptation to a higher moral plane as a result of learning the sometimes harsh lesson of giving in to temptation. The story usually ends with atonement, reconciliation, and forgiveness.[17]

In the movie *Fatal Attraction* (1987), happily married New York lawyer, Dan Gallagher (Michael Douglas), yields to temptation and has a one-night stand with a colleague, Alex Forrest (Glenn Close) while his wife (Anne Archer) and daughter are away. But Alex will not let go of him, and begins to terrorize him and his family. She calls the house, but just stays silent when Dan's wife answers. Then Alex murders a family pet. Dan becomes truly sorry for his indiscretion, and in the end overcomes Alex, who attempts to murder his wife. Dan's wife, of course, forgives him.

11. Metamorphosis. This plot is about change—the actual physical characteristics of the protagonist as well as his behavior. The protagonist may start out as an animal and end up a gorgeous, young man of marriageable age or the reverse may be true in the case of "The Wolfman" in which a man turns into a wolf at the times of the full moon. He desperately wants to be released from the curse. The cure for the curse in metamorphosis plots is always love. The protagonist may get the chance for salvation, restoring the good within him.

If the curse is so profound that only death can release the character from his state, he seeks death. The terms of release are usually carried out by the antagonist who may do such things as shoot the Wolfman with a silver bullet or drive a wooden stake through the vampire's heart. The metamorphosis plot is a character plot; consequently we care more about the metamorph than we do his actions.[17]

12. Transformation. This plot deals with the process of change in a protagonist as he moves through a particular stage of life. He is a different person at the end of the story than he was at the beginning.[17]

In Steven Crane's *The Red Badge of Courage* (1895),

Confederate soldier, Henry Fleming, deserts his regiment in the heat of battle. After a time, Henry joins a column of wounded soldiers winding down the road. He is deeply envious of these men, thinking that a wound is like "a red badge of courage." He eventually teams up with a wounded friend, Jim Conklin, who subsequently dies from his injuries. Henry rejoins the battle and in a rage thinking about Jim fights like a lion, transformed from a coward to a war hero.[30]

13. Maturation. Unlike the transformation plot which deals with an adult going through a change, the maturation plot deals with a child who is in the process of growing up. There are lessons to learn, and they may be difficult, but in the end the character becomes a better person for it.[17]

Great Expectations by Charles Dickens appeared in serial form between 1860 and 1861 and concerns a young boy, Pip, and his development through life. Crucial to his development as an individual is his introduction to Miss Havisham, an aging woman who has given up on life after being jilted at the altar. Cruelly, Havisham has brought up her daughter, Estella, to revenge her own pain, and so as Pip falls in love with Estella she tortures him in romance. Aspiring to be a gentleman despite his humble beginnings, Pip seems to achieve the impossible by receiving a fund of wealth from an unknown source. However, he eventually loses everything and Estella marries another. He realizes that his future existence is based on outgrowing his great expectations and returning to his roots.[31]

14. Love. A good love story is more about characters than the actions. It is a story about love denied and either recaptured or lost. The prospect of love is always met with a major obstacle. The lovers may be ill-suited in some way. They may come from different social classes or one may be blind or otherwise handicapped. Emotion is an important element in writing about love, often consisting of a full range of feelings—fear, loathing, disappointment, sadness, happiness, and so forth. Love stories don't have to have a happy ending.[17]

Love Story (1970) by Erich Segal is a classic romance. It is about Oliver Barrett IV, a rich jock from a stuffy family who is on his way to a Harvard degree and a career in law. He meets Jenny Cavilleri, a wisecracking, working-class beauty who is studying music at Radcliffe. They are immediately attracted to each other, sharing a love that defies everything. When the couple decides to get married, Oliver's father (Oliver Barrett III) threatens to disinherit him from the family will. Ultimately, Jenny becomes ill and suffers an untimely death at age 25.[32]

15. Forbidden Love. Forbidden love is any love that goes against the conventions of society. Adultery is the most common form of forbidden love. Others include marrying outside one's own faith, race, or social class. Also, one shouldn't marry another who is too old or too young, who is a close relative, or who is too ugly or physically handicapped. In the past, homosexual love has been a topic of forbidden love.[17]

Harold and Maude (1984) by Colin Higgins is about the unlikely romance between a death-obsessed 19-year-old named Harold and a life-loving 79-year-old widow named Maude They meet at a funeral and eventually become lovers, which brings Harold out of his fatalistic depression His parents are, of course, mortified and oppose the relationship. In the end, Maude commits suicide because she doesn't want to live past 80 and suffer the infirmities that old age brings. She wants death to be on her terms. Her dying message to Harold is "Go out and love some more." We are left with the impression that he plans to do just that.[33]

16. Sacrifice. In a sacrifice plot, a person sacrifices himself for an ideal, such as love, honor, charity, or for the sake of humanity. The sacrifice always comes at a great personal cost. The character undergoes a major transformation during the course of the story, moving from a lower moral state to a higher one, and facing a strong moral dilemma at the center of the story.[17]

In the classic western movie *High Noon* (1952), Will Cain (Gary Cooper), a sheriff of a small town in New Mexico, has just gotten married to Amy (Grace Kelly). Amy is a Quaker and hates violence. In deference to her pacifist beliefs, Will is turning in his badge. But just as the newlyweds prepare to leave town for a new life, Will learns that a criminal, Frank Miller (Ian MacDonald), who he put behind bars is being paroled and arriving in town on the 12-noon train for a showdown. Amy begs Will to leave with her, but he knows he can't run away. It's a matter of honor. Will finds himself alone in the battle as everyone in town, including his deputy sheriff, deserts him. In the face of such odds, Amy takes up a rifle to protect her husband, even though it goes against her strongly-held beliefs. She sacrifices her religious beliefs for love.

17. Discovery. The discovery plot is a character-oriented plot in which a character undergoes a quest to understand something fundamental about himself. It is a plot about discovering and dealing with life. The characters and the circumstances speak for themselves. The reader is allowed to draw his own conclusions based on the events of the story.[17]

In Eudora Welty's *Death of a Traveling Salesman* (1936), R. J. Bowman has been off work for some time due to a bad bout of influenza that has damaged his heart—a heart that is empty and seeking to be filled. He is back on the road as a shoe salesman before he is fully recovered. His car falls into a ravine, and he goes to the nearest farmhouse for help. The woman there assures him that her husband will help him. She is pregnant, dowdy, frumpy, and prematurely aged—no one that the more cosmopolitan salesman would find attractive, but he recognizes that within her there is life as well as the evidence of having been loved. Within him there is nothing. The next morning, back on the road alone as always, he has been profoundly changed by his meeting with the farm couple. He has discovered the necessity of love and of roots, and possibly that he needs to reform his life. But he keeps the emotion bottled up inside him until he has a heart attack and dies.[34]

18. Wretched Excess. This plot is about the psychological decline of a character, either because he is mentally unbalanced or because he has been trapped by circumstances that made him behave differently than he would under normal circumstances. The tension in this plot comes from convincing readers that whatever the excess it could happen to them too. The battleground can be alcohol or other drugs, greed, ambition, jealousy, or any number of other difficulties. Things happen because the character does, or does not do, certain things.[17]

In *The Lost Weekend* (1944) by Charles R. Jackson, Don Birnam, a would-be writer and long-time alcoholic, daydreams of himself as a genius, but his loneliness, his need to drink, his dangerous hangovers, and his actual nightmares combine to form a terrible experience. His brother, Wick, has managed to keep him sober for the 10 days, and he seems to be over the worst, but his craving becomes more insidious. Evading a country weekend planned by his brother and Don's girlfriend, Helen, Don begins a three-day bender. In flashbacks, readers see past events, all gone wrong because of the bottle. This bout looks like his last.[35]

19 and 20. Ascension and Descension. These are the rags-to riches and riches-to-rags stories. Sometimes the two are combined—rags-to-riches-to-rags or the other way round. Usually the personality traits that allowed the character to reach prominence (ambition, aggressiveness, courage, and so forth) are the same traits that cause his downfall. The focus of the story is a single character who is strong-willed, charismatic, and seemingly unique. Everything relates to him. He also suffers from an overblown ego, which may be the cause of his ultimate downfall.[17]

Leo Tolstoy's novella *The Death of Ivan Ilyich* (1886) is an excellent example of an ascension to descension plot. Ivan works hard to attain a solid position in the Russian court system, and from the outside seems to have everything a man could want, but we learn that he doesn't love his wife because she drives him crazy with her constant demands and petty jealousies. In fact, one of the reasons he was able to attain such a high position in the Court of Justice was that he spent almost no time at home. Then a minor injury turns troublesome. He goes to a series of doctors who cannot agree on a diagnosis. His steadily worsening condition is made even more disturbing by his wife who seems to feel that she is the one who is suffering because of his annoying moaning. Ivan begins to ask questions of himself. What is the meaning of life? Was there more he should have done? Did he miss the whole point? He finally concludes that he did, but by then it is too late; he dies in agony, partly from physical pain, but equally from the knowledge that he wasted his whole life.[36]

PLOT SUMMARY

It should be possible to state a plot in one or two sentences. If a plot requires more than a few dozen words to describe, it is probably too complex. The plot should be simple, even if the story is complex.[37]

- After twenty years at war, a king battles the elements, the gods and himself to get home, only to find that his kingdom is overrun with usurpers and his wife doesn't recognize him (*The Odyssey* by Homer, 800 B.C.).[38]

146

- Ahab, a whaleboat captain bent on revenge against the white whale that mauled him, spurs a tired crew across the ocean in a grand hunt. Ignoring the dangers of the sea, he becomes consumed with revenge and will do anything to kill the whale (*Moby Dick* by Herman Melville, 1851).[39]

OUTLINING

When it comes to outlining the plot, every writer is different. Some feel that outlines torpedo their creativity; others love them and can't write without them. Some writers always write with a detailed plot outline worked out on a chapter by chapter basis, while others use a less detailed outline, and yet others outline only as far ahead as the next scene. A very few writers say they just start writing and see where it takes them.

Logically, you do need at least some idea of where you are going, even if it's just a rough outline in your mind, otherwise you end up with a random set of events and a lot of dead ends. Plot-oriented stories, like murder mysteries, can benefit from having a clearly-drawn outline right from the beginning. In stories with parallel or subplots, a good outline will help you keep track of the interactions between these and the main plot.[6,9]

Rich Hamper identifies a number of benefits of plot outlining that he says work for him:

- *You'll have a framework on which to base your story, which gives you direction as you write.*
- *If you're writing a multi-threaded plot, you'll find it easier to keep track of those threads.*
- *You'll know early on if you need to shore up the middle of your story.*
- *The outline itself can become a mechanism for creative plotting. You can bury questions and thoughts right along with your plotline in the outline.*
- *An outline provides an easy mechanism for tracking your progress; you'll know where you are and have a pretty good idea of how much of your story has yet to be written.*
- *A story synopsis is much easier to write if you have a story*

outline in hand.[40]

For those writers who use an outline, it's a tool and nothing more. Flexibility is essential. Outlines change as the story is written and have to be revised from time to time, but at least the writer knows where he's going at any given time. The story is allowed to flow in the direction the writer's creativity drives him. The outline becomes more detailed over time as the plot evolves. The idea here is to maintain enough flexibility to be able to change things; in other words, don't box yourself in with excessive details. Let the writing give rise to the details. All that said, you'll need to find out what works best for you.[6,8]

References

1. Silvester, Niko, Writing Fiction: A Beginner's Guide, Creative Writing for Teens, http://teenwriting.about.com/library/weekly/aa111102a.htm.
2. Swain, Dwight V., Techniques of the Selling Writer, University of Oklahoma Press, Norman, 1974.
3. Ingermanson, Randall, Writing the perfect scene, http://www.rsingermanson.com/html/perfect_scene.html.
4. Kilian, Crawford, Advice on novel writing, http://www.steampunk.com/sfch/writing/ckilian/#6.
5. Lake, Lori L., Plot ... Part Two, Navigating dangerous terrain, http://www.justaboutwrite.com/A_Archive_Plot2LL.html, 2003.
6. Writing a good plot outline, PageWise, http://meme.essortment.com/writingplotout_rtuj.htm, 2002.
7. Writing: Plot & Sub-plot, One of Us, http://www.oneofus.co.uk/writing_tips/plot_and_subplot.htm.
8. Cook, Robin, Chromosome 6, Berkley Books, New York, 1998.
9. Dibell, Ansen, Plot, Writer's Digest Books, Cincinnati, 1999.
10. Milhorn, H. Thomas, Caduceus Awry, Writer's Showcase, San Jose, 2000.
11. Conflict, Mrs. Dowling's literature terms, http://www.dowlingcentral.com/MrsD/area/literature/Terms/conflict.html.
12. Bishop, Leonard, Daring to be a great writer, Writer's Digest Books, Cincinnati, 1992.
13. The seven basic conflicts, EveryThing2.com, http://everything2.com/index.pl?node_id=1435775.
14. Terminology, English 1302,

http://www.odessa.edu/dept/english/dlane/eng1302r/pages/Terminol
ogy.html.
15. Junger, Sebastian, The Perfect Storm: A True Story of Men Against
the Sea, HarperPaperbacks, 1998.
16. Bokesch, Laura, Literary terms, Literary elements, Literary Terms,
Academy of the Arts,
http://www.orangeusd.k12.ca.us/yorba/literary_elements.htm.
17. Tobias, Ronald B., 20 Master Plots, Writer's Digest Books,
Cincinnati, 1993.
18. Archer, Jeffrey, Fourth Estate, HarperCollins, New York, 1997.
19. Freshman English, Conflict,
http://falcon.kcsd.k12.or.us/freshman%20eng%20ret/Unit%201%20
Short%20Stories/conflict.htm.
20. Solzhenitsyn, Aleksandr, A Day in the Life of Ivan Denisovich
(1962), Britannica.com,
http://www.britannica.com/nobel/micro/734_2.html, 1997.
21. Irving, Washington, The Legend of Sleepy Hollow (1917),
Bartleby.com, http://www.bartleby.com/310/2/2.html.
22. Noble, William, Conflict, Action & Suspense, Writer's Digest
Books, Cincinnati, 1994.
23. Morgan, Tina, Conflict and suspense, Fiction Factor,
http://www.fictionfactor.com/articles/conflict.html.
24. Morgan, Tina, How to keep them reading: Part one,
http://www.fictionfactor.com/articles/keepthemreading.html.
25. Creating suspense, Writer's Guide,
http://writersguide2002.tripod.com/guide/id37.html.
26. Swiniarski, Steven, Basic plotting for science fiction, Sci Fi Editor,
http://www.scifieditor.com/Swiniarski.htm, 1996.
27. Ottewell, Wanda, Are you a character-or plot-driven writer?,
eHarlequin.com,
http://www.eharlequin.com/cms/learntowrite/ltwArticle.jhtml?pageI
D=021101wo08001.
28. Brown, Dan, The Da Vinci Code, Doubleday, New York, 2003.
29. Poe, Edger Allan, The Purloined Letter (1917), Twenty Great
American Short Stories,
http://www.americanliterature.com/SS/SS10.HTML.
30. Crane, Stephen, The Red Badge of Courage (1895), American
Literary Classics,
http://www.americanliterature.com/RBC/RBCINDX.HTML.
31. Dickens, Charles, Great Expectations (1860-1861), bibliomania,
http://www.bibliomania.com/0/0/19/37/.
32. Segal, Erich, Love Story, HarperCollins, New York, 1970.
33. Higgins, Colin, Harold and Maude, Gallimard, Paris, Paris, 1984.
34. Welty, Eudora, Death of a Traveling Salesman (1936), The

Mississippi Writers and Musicians Project of Starkville High School, http://www.shs.starkville.k12.ms.us/mswm/MSWritersAndMusician s/writers/Welty.html#works.

35. Jackson, Charles, The Lost Weekend, Syracuse University Press; Reprint edition, Syracuse, 1996 (Originally published in 1944).

36. Tolstoy, Leo, The Death of Ivan Ilyich (1886), http://endeavor.med.nyu.edu/lit-med/lit-med-db/webdocs/webdescrips/tolstoy352-des-.html.

37. Schnelbach, Susan D. and Christopher Scott Wyatt, Tameri Guide for Writers, http://www.tameri.com/edit/gramerrors.html, June 15, 2005.

38. Rasley, Alecia, 13 prime plot principles, http://www.sff.net/people/alicia/art13.htm, 2000.

39. Heisler, Jeff, Plotting, http://www.talewins.com/plotting.htm.

40. Hamper Rich, Should you outline your story plots?, Fiction Writing, http://home.comcast.net/~rthamper/html/body_outline_benefits.htm, 1989.

Chapter 9

Structure

Structure is a way of arranging story material so that it is organized in both a logical and a dramatic manner. The structure of genre novels can be broken down into a number of parts: (1) Title, (2) prologue, (3) beginning, (4) middle, (5) end, and (6) epilogue.

All novels have titles, a few have prologues, fewer have epilogues, and even fewer have both prologues and epilogues. As a general rule, all stories have a beginning, a middle, and an end.

A story begins with a change of some kind, which leads to a goal, which raises a story question in the reader's mind—will the goal be attained? The story ends by answering the story question. The middle deals with multiple failed attempts to attain resolution of the story question. The movie *Fatal Attraction* (1987) demonstrates this quiet well.

- *Beginning.* Dan Gallagher (Michael Douglas) meets Alex Forrest (Glenn Close) and over the weekend the two have a sexual encounter while his wife Ellen (Anne Archer) is out of town. When Dan tries to go home, Alex becomes emotionally disturbed.
- *Middle.* A series of complications take place in which Alex begins to interfere with Dan's life in small ways, such as

telephone calls and surprise visits. As Dan continues to push her away, her actions become increasingly more hostile and desperate. The escalations continue and Alex's actions become more and more violent, including the killing of the family rabbit and placing it in a pot of boiling water on the family's stove. Then the deranged Alex kidnaps their daughter, and Ellen in panic has a bad car accident.

- ***End.*** Alex invades their home and tries to kill Ellen. Dan, Ellen and Alex battle it out in a terrifying scene that culminates in Alex being killed.

Notice how the action and the stakes in the middle grow larger and larger. The effect of the action is to snowball, increasing tension and conflict from the simple story of a man who cheated on his wife to one who is battling a crazed woman who is willing to kill his family to get what she wants.[1,2]

TITLE

Sometimes a good *title* just pops into a writer's head out of nowhere. Other times, the writer may only discover the perfect title in the midst of writing, after the manuscript is finished, or even after it is edited or re-edited. Then once he has decided on the perfect title, the editor may decide to change it.

Many writers use a working title when composing a story. The working title gives the writer a way to refer to the work as something other than "untitled." The working title, of course, may end up being the actual title. The title usually achieves meaning to readers as they gain insight while they read the novel, or even after they finish it.[3,4]

Categories

You can choose almost anything you want as a title as long as it isn't overly long. It certainly can't be overly short. Many titles consist only of one word. Some categories of titles that have been used include:

- *Character Attributes.* The Wonderful Wizard of Oz (1900) by Frank Baum.
- *Names of Characters.* David Copperfield (1849-1850) by Charles Dickens.
- *Names of Events.* When Worlds Collide (1997) by Robert N. McCauley.
- *Names of Objects.* The Sword in the Stone (1938) by T. H. Stone.
- *Names of Places.* Red Mars (1993) by Kim Stanley Robinson.
- *Text.* The King Must Die (1958) by Mary Renault.
- *Themes.* Pride and Prejudice (1813) by Jan Austin.
- *Times.* 1984 (1949) by George Orwell.[3,4]

Importance

There are two differing opinions about the importance of a title: (1) It is very important and (2) it's not important at all.

Important

The title of a work can have a huge impact. A bad title can confuse the reader, ruin the suspense, or discourage a reader from even buying the novel. On the other hand, a great title can add depth and meaning to a work, hint at important themes, or just sound so intriguing it makes the reader want to buy the novel and start reading right away. Furthermore, since the title is the first thing a reader sees, it needs to make the right impression.[3,4]

Unimportant

The title doesn't tell the reader anything about the content of the novel. *The Devils Waltz (*2003) by Jonathan Kellerman, for instance, doesn't provide any information about the content of the novel in which psychologist, Alex Delaware, pursues the possibility that 21-month-old Cassie Jones is the victim of Munchausen's Disease by Proxy, a complex syndrome in which a parent, usually the mother, secretly causes the medical symptoms that endanger the child.[5]

Which opinion is correct—important or unimportant? Got me!

I personally pay little attention to titles when I'm picking out a book to read. I read the author's name, the story summary on the cover, and the first page of the novel. Once I've started reading the novel, I couldn't tell you what he title is if you asked me without closing the book and reading it off the cover. Others pay a lot of attention to titles.[3,4]

PROLOGUE

A *prologue* serves three functions: (1) It directly or indirectly foreshadows what the novel will be about, (2) it is a source of reference from which the writer draws material to use in the body of the novel, and (3) it establishes continuity between the past and the present.

Unnecessary prologues can turn the reader off or cause the reader to simply ignore them. So if you are thinking about using a prologue, make sure it is essential; that is, be sure it will contribute to the plot. To be essential it has to reveal significant, relevant facts that will be vital to the understanding of the story. It should also make a strong promise of conflict to come.[6,7]

In the prologue of *Jurassic Park* by Michael Crichton (1990, a construction worker is severely mauled in Costa Rica by an unidentified animal, foreshadowing future events. In the body of the novel you learn that the animal was a dinosaur. Engineers, in fact, have cloned 15 species of dinosaurs and established an island preserve where tourists can view the large animals. All hell breaks loose when a rival genetics firm attempts to steal frozen dinosaur embryos, and it's up to two kids, a safari guide, and a paleontologist to save the day.[8]

A prologue gives you the chance to begin your story twice, at two different points. This can be an advantage or disadvantage depending on how you look at it. A prologue, followed by chapter one, can avoid what otherwise might be a jolting transition between two scenes widely separated by time or space or which have different narrators. The reader expects to start over again after a prologue.

The prologue should start with a strong and intriguing hook as if it were the beginning of the novel. This does not exempt the first chapter from beginning with an equally strong and intriguing hook.

Occasionally a prologue consists of a real or fictional document, such as a court summons, a last will and testament, a newspaper article, or a personal letter that prepares the reader for the drama to come.[6,7]

Types of Prologue

Lila Talmor points out four major types of prologue: (1) Background, (2) different point of view, (3) future protagonist, and (4) past protagonist.[7]

Background. A *background prologue* usually can be found in science-fiction and fantasy genres where the settings may differ so wildly from our own world that, without a proper explanation, readers might get lost. Trying to explain such settings as you go along in chapter one might slow the pace to a crawl. On one hand, you cannot require readers to wade through an essay of history (or future-history) in a prologue as soon as they pick up the novel. On the other hand, you can't throw them into deep space with no information. The key is to create a balance between information and interest. You can do this by telling a simple story which demonstrates to the reader the mechanisms of that world.[1,7]

David Morrell in *The Fifth Profession* (1990) uses a three-part prologue to introduce the background information needed to understand the mind and profession of his protagonist, Savage. In part one of the prologue he explains the first four professions, which have to do with gaining something, whereas the fifth profession has to do with protecting it once it's been gained. In the second part, he introduces the concept of comitatus—men who, under a Germanic code of absolute loyalty, defended tribal chieftains 400 years after Christ. In the third part, he introduces the samurai, the Japanese equivalent of the comitatus. These protective warriors came into being 1100 years after Christ when provincial chieftains needed fiercely loyal bodyguards. Readers find out in Chapter 1 that Savage, in the mold of comitatus and samurai, is a hired protector of wealthy clients.[9]

Different Point Of View. A *different point-of-view prologue* describes an event from a point of view different than that of the main characters. The event may occur in the same time-frame as the plot, or years before or after. Its relevance may be made clear in the course of chapter one or later chapters.

A different point-of-view prologue may be written in third-person, even though the novel is written in first-person, or vice versa. This type of prologue allows you to introduce a danger to the protagonist which the reader should know, but the protagonist shouldn't—at least not yet.[1,7] Michael Crichton uses a different point of view in the prologue to *Jurassic Park* (1990) than he does for the rest of the novel.[8]

Future Protagonist. The *future protagonist prologue* shows the protagonist some time after the main part of the story has taken place, and is written in the same point-of-view and style as the rest of the novel. The prologue gives the end of the story, while the novel itself explores how things came to pass. In this type of prologue, you may find the protagonist writing a memoir or explaining why one must be written or told. The emphasis is on the protagonist's own impression of the past.[1,7]

In the prologue to *Rebecca* (1938), Daphne du Maurier has the scene take place in present time with the rest of the novel as a flashback. The story centers on a young and timid heroine who is un-named. She narrates the story about how her life was made miserable by her strangely behaving husband, Maxim de Winter, whom she had just married. Maxim is a wealthy widower whose previous wife, Rebecca, died in mysterious circumstances. His house is ruled by Mrs. Danvers, the housekeeper, who has made Rebecca's room a shrine. Du Maurier focuses on the fears and fantasies of the new wife about Rebecca. Eventually, the new wife learns that her husband did not love Rebecca, who was a cruel, egoistical woman.[10]

Past Protagonist. The *past protagonist prologue* is generally used when the protagonist has a defining moment in his past which must be known to the reader for him to understand the character. An example of this is the movie *Batman Begins* (2005). The story begins with young Bruce Wayne standing bewildered over the bodies of his parents. Afterward, the disillusioned industrial heir travels the world seeking the means to fight injustice. Prologue completed, Wayne returns to Gotham and unveils his alter-ego, Batman (Christian Bale)—a masked crusader who uses his strength, intellect, and an array of high tech deceptions to fight the sinister forces that threaten the city.[7]

Prologue Test

To make sure your prologue works well you can put it to a simple two-step test: (1) Try to leave it out and see if anything important is missing and (2) try to change its title to "Chapter One," and then check to see if the plot integrity is damaged. If you answered both questions with a "yes," then your prologue is acceptable.[7]

BEGINNING

Editors at major publishing houses get hundreds more manuscripts every year than they can read, much less publish. So your first couple paragraphs need to grab the attention of the editor before he puts it down and moves on to the next manuscript. If, in these first two paragraphs, you can convince the editor your novel is worth reading, you will have overcome the first and perhaps the largest hurdle in getting your novel published.

The opening of a novel also sets the overall mood of your story; that is, whether it will be sad, happy, exciting, humorous, tragic, gloomy, violent, or whatever. If your story on a whole is a violent one, then the initial scene should resonate with that feeling.

Novels usually open with a scene. If you chose to begin with something other than a scene, you will have to make it especially striking and powerful—something that's not always easy to do.[1,11-13]

As an example of a novel that doesn't start with a scene, consider Jeffrey Eugenides' *The Virgin Suicides* (1993) which successfully begins with a narrative in which the reader is told immediately that all five sisters in one suburban family committed suicide, and then the rest of the book is spent exploring how and why this happened. The following is the first sentence of the novel:

- *On the morning the last Lisbon daughter took her turn at suicide—it was Mary this time, and sleeping pills, like*

Therese—the two paramedics arrived at the house knowing exactly where the knife drawer was, and the gas oven, and the beam in the basement from which it was possible to tie a rope.[14]

Every beginning makes a promise to readers: A romance novel promises to entertain and titillate them, a mystery novel makes a promise to intellectually challenge them, a thriller novel makes a promise to excite and keep them wondering what's going to happen next, and a horror novel promises to scare them. You must keep your promise or readers will be sorely disappointed and never buy any of your future novels, if there are any.

The beginning of a story is almost always about change. Something is different in the protagonist's usual day—an unexpected arrival, a snow storm in May, a death, a birth, or whatever. To build the beginning of a story around change you need four things: (1) An existing situation, (2) a change in that situation, (3) a character affected by the change, and (4) continued consequences triggered by the change; that is, a chain-reaction of stimuli and responses.

So where do you begin? There are three choices: Start just before the change (the protagonist's concern about the report of tornados in the area), just as the change takes place (a tornado swoops down on the protagonist), or just after the change (the protagonist explores the damage caused by the tornado). You should note that all three choices are in the immediate vicinity of the change.

In the beginning, you may want to foreshadow the major conflict that is to occur toward the end of the novel. This can be done by showing the protagonist in a situation similar to that of the end of the novel, but with the opposite outcome. For instance, if the protagonist is afraid of heights but must overcome that fear to resolve the conflict at the climax of the novel, at the beginning he might be in a situation where the fear is not only made apparent but also gets the best of him.

The opening scene usually does three things: It gets the story going and tells what kind of story it's going to be, it introduces and characterizes the main characters, and it engages the reader's interest in reading on. Some beginnings do more than this, but none should do less.[1,11-13]

Story Question

Readers like to worry about how the story is going to turn out in the end. To make the readers worry, you must establish a *story question* for them to worry about. The story question is the main thing the readers will be concerned about throughout the story. Will the protagonist finally rescue the heroine from the clutches of the antagonist, will the detective solve the mystery, will the lovers overcome adversity so they can live happily ever after, will the protagonist save the world from alien invasion or the mad scientist?

The story question should be introduced early, the key elements of the story must relate to it, and you must answer the question at the end of the novel.[15,16]

Questions Readers Ask

Dwight Swain states that at the beginning of every story the reader subconsciously asks: (1) Where am I, (2) what's going on, (3) who's involved, and (4) whose skin am I in? Your job is to provide answers to these questions. Without the answers, readers become confused.[14]

Where Am I?

The reader needs to know the locale. Characters can't operate in a vacuum. Does the story open in a ballroom in New York City, a barn in Minnesota, or a bedroom in Paris? Is it midnight, dawn, 1860, or 2045? Is it in the middle of a frigid ice storm or in oppressive heat in the desert?[1,11-13]

What's Going On?

"What's going on?" means "What's happening right now?" You present the beginning of the novel in such a manner that the reader becomes aware that you are leading up to something. Therefore you must state or imply one of the following:

Uniqueness. Uniqueness means to be one of a kind. To call attention to uniqueness is to make your reader wonder what you're up to (He was the only two-headed man in Manhattan. At three feet in height he was the tallest man in his universe. He had the highest I.Q. of anyone in the world.)[1,11-13]

The Unanticipated. The beautiful blonde walks in front of the church's alter and let's her fur coat fall to the floor, revealing her naked body. A newborn baby falls from the sky. A man's wife reveals herself as an alien creature.[1,11-13]

A Deviation from Routine. Instead of getting off the elevator on the third floor as he has done every day for the past ten years he rides it to the sixth floor and gets off when he's sure no one is looking. Jake, a teetotaler, stops at a local bar at happy hour. A dedicated surgeon doesn't show up for a scheduled surgery.[1,11-13]

A Change about to Take Place. Storm clouds gather on the horizon. A man's doctor calls and tells him he needs to come to the clinic as soon as possible. A woman's husband is packing his suitcase.[1,11-13]

Inordinate Attention to the Commonplace. Describe any object in great detail and readers will assume there must be some reason for it. For instance, describe a doorknob in great detail and readers will anticipate that someone or some thing is going to come through the door. Describe a gun hanging in a holster on the wall and the reader will wonder if it is going to be used and on whom. Describe a bent paper clip in great detail and the reader will wonder what the hell is going on.[1,11-13]

Who's Involved?

To answer the question "*Who's involved?*" you introduce your main story person to your reader. The first time this character appears he should perform some act that characterizes him. If he is a thief, show him stealing money. If he's cruel, show him kicking a dog. If he's honest, show him returning money that was paid to him in error.

To help the reader remember the characters and keep them separated from one another, give each of them one or more descriptive tags—something that sticks out like a sore thumb (buck teeth, big ears, bright red hair). And bring your characters on in action—doing something exciting.[1,11-13]

Whose Skin Am I In?

Point of view is the unfolding action as someone sees it. The point of view may be through the eyes of one or more characters in the story or from a narrator who is not a character in the story.[13]

Components of the Beginning

The beginning is composed of an initial setup and a big event. These usually are covered in the first page or so of a short story and the first few pages of a novel.

Initial Setup

The *initial setup* usually consists of (1) the necessary background (exposition), (2) a hook to pique the reader's curiosity, (3) an introduction of the main character, and (4) establishment of the setting of the opening. Rather than existing as individual parts, these elements are entwined in the opening of the story.

Exposition

Exposition shows what the main characters and their world were like before the beginning of the novel; that is, it explains who the characters are and how they got into such a mess. It can be handled in the author's voice or in the voice of one of the characters. *In Kramer vs. Kramer* (1978) by Avery Corman, the story opens in the delivery room during the birth of the couple's first child, Billy. The next few scenes are backstory about the course of the pregnancy, both partners' reactions to it, and the acquiring of a crib and other necessities. All of this shows how happy their lives were prior to the mother abandoning them.[17]

Since exposition slows the forward progress of the story, it should be kept to a minimum, and only that which is absolutely necessary should be presented. To write successful exposition, you must motivate readers to want to know the past; that is, you must make it important to them.[1,12,13] Exposition was discussed in Chapter 3.

161

Hook

Hook is a term that refers to the opening sentence, paragraph, or scene that convinces a reader to keep on reading. Therefore, beginnings need to be intriguing and energetic. Readers are impatient. They don't read far if their attention is not engaged almost immediately. With the first words you must make the reader care about issues, characters, or story.

The opening usually introduces setting and characters and raises a question about the character's status and subsequent actions. Something has happened, is happening, or is about to happen that will cause dramatic consequences in the life of the character. You want the browser who picks up your book in a store and scans the first page to simply feel he must know what is going to happen next.

How many times have you opened a book, read the first few sentences, and made a snap decision about whether to buy it or not? As a writer, producing those first few sentences (a hook) is one of your most important tasks. So, how do you go about doing it? Questions that require answers is what keep readers going, and the place to start raising those questions many times is with your very first sentence.

In her book *Hooking the Reader: Opening Lines that Sell* (2001), Sharon Rendell-Smock gives a multitude of opening lines from the literature that were designed to hook the reader.[18] Successful novels have opened with hooks using description, emotion, weather, and a number of other topics, while still others have opened with something known as universal assumptions.[12,13,18] Consider some openings given below from published novels.

Description. Writers have begun novels with the description of a variety of things, including a character, a crowd, money, a room, and many others.

- ***Character.*** *He was an inch, perhaps two, under six feet, powerfully built, and he advanced straight at you with a slight stoop of the shoulders, head forward, and a fixed from-under stare which made you think of a charging bull.* (*Lord Jim*, 1900, by Joseph Conrad).

Lord Jim obviously is an intense man, and powerfully built. He doesn't sound like someone you would want to cross. Often the description of a character immediately precedes him experiencing a life-changing event.[11,18]

- *Crowd. A throng of bearded men, in sad-colored garments and gray, steeple-crowned hats, intermixed with women, some wearing hoods, and others bareheaded, was assembled in front of a wooden edifice, the door of which was heavily timbered with oak, and studded with iron spikes.* (*The Scarlet Letter*, 1850, by Nathaniel Hawthorne).[18]

Why is the crowd assembled? There must be something significant about the door for it to be so strongly built, or at least it would appear so.

- *Money. They were old hundred-dollar bills, a little limp now, even a little greasy, and one of them had a rip in it that somebody had neatly mended with a strip of Scotch tape.* (*The Porkchopper*, 1972, by Ross Thomas).[18]

Why is this money important and why is it in such bad condition? One immediately wonders if it was obtained for having done some illegal act.

- *Room. Cassia's eyes slowly fluttered open. The room was dark and shadowed, lit only by a faint fire burning in the blackened stone hearth. Tiny bits of shattered glass littered the area around her. A chair lay on its side at her feet, one of its slender, spiral-turned legs snapped and splintered. The flickering flames had set eerie shapes dancing across the paneled walls that surrounded her, adding to the already hellish atmosphere of the room.* (*Chasing Dreams*, 1995, by Jaclyn Reding).[18]

Obviously something bad has happened here—a robbery, a fight, spousal abuse, a tornado? I certainly would keep on reading to find out what.

Dialogue. Novels also have begun with dialogue; that is, a question or a statement. Occasionally a novel begins with a character thought.

- **Question.** *What can you say about a twenty five year old girl that died? (Love Story, 1970,* by Erich Segal).[12]

What can you say about a 25-year-old girl that died? Obviously, from the question we expect that there is something to say and most likely something interesting.

- **Statement.** *I feel compelled to report that at the moment of death, my entire life did not pass before my eyes in a flash. ("I" is for Innocent,* 1992, by Sue Grafton).[18]

If private detective Kinsey Millhone died, how does she manage to be telling us that her entire life did not pass before her eyes? Something strange is going on, but what?

Emotion. Many novels have begun with a character's emotions, including anticipation, confusion, envy, fear, and love.

- **Anticipation.** *At approximately ten-forty-five, Della Street nervously began looking at her wrist watch. (The Case of the Stepdaughter's Secret,* 1963, by Earl Stanley Gardner).[18]

Della is obviously anticipating something that will or will not happen—most likely something bad.

- **Confusion.** *He had had hangovers before—on occasion terrible ones—but this one didn't make any sense. He had consumed only three drinks at most the night before. Or was it four? It was hard to think clearly. His thoughts were jumbled. (Caduceus Awry,* 2000, by H. Thomas Milhorn).[19]

What happened the night before? Clearly Mark Valentine has no idea. What did he do in an alcoholic blackout and what consequence will it have for him?

- **Envy.** *One day, Linc Marani vowed to himself he would drive*

*a car like Kyle's and wear five-hundred-dollar suits. (Outward
Bound,* 1999, by James P. Hogan).[18]

What kind of man is Marani? Does he come from a poor
background? Where does Kyle get his money? Bet you it's from
an illegal activity, but then, who knows.

* **Fear.** *Regina Dalton snapped awake the instant the coffin lid
  closed. Darkness pressed around her like a smothering
  blanket. Not a sliver of light penetrated. The dense air smelled
  of old dust and ancient velvet. The side walls seemed to
  contract, so she was supremely aware of her left shoulder
  wedged against padded wood while her right nestled beneath
  unyielding solid flesh and bone. Warm flesh and bone. (Kane,
  1998,* by Jennifer Blake).[18]

Wow! Now that's scary. Bad enough to wake up in a coffin,
but what about the person next to her—if it is a person?

* **Love.** *There are some men who enter a woman's life and
  screw it up forever. Joseph Morelli did this to me—not
  forever, but periodically. (One for the Money,* 1995, by Janet
  Evanovich).[9]

How exactly did Morelli screw up her life? Why did she
permit it to happen—more than once? Is she a victim or a willing
participant? So we read on to find out the answers.

Weather. Weather also seems to be a popular way to begin a
novel, including fog, rain, sunshine, and snow.

* **Fog.** *The night it all began, a thick fog rolled down the dale
  and enfolded the town of Eastvale in its shroud. (Innocent
  Graves,* 1996, by Peter Robinson).[18]

That's shroud, as in funeral shroud. Obviously, something
eerie is about to happen. Wonder what?

* **Rain.** *Lightning stroked the night, the glare flaring through
  the narrow windows, thunder rolling after. As if summoned by
  the flash, a blast of rain hammered down on the small,*

ramshackle, dockside tavern, while the wind rattle door and sideboards and slammed a loose shutter to and fro, and Waves roared against the pilling "neath." (*The Dragonstone*, 1996, by Dennis L. McKiernan).[18]

Again, something is about to happen, and based on the setting it's probably not going to be good. In fact, I would guess that it's going to be very, very bad.

- *Sunshine. It was morning, and the new sun sparkled gold across the ripples of a gentle sea.* (*Jonathan Livingston Seagull*, 1970, by Richard Bach).[18]

What a beautiful scene. We can only expect a beautiful story to follow.

- *Snow. Snow was falling on Riverside—great white feather-puffs that veiled the cracks in facades of its ruined houses, slowly softening the harsh contours of jagged roof and fallen beam.* (*Swordspoint*, 1987, by Ellen Kushner).[18]

Ruined houses, jagged roof, and fallen beam. Why the destruction? Are the houses simply decaying from old age and neglect, or has something more sinister happened?

Other. Of course there are many other ways to begin a novel, including action (very popular), animals, change (maybe the most popular), discovery, exposition, figurative language, foreshadowing an event, memory or recollection, a realization, one of the senses, sex, something different, a universal assumption, an unusual situation, work, or a combination of any of these.

- *Action. Louvre Museum, Paris, 10:46 P.M.: Renowned curator Jacques Saunieàre staggered through the vaulted archway of the museum's Grand Gallery. He lunged for the nearest painting he could see, a Caravaggio. Grabbing the gilded frame, the seventy-six-year-old man heaved the masterpiece toward himself until it tore from the wall and Saunieàre collapsed backward in a heap beneath the canvas.* (*Da Vinci Code*, 2003, by Dan Brown).[20]

Something obviously bad has happened to the curator. Did he have a heart attack? Has he been shot, stabbed, hit with a baseball bat? Why did Saunieàre tear this particular picture off the wall and clutch it to his chest, and what will happen next. The fact that the Louvre was chosen as the site of the action raises the question of why this particular place?

- ***Animals.*** *When Ellen Wainwright was married to Richard Lancy in July, 1873, the day was so hot that the church doors were left wide open, and towards the end of the ceremony, a stray dog ran in and stood howling in the central aisle. (Cast a long shadow, 1977, by Mary Pearce).*[18]

The fact that the day was so hot that the church doors had to be left open tells us immediately that something is different about this day. In folklore and fiction, a howling dog is a predictor of bad things to come, so we are left to wonder what horror lies ahead for these happy people.

- ***Change.*** *After nearly a quarter of a century of marriage, Rickie Meyers, my husband, told me to call him Rick. The he started slicking back his hair with thirty-five-dollar-a-jar English Promande. (After All These Years, 1993, by Susan Isaacs).*[1]

Do you think Rickie is having an affair? Maybe there's some other reason for this change in behavior. I guess we'll have to read the novel to find out.

- ***Discovery.*** *It was a hot June day when I discovered my father's secret, which was to change the whole course of my life as well as his. (The Demon Lover, 1982, by Victoria Holt).*[18]

It must have been one hell of a secret to change the lives of two people. I wonder what it was and why it would have such an effect.

- ***Exposition.*** *It must have been a little after three-o'clock in the afternoon that it happened—the afternoon of June 3rd, 1916.*

It seems incredible that all that I have passed through—all those weird and terrifying experiences—should have been encompassed within so short a span of time as three brief months. (*The Land That Time Forgot*, 1924, by Edgar Rice Burroughs).[18]

Weird and terrifying experiences, all occurring in a three month period. Now that's worth reading some more in hopes of finding out what they were.

- ***Figurative Language.*** *The world had teeth and it could bite you with them anytime it wanted.* (*The Girl Who Loved Tom Gordon*, 1999, by Stephen King).[18]

Personification is used here (giving human qualities to an object), but it just as easy could have been a metaphor or simile, or whatever.

- ***Foreshadowing.*** *The last day of pretty sixteen-year-old Sally Ander's life began much as any other.* (*A Death in a Town*, 1990, by Hillary Waugh).[21]

The last day of her life. Why? What's going on? What's going to happen to her?

- ***Memory/Recollection.*** *Her memory of that day never lost clarity. Eighteen years later, it was still there, every odor, every work and image, the exact heft of the pistol, each decibel of the explosion detonating again and again in the soft tissue of memory.* (*Body Language*, 1998, by James W. Hall).[18]

Did she kill someone? If so, who, and why? How has it affected her life since?

- ***Realization.*** *My decision to become a lawyer was irrevocably sealed when I realized my father hated the legal profession.* (*The Rainmaker*, 1995, by John Grisham).[18]

Obviously, he and his father didn't get along. Why not? What kind of person would go to law school just to spite his father?

How did it turn out?

- **Sense of Smell.** *The studio was filled with the rich odour of roses, and when the light summer wind stirred amidst the trees of the garden, there came through the open door the heavy scent of the lilac, or the more delicate perfume of the pink-flowering thorn.* (*The Picture of Dorian Gray*, 1891, by Oscar Wilde).[18]

I don't have a clue what this has to do with a picture of a man that ages, but it's an interesting opening.

- **Sex.** *When I was a little girl I used to dress Barbie up without any underpants.* (*High Five,* 1999, by Janet Evanovich).[18]

What kind of woman is this? Obviously she's one that's interested in sex. Barbie without underpants conjures up an image of some sexy lady not wearing the same. Maybe I should get to know her better. I think I'll read on.

- **Something Different.** *When I picked up the mail at the post office, I found one first-class envelope in with the usual junk.* (*Daughter of the Stars*, 1994, by Phyllis A. Whitney).[18]

Okay, it goes without saying; the first-class envelope is important, either bringing good news or bad news. I guess I'll have to keep reading to find out what's going on.

- **Unusual Situation.** *Granted: I am an inmate of a mental hospital; my keeper is watching me, he never lets me out of his sight; there's a peephole in the door, and my keeper's eye is the shade of brown that can never see through a blue-eyed type like me.* (*The Tin Drum*, 1959, by Gunter Grass).[18]

Now that's really spooky. How did the person get into a mental institution? What's wrong with him? What is the relationship between him and his keeper? What is the significance of their eye colors?

- **Work.** *He had been on the job only a week but he had got used to sitting in a dead man's chair. (Dead Fall*, 1954, by Dale Wilmer.)[18]

Who has been on the job a week? What kind of job is it? Who died, and why?

Universal Assumption. Beginning a novel with a sweeping expository statement—telling us something in the grand abstract—can be an effective attention getter if it raises questions about the story to come.

- *It is a truth universally acknowledged, that a single man in possession of a good fortune must be in want of a wife. (Pride and Prejudice*, 1817, by Jane Austen).[22]

Is that really true? The story is obviously about a rich man looking for a wife—or is it?

Combination. To this point we have considered only single-type openings. You can of course combine two or more of these into one opening, such as character description and weather.

- *Marshal Frank Seeger brought the bad news from Deep Bend to the Deen spread at Middle Creek, riding in with his long frame hunched inside a shiny yellow slicker as the first ice-cold splatters of rain blew in from the east. (Bury Him Deep in Tombstone*, 1977, by John Paxton Sheriff).[23]

Want to see how hundreds of successful authors begin their novels? Then have a look at a New York Times website that gives the first chapters of hundreds of books. Read and study as many first chapters as you wish: *www.nytimes.com/pages/books/-chapters/index.html.*

Main Character

The *main character* should be introduced, and ideally he should be doing something that is basic to that character. If he is a doctor, show him doing something medical. If he is a lawyer, show him doing something in the legal profession. If he's a plumber, show him plying his trade.

Don't bog your opening down with too much character description. Sometimes how a character looks is not as important as how he behaves, thinks, reacts, and talks. And even if your character's appearance is important, the beginning may not be the best place to describe it in detail. You can develop character appearances as the story goes on. [13,23-26]

Setting

Does the story open in Alaska in the current decade, London in the 1800s, New York at the turn of the century, or three o'clock in the morning in Hoboken? Where and when you have the action take place tells the reader a lot about the action and the people involved.

What is the mood—happy, sad, fearful, apprehensive, hostile? The middle of a loud, bustling country fair at noon is a far cry from a dark, spooky cemetery at midnight. Again, go easy on the details of the setting. This can be added in minor chunks if needed as the story progresses. [13,23-26] Setting was discussed in detail in Chapter 6.

Big Event

The *big event* begins when the protagonist is thrust by circumstance into the action—a murder, a kidnapping, winning a lottery, a rich woman learning her prospective daughter-in-law is a reformed prostitute, or a police detective being dared by a serial killer to track him down.

Should you open with a bang (a car chase, a lusty love scene, a building exploding in a fireball)? Some stories do, but a word of caution; a story with such an opening tells readers they can expect nonstop action and suspense the rest of the book. Such an opening gets the readers' attention, but it's a hard act to follow. The opening scene should mirror the overall conflict of the novel in some way, since your first scene sets the tone for the rest of the book. For instance, if the novel is about the protagonist getting revenge for a murder, then a good way to start might be a scene about the murder taking place.

Conflict must be present in your start (man versus man, man

versus nature, man versus the supernatural, and so forth). Make sure something that the protagonist feels an attachment to and cares for very much is threatened. Blood doesn't have to be shed and people do not have to die, but something significant does have to be at stake.

Because of a personal stake, the protagonist is motivated to deal with the conflict. For example, if your protagonist is a father, have a despicable character threaten to kidnap the child he cares about more than life itself. Then have him storm off to find and confront the person.[5,12.23,24,26-30]

Wide and Narrow Beginnings

There are two classic beginnings for a novel—wide and narrow. These can be modified, varied, or combined. The two openings can also be alternated, first wide then narrow then wide again, or vice versa.[6]

Wide Beginning

With a wide beginning, an important event has already taken place, which drastically affects the lives of a set of characters. The event has happened outside their lives, and the characters were not responsible for it. Such a beginning, for instance, might involve a war (the event) that is going on and the characters are drafted into service of their country. The focus is wide because the event happens first. The view then gradually narrows from the overall war as the important characters appear and begin to act out their lives.[6]

Narrow Beginning

With a narrow beginning a set of characters has committed an act that has caused an event to occur. Their roles in the novel stem from the incidents caused by the event. For instance, the characters become bored and decide that joining the navy during the war would be exciting (the event). The opening is narrow because the characters have to move outward to incorporate themselves into the war. The view gradually widens as the full meaning of the event emerges through their lives.[6]

Beginnings to Avoid

Leonard Bishop gives four beginnings to avoid: (1) Starting the plot too early, (2) starting with a flashback, (3) starting with a dream, and (4) presenting too many characters.

Starting too Early. You should rarely start a plot at the beginning of the story. Doing so makes the plot too slow getting off the ground. For example, don't tell how the protagonist decided to go out and buy some dynamite, how much it cost, how he brought it home and stored it, and the details of how he made it into a bomb. Begin after all this has happened—when he lights the fuse. This way the reader will see a big bang coming and read on to find out what blew up and why and if anyone was hurt in the explosion, and if so who. In other words, start with something threatening, and nothing is more threatening than change—a bus comes to town and a stranger gets off, a telegram is delivered to someone's door, a storm of epic proportions is on the horizon.

A cliché situation that novice writers sometimes use at the beginning of a manuscript involves the protagonist waking up, getting dressed, and then traveling somewhere by car, bus, train, or plane. During the travel time, background information is filled in. The action only starts once he has arrived at his destination. This opening will assure that your manuscript never gets past an editor. Like other cliché situations, this one also has a solution. Start the story after the protagonist arrives—once the action has begun. Fill the background material in bit by bit after that.[1,6,22]

A Flashback. The purpose of a flashback is to contribute information that the present relationships and conflicts cannot provide. Before the past can contribute, however, a present must first exist. Until readers know who the present characters are and what the conflict is they have no reason to care about the past. Besides, once the flashback is over there is nothing to return to, since the present doesn't yet exist. Only after the present is firmly established should you even consider a flashback.[6] Flashbacks were discussed in Chapter 3.

A Dream. You shouldn't open with a dream because an opening dream can be misunderstood. The reader has no idea who is doing the dreaming, and there is no way of knowing where, when, and why the dream is happening. The circumstances of the present are unknown and have to be delayed until the dream is over. If the dream is done realistically, the reader might mistake the dream for reality. Instead of opening with a dream you should first begin the novel with a situation in reality, and then if you absolutely have to have a dream, let the character have it after that.[6]

Too Many Characters. Don't introduce all your important characters in your opening chapter. The reader will have a hard time remembering which character is which and why each is important. Readers will have to keep turning back to refresh their memories about which name belongs to which character and who is involved in which situation. I have read a few novels in which I had to resort to keeping a list of the names of the characters and what their roles were in the story to keep up with them. It's frustrating.

You should use the opening chapter to name and define only the major characters and show their situations. And don't tell all you know about them. Give only the information that is important to know at the time. Save other information for later, after the storyline has been established. And don't include the secondary characters until their roles become important in the plot.[6]

MIDDLE

The Middle increases conflict, further develops the main characters, introduces other characters, and usually raises the stakes. By the end of the middle, all the various forces that will collide at the story's climax should have been put in place. The beginning should seamlessly become the middle, with no obvious dividing point.[14,31]

The biggest problem most new writers have with the middle is "Oh my God, how do I fill up all those pages with interesting and exciting material?" This is a realistic question. The middle makes up the major part of any novel in regard to length. In Margaret Mitchell's 63-chapter novel, *Gone with the Wind* (1936), the beginning consists of six chapters and the end consists of one chapter. This means that 86 percent of the novel (56 chapters) makes up the middle. So, therefore, the middle is an extremely important part of your novel.[32]

A fundamental purpose of the middle is to develop the characters, especially the protagonist, so that their motivations are understandable and their actions clearly seen as furthering the plot. This is also where you should develop the relationships between the protagonist and other characters, since their interactions cause many of the important events—the conflicts, the alliances, the rivalries—that move the plot along. The middle also has the purpose of exploring the setting and its effect on the characters and events in the story, examining the protagonist's relationship to the society in which he lives, and developing the values that drive him.

During the development of the middle, the protagonist should change, sometimes physically, depending on the timeline, but certainly internally, almost always becoming a better person for his experiences.

Of considerable importance is the evolving of the problem that drives the plot to set up the end so that when the end arrives it will be plausible. If you're writing a mystery, for instance, the middle assembles the evidence that will eventually solve the problem; that is, answer the story question.

The middle is usually divided into (1) complications in which things get worse for the protagonist and (2) a crisis in which the protagonist must make a decision that can lead to either success or failure in achieving his story goal.[13,28,31]

Complications

The *middle* of the novel is characterized by *complications*, which are things that make the protagonist's situation worse—things that endanger his chances of attaining his story goal.

As the protagonist tries to achieve his goal, obstacles are introduced, usually by action of an antagonist. The protagonist then reacts in someway to these obstacles, leading to further conflict. You should have him attempt one course of action after another as he faces each obstacle, only to discover that each in its turn is a dead end.

Let your protagonist find himself going from good fortune to bad, and back again, only to repeat the cycle a number of times as the result of his choices and actions. Make each challenge he faces more difficult than the last one, and make the consequence of responding to each challenge greater than that of the last challenge. In other words, make it more difficult for him to achieve his goal. Be sure that tension steadily increases from the beginning of the middle through to its end until eventually your novel reaches the climatic peak.

In the Wonderful Wizard of Oz (1900) by Frank Baum, Dorothy wants to go home, but to get to the Wizard of Oz who can grant her wish she must first overcome a complication; she must do battle with the dangerous Wicked Witch of the West and her flying monkey-like guards.

Complications are also known as *plot points* or *reversals*.[14,27]

Disaster

A *disaster* is a failure of your protagonist to reach his scene goal. Once he does reach his scene goal the scene is over. So you can't let him reach it without first making a heroic effort. When a scene ends with victory, your reader feels no reason to turn the page; so make it as difficult as possible for your character. Hang him off the proverbial cliff and readers will turn the page to see what happens next.[13,26]

Murphy's Law

Murphy's Law states that "If anything can go wrong, it will." This concept certainly applies to the fate of most protagonists in the middle of novels. Murphy's Law and three of its corollaries seem to fit here.

Corollary 1. *That which goes wrong will go wrong at the most inopportune time.* Again, the unexpected. The protagonist thinks he's got the problem fixed, only to have it flare up again when he least expects it.

Corollary 2. *If there is a possibility of several things going wrong, the one that will cause the most damage will be the one to go wrong.* The problems characters face, for the most part, should be the big ones.

Corollary 3. *If you perceive that there are four possible ways in which something can go wrong, and circumvent these, then a*

176

fifth way, unprepared for, will promptly develop. No matter what effort the protagonist makes, just when he thinks he's got all bases covered someone tries to steal home plate.[33]

Simple and Complex Complications

There are two basic forms of complication in a novel: The simple and the complex. The *simple complication* is quickly resolvable and final. It provokes a few incidents and ends. The *complex complication* is continuing and open-ended. It continues for a longer period of time before it is resolved, only to provoke the existence of another complex complication. Consider the following examples from Leonard Bishop:

- **Simple Complication.** *A young couple gets married, certain that their families will not follow through on their promise to cut them off financially if they do. They were correct. Their families were just testing them.*[6]
- **Complex Complication.** *A young couple gets married, certain that their families will not follow through on their promise to cut them off financially if they do. They were wrong. The families cut them off. Their financial hardships cause rifts in their marriage. They separate and begin to see other people. And on and on.*[6]

All major characters during the course of a novel should have several complex complications and many simple ones. Simple complications tend to come from outside the character, from external circumstances. Complex complications tend to come from within the character, from inner conflicts.[6]

Crisis

Crisis begins the moment the protagonist faces the fact that there must be a final showdown or climax. He must make a decision to continue the quest for a victory, despite knowing there is a risk, and most likely a very big risk. The decision to face the final conflict is a difficult one. The protagonist should experience fear, doubt, and other troubling emotions. He agonizes and does much soul searching and wringing of hands. Readers should have to wonder if he will rise to meet the challenge."

Once the decision is made to move ahead, the point of no return is reached. Usually there is more than one possible choice, but all have the potential for serious consequences. The one the protagonist chooses will reap the greatest reward, but undoubtedly will carry the greatest risk.

The true natures of the various characters are revealed during the crisis. We see why the protagonist is heroic and why the antagonist cannot see that he is wrong. Also, during the crisis an *epiphany* occurs—a moment of startling, sudden insight gained by the antagonist as a result of the unfolding events in the story. This epiphany is sometimes called the *revelation*. The crisis is sometimes called the *pinch*.[29]

The Sagging Middle

We've already seen that the middle, by far, comprises the greatest part of a novel. The beginning and the end by contrast are complex, but short and much easier to deal with as a writer. By its shear weight the middle can wear the writer out and become tedious. No wonder it sometimes begins to sag.

Reasons for Getting Stuck

Nancy Kress in her book *Beginnings, Middles & Ends* (1993) points out four common reasons for getting stuck in the middle of writing a novel: (1) Fear of failure, (2) fear of success, (3) writer's block, and (4) wrong direction.[22]

Fear of Failure. *Fear of failure* involves writing the first half of your story, reading it over, and immediately becoming discouraged because it's not as good as the stories you read every day. This is know as the *Tolstoy Syndrome* because, after all, how many of us can write as good as Leo Tolstoy?

A technique that works for some with Tolstoy Syndrome is to convince yourself that you are not really writing a story, but a simulation of a story. In writing a simulation, you aren't competing with Tolstoy, or anyone else for that matter. If you get stuck because nothing you write measures up to your high standards, you aren't practicing your craft because you are not already good at it. Sounds like circular reasoning to me.[22]

Fear of Success. *Fear of success* involves the never-ending story. "If I finish the novel I'll have to start another one, and I don't have another idea. And maybe the other story won't go as good as this one." So instead of finishing you spend your time polishing what you've already written, or planning various endings, or rewriting the opening.

Sometimes fear of success takes a different form. You finish the story, but you never mail it because "it's not good enough." You take it to an endless series of workshops to avoid testing yourself in the marketplace.

It's important to realize that many published authors had first works rejected, sometimes many times, only later to achieve success. Among these are Jane Austen, Earl Stanley Gardner, Pearl Buck, and John Grisham. So put the manuscript in the mail and immediately start your next novel.[22]

Writer's Block. Sometimes reluctance to work on a manuscript comes from the fact that you can't figure out what's supposed to happen next in your story—a condition known as *writer's block* or *literary fogginess*. As an approach to this problem, instead of forcing yourself to work on your next scene, let the keyboard sit idle and invest some time thinking about your characters and plot. Go back to the beginning of your story. What other direction can your plot take? Are there any new characters that are more interesting to you, including minor characters that you might consider elevating to major character status? When you come up with something interesting, start writing again. You might have to abandon much of what you've already written, but your original vision had a problem anyway; it was foggy.[22]

Wrong Direction. When you started writing you were very excited about your idea and your outline of the plot. Then something happened. You stuck to your outline, but you lost interest in writing. Your characters had to say what they said to explain what they were doing and why they were doing it. Without these explanations the reader wouldn't understand your characters' actions.

Characters who feel a need to explain what they are doing and why generally do so because the situation itself isn't as interesting as it should be. As a result, you've had your characters over compensate in an attempt to make it more interesting.

If you are having your characters do things out of character, either your plot is wrong for your characters or your characters are wrong for your plot. Obviously your outline isn't working. You have two choices: (1) Abandon your plot and see where the characters take you or (2) back up and start afresh from the last place where you were genuinely interested. From that point on discard everything beyond it, and then built a new plot from there.[22]

Shoring It Up

Kristen Kyle discusses a number of ways to shore up a sagging middle.[34] These include the following:

Change Point of View. If a scene seems to be dragging, try switching the viewpoint character. Choose the person with the most at stake during the scene, emotionally or physically.

Create Cliffhangers. End a chapter or a scene in a way that tempts the reader to turn the page and keep going. Stop a scene or chapter in the middle of a crisis, or when a decision has been made that will change the course of the adventure, or when plans have been made but not put into effect, or any place that leaves the reader itching to know more.

Demand Action. Put the protagonist in a situation where he doesn't have a choice. He must take action. Directly challenge his fears or flaws, or both at the same time.

Eliminate Scenes or Sequels. Cut out scenes that do not advance the plot or contribute something new to characterization or relationships. Don't hang on to a scene just because it took you three days of precious time to write it. You also can eliminate sequels or connect two scenes with a transition instead of a sequel.

Foreshadow. Hint at things to come, such as an approaching danger that threatens to tip the scales against your protagonist.

Heighten Conflict. You can beef up the existing conflicts by inserting further complications for the characters as they continue on in their journey toward the answer to the story question. Think of situations that will create a strong reaction in one or more characters. Aim for scenes involving strong emotions—anger, frustration, jealousy, joy, passion and so forth.

New Barrier. Throw in a new barrier that threatens the life of the protagonist or prevents him from obtaining his goal or threatens his relationships. The resulting setback provides an opportunity for renewed conflict.

Secrets. Add suspense by revealing a character's mysterious past in teasing little tidbits. You also can build suspense by letting the reader know something that the character doesn't, such as a decision that will lead to serious consequences. Then have the character make the wrong choice, or let the reader peek in on the antagonist during a planning scene as he plots the next assault on your protagonist.

Show Characters Interacting More. Showing the characters interacting more increases the reader's interest.

Show Don't Tell. Because blocks of narration slow down the pace, look for places where you can change narration to more interesting dialogue and action.

Time Pressures. If your story lacks a sense of urgency, create a deadline of some sort, either physical or emotional, with definite consequences if your character fails.

Something New. Introduce new and more interesting characters. You can also introduce new and more interesting subplots or boost the importance of existing subplots.

Up the Stakes. Make the goal more difficult to achieve, or the consequences of failure even higher. Think of plot twists where you can combine more than one thing going wrong at the same time. [28,31,34]

END

The story narrows down as the end approaches so the ending can take place clearly and decisively. If you have parallel plots, they should have converged already into a single plot line. All the subordinate characters should be "offstage," their work done, to leave the main characters alone in the "spotlight" to do the final battle. The end then answers the story question.

Don't introduce new or complex settings for the end if it's going to mean stopping the story for description. If the place is new but simple, such as a supermarket, then it won't need much description. Just cite a few details. Readers can fill in the rest. The moment the final situation is over and things have assumed their final shape, that's the end of the story. [30,35]

The end consists of two parts: (1) the climax and (2) the resolution.

Climax

The *climax*, also known as the *showdown*, is the decisive event that resolves the conflict. Although a novel has a number of high points of tension and action, the climax is the highest point. Everything in the story up to this point has been leading to the climax. If a character is going to change, this is the experience that finally demonstrates that change. If the major problem is going to be resolved, this is where the protagonist resolves it. And this is where the antagonist makes his last big fight, where the lovers are united, or where the quest reaches its goal.

The climax should be the hottest action scene or the most intense suspense scene. For instance, in the climax to the movie *Star Wars*, the Rebels, including Luke Skywalker (Mark Hamill), make an attack on the Empire's most powerful and ominous weapon, the Death Star, which is capable of destroying entire planets. It is aimed and ready to wipe out the rebel base. After a great battle and the deaths of some rebel pilots, Luke successfully fires his missile into the death star's vulnerable spot and destroys it, saving the rebel forces. Climax over.

The climax must be in proportion to the length of your story. In a novel, the climax usually occupies at least one chapter and may take up several.[22]

Resolution

Once the climax is completed, the falling action leads quickly toward the story's *resolution,* which is the final explanation of events. Its function is to wrap up the story.

The final scene should show the new order after the upheaval of the climax. It should show that the characters' worlds have not been thrown permanently off-kilter, but that the protagonist's courage in facing the conflict has prevented a disaster.

Whereas the climax usually resolves the external conflict, the resolution usually resolves the internal or psychological conflict. This provides closure on those essential storylines. In the resolution of *Caduceus Awry* (2000), a police detective, Sam Kincaid, explains to Dr. Mark Valentine how they cleared him of the murder of his ex-wife, names the person who actually committed the murder, and explains how they caught him. Also, it becomes evident that Mark has come to grips with his aversion to the Caduceus Club, a meeting of doctors with substance abuse problems, which has already been foreshadowed as the key to him maintaining sobriety. The theme of "man can overcome his personal demons" has been fulfilled, or at least its fulfillment has been hinted at.

A successful resolution has three characteristics: (1) Closure, (2) brevity, and (3) dramatization. *Closure* means you give the readers enough information for them to feel that the book is over. *Brevity* is important to the resolution because if it goes on too long it will leach all emotion from the climax. *Dramatization* ensures that your resolution feels like part of the story, not a chunk of narrative tacked on after the story is over. Try to show what happens to your characters after the climax by showing them in motion.

Resolution is also known as the *denouement*, which literally means "unknotting."[22,30,36]

Types of Endings

Endings come in two types—circular and linear. Within these two types, endings can by happy, sad, satisfying, or seem not to exist.

Circular Ending

A *circular ending* involves a trip away from home and then a return. Quest-adventure stories often have this pattern. The major character sets out to find something, passes through a number of trials along the way, and finally succeeds, often at great personal cost, and then returns home, in part to be rewarded and in part to share the benefits of his experience with his family, tribe, or nation. The experience may be tangible (treasure) or intangible (insight and wisdom).[12,29,30,35,36]

The *Wonderful Wizard of Oz* (1900) by Frank Baum is an

example of a circular plot. Dorothy dreams of a better place, without torment of her dog, Toto, by a hateful neighbor spinster, so she plans to run away. A cyclone appears and carries her to the magical Land of Oz. After a run in with the Wicked Witch of the West and her flying monkey-like creatures, Dorothy and her three traveling companions—the lion, the tin man, and the straw man—finally reach Oz and the wizard. In the end, they all learn that they already have that which they wish for. With the quest over, Dorothy returns home to Kansas, having learned "There's no place like home."[37]

Linear Ending

With a *linear ending*, the story is a jagged, uphill journey with building suspense until at last it reaches the highest point of conflict. Minor characters have come and gone, and finally it's just the two opposing forces left. Once the result of the conflict is known, the story is over. Most genre fiction, particularly mystery, adventure, and suspense, follow this pattern.[12,29,30,35,36]

In the movie *The Maltese Falcon* (1941), Sam Spade (Humphrey Bogart) is a partner in a private-detective firm. He finds himself hounded by police when his partner, Miles Archer (Jerome Cowan), is killed while tailing a man. The woman, Brigid O'Shaughnessy (Mary Astor), who hired Sam and Miles turns out not to be who she says she is, and is really involved in something to do with the "Maltese Falcon," a gold-encrusted life-sized statue of a falcon, the only one of its kind. The story ends with a final confrontation between Sam and Brigid in which Brigid is unmasked as the liar and killer she is, and the circumstances of Archer's death is revealed. Story over.

Happy, Sad, and Satisfying Endings

A *happy ending* is one in which the main character gets the ending he has earned by his actions during the story. A *sad ending* is one in which he does not. Most genre fiction tends to end on a positive note—the murderer caught, the lovers reunited, or the kidnapped child rescued. However, the important thing is that the ending is *satisfying* to the reader. For example, in *A Tale of Two*

Cities (1859) by Charles Dickens, the satisfying ending is peace of mind. The protagonist, Sydney Carton, dies, giving his life in the place of his look-a-like who is the husband of the woman he loves. His happiness is the fact that he has saved her happiness. His last words, spoken on the Guillotine, are the last line of the book?[12,29,30,35,36,38]

- *"It is a far, far better thing I do, than I have ever done; it is a far, far better rest that I go to, than I have ever known."*[38]

No Ending

Unfortunately, stories with seemingly *no ending* do get published, sometimes by famous authors. How many novels have you read where you turned the page to see what happens next only to find a blank page? In such stories there's no final resolution, nothing that seems worth all the build up—just a disappointed and cheated feeling by the reader.

Stated Goal versus True Goal

A common assumption among new writers of fiction is that the thing the protagonist gets must match the goal he seeks. This is not necessarily true. There's a vast difference between a stated goal and a true goal. The protagonist usually is unaware of this and believes, for instance, that if he seeks a million dollars, obtaining it will make him happier than anything else. His real need may be for an inner sense of his own self worth, which he mistakenly believes the money will supply. In the end, he becomes aware of this, and sees the true path to obtaining his real goal.[13] Consider the following example:

- Joe Blow is unhappy with his marriage and family life. He feels overwhelmed by the bills, which he has trouble paying. He longs for financial security and sees the solution to his problem as somehow obtaining a million dollars. He abandons his wife and two young children and sets off on the quest. By hook and by crook, mostly the latter, he eventually obtains a huge some of money, only to end up in prison. In prison, he thinks back about his wedding, the birth of his children, and the happy times in his marriage. He watches a TV program about financial management and comes to the realization that the problem was not insufficient money, but over-spending to make it appear that he was wealthier than he truly was. Enlightened, he longs for the happy relationship with his family that he had abandoned.

Clearly, Joe Blow's stated goal is wealth. In the end it turns out that his true goal is satisfaction with his marriage situation. Will Joe Blow ever be reunited with his family? Who knows for sure? A definite answer is seldom given. However, usually a hint of some kind is, leaving the reader with an impression of how it will turn out.[13]

Deus ex Machina

Whatever you do, avoid the *Deus ex Machina* (God from a machine) ending. It happens when the protagonist is overwhelmed and there doesn't seem to be any possible way out. Then suddenly an improbable event occurs that bails him out. Consider the following example:

* John hero is in the throws of the biggest battle of his life—a dagger to dagger fight with Sam Villain. The battle takes place at the edge of a bottomless pit. Hero is no match for Villain who is twice as big and four times as strong. Hero quickly becomes overwhelmed and falls backward to the ground. Villain quickly straddles him and presses the tip of his razor-sharp dagger against Hero's chest. "Die you weakling," Villain snarls as he prepares to plunge the dagger deep into Hero's heart. Hero is totally exhausted—too weak to resist. Death seems certain. His life starts to flash before his eyes. Villain draws the dagger back to make the fatal plunge. Suddenly, an eagle swoops down and smashes into Villain, knocking him over the edge into the bottomless pit. Hero is saved. Villain is vanquished.

The Deus ex Machina device originated in the ancient Greek

theater. Playwrights arranged for characters at the end of the play to become so enmeshed in irresolvable situations that they were doomed to failure. Then suddenly a machine was lowered onto the stage and one of the Greek gods stepped out. In his divine manner, the god resolved what the mere mortals could not.[6,39]

Symbolic Event

Sometimes stories end with a *symbolic event* in the form of a *punch line* that symbolizes fulfillment. It's an indication that your characters have a future. To create a situation where a punch line will be effective you establish early on that a particular event represents fulfillment for the protagonist, and then at the end you spring the punch line.

At the end of *Caduceus Awry* (2000), Dr. Mark Valentine has rescued his daughter, Lisa, from the clutches of the crime boss who kidnapped her. The loose ends in the story have been wrapped up except whether or not Valentine will finally get control of his alcoholism.

Throughout the novel, Mark had tossed things at wastebaskets and missed, on one occasion comparing his misses to the sorry state of his life. The following is the last paragraph of the novel (Angela and Kincaid are two other prominent characters in the novel):

* *"I'll be damned," Mark said. He gave Angela one last look, then turned to leave the room. When he and Lisa reached the door, he stopped, took the nearly full pack of cigarettes from his shirt pocket, and tossed it at the wastebasket in the corner of the room. The pack hit the basket dead center. Then he turned back to Kincaid and smiled. "Two points," he said, holding up two fingers in a victory sign.[19]*

By finally hitting the basket dead center a making the victory sign he signaled to the reader that all is finally going to be right with his life, including resolution of his alcohol problem.

EPILOGUE

An *epilogue*, also called an *afterword*, is a small addition or concluding section at the end of a novel. It often deals with the future of its characters. Contemporary novelists seldom use an epilogue, and when they do it is usually added to the resolution only if it differs significantly from the main story in time or place or if it's going to use a radically different narrative style. Putting this material in an epilogue alerts the reader that something different is coming, which softens the transition.

The narrative in the epilogue of Michael Crichton's *Jurassic Park* (1990) takes place off the island in a city more than 20 miles away, days after the destruction of the island dinosaurs. And in the epilogue of John Irving's *The World According to Garp* (1978), the narrator warns us about the futures of 14 characters.[8,40]

The epilogue may hint at future action, thus allowing the reader an opportunity to imagine what is not written; that is, leaving a question or two unanswered. For example, after the vicious serial killer has been captured and put away you might show him contemplating his escape from prison.[22,29]

STRUCTURE CHART

The following *structure chart* illustrates the main points of a novel as described in this chapter. When writing your novel, it may be helpful to create a similar chart and fill in the details.

Title	-	• No real rules, except don't make it too long. Many titles are just one word.
Prologue	-	• Four types (background, different point of view, past protagonist, or future protagonist) • Prologue test
Beginning	Initial Setup	• Exposition • Hook

		• Main characters • Setting
	Big Event	• The situation that launches the story (protagonist is thrust into the action) • Involves conflict • Establishes the story goal • Establishes the story's direction
Middle	Complications (plot points, reversals)	• Protagonist tries to achieve his goal • Obstacles are introduced • Disasters occur
	Crisis (Pinch)	• A showdown becomes inevitable. • Protagonist comes to realize that he must take a stand. There are only two choices. • He agonizes over which of the two courses of action to take. • He makes his decision. • Epiphany (revelation) • He sets out to do final battle (the climax).
End	Climax (Showdown)	• The final and biggest "battle" • Highest point of tension • Decides overall winner and loser • Protagonist demonstrates internal change
	Resolution (Denouement)	• Climax is over and story goal is answered • Winners and losers are known • Loose ends are wrapped up • Characters have gained new insights that reflect their growth • Theme is reinforced • Symbolic event
Epilogue (Afterword)	-	• Seldom used • Often deals with futures of characters

		• Differs significantly from the main story in time or place or narrative style

Based on Susan D. Schnelbach and Christopher Scott Wyatt[29]

References

1. Kress, Nancy, Beginnings, Middles & Ends, Writer's Digest Books, Cincinnati, 1999.
2. Tobias, Ron, 20 Master Plots, Writer's Digest Books, Cincinnati, 1993.
3. Clough, B. W., Theory and practice of titles, http://www.sfwa.org/bulletin/articles/clough.htm, 1995.
4. Silvester, Niko, Creative Writing for Teens, http://teenwriting.about.com/library/weekly/aa111102a.htm.
5. Kellerman, Jonathan, The Devil's Waltz, Ballantine Books, New York, 2003.
6. Bishop, Leonard, Dare to be a Great Writer, Writer's Digest Books, Cincinnati, 1992.
7. Talmor, Lital, Where to Begin? When, Where and How to Write a Prologue, Writing-World.com, http://www.writing-world.com/fiction/prologue.shtml, 2004.
8. Crichton, Michael, Jurassic Park, Knopf, New York, 1990.
9. Morrell, David, The Fifth Profession, Warner Books, New York, 1990.
10. Du Maurier, Daphne, Rebecca, Doubleday; Reissue edition, New York, 1938 (Originally published in 1938).
11. Article: In the Beginning, Writing and Publishing, Suite101.Comhttp://www.suite101.com/article.cfm/novel_writing/18290/1.
12. Dibell, Ansen, Writer's Digest Books, Cincinnati, 1989.
13. Swain, Dwight V., Techniques of the Selling Author, University of Oklahoma Press, Norman, 1974.
14. Eugenides, Jeffrey, The Virgin Suicides, Warner Books; Reprint edition, New York, 1994 (Originally published in 1993).
15. Bickham, Jack M., Scene and Sequel: Two Keys to a Strong Plot, In The Writer's Digest Book of Novel Writing, Ed. By Tom Clark, William Brohaugh, Bruce Woods, Bill Strickland, and Peter Blosksom, Writer's Digest Books, Cincinnati, 1992.
16. Bickham, Jack, M., Scene and Structure, Writer's Digest Books, Cincinnati, 1993.
17. Corman, Avery, Kramer vs Kramer, Signet, New York, 1978.

18. Rendell-Smock, Sharon, Hooking the Reader: Opening Lines that Sell, Morris Publishing, Kearney, NE, 2001.
19. Milhorn, H. Thomas, Caduceus Awry, Writer's showcase, San Jose, 2000.
20. Brown, Dan, The Da Vinci code, Doubleday, New York, 2003.
21. Ocork, Shannon, How to Write Mysteries, Writer's Digest Press, Cincinnati, 1989.
22. Kress, Nancy, Your opening quest, WritersDigest.com, http://www.writersdigest.com/articles/kress_opening.asp?secondarycategory=Fiction+Subhome+Page.
23. Greenway, Will, Dynamic beginnings: Getting your story off to a great start, http://www.writing-world.com/fiction/greenway1.shtml, 2000.
24. Elements of a successful story, The Fiction Writer's Page, http://www.capcollege.bc.ca/dept/cmns/story.html.
25. Kilian, Crawford, Advice on novel writing, http://www.steampunk.com/sfch/writing/ckilian/#2.
26. Simon, Rachel, The Writer's Writing Guide: Beginnings, Middles and Ends, http://www.rachelsimon.com/wg_begmidend.htm, 2002.
27. Kittredge, Mary, Hot to Plot! A Plotting "System" That Works, In The Writer's Digest Handbook of Novel Writing, Ed. By Clark, Tom, William Brohaugh, Bruce Woods, Bill Strickland, and Peter Blocksom, Writer's Digest Press, Cincinnati, 1992. pp 56-61.
28. Rasley, Alecia, Tightening the sagging middle, The Writers Corner, http://www.sff.net/people/alicia/artmid.htm, 2000.
29. Schnelbach, Susan D. and Christopher Scott Wyatt, Plots and Stories, Tameri Guide for Writers, http://www.tameri.com/write/plotnstory.html.
30. Lake, Lori L., Plot: Part Two, Navigating dangerous terrain, http://www.justaboutwrite.com/A_Archive_Plot2LL.html, 2003.
31. Hinze, Vicki, Sagging middles, Fiction Factor, http://www.fictionfactor.com/guests/middles.html, 2003.
32. Mitchell, Margaret, Gone with the Wind, Scribner Reprint Edition, New York, 1936.
33. Murphy's Laws Site, http://www.murphys-laws.com/.
34. Kyle, Kristen, Curing the sagging middle, http://www.kristenkyle.com/sagpace.html, 2004.
35. Rasley, Alicia, End Thoughts, Writers' Corner, http://www.sff.net/people/alicia/art1.htm, 1997.
36. Collier, Oscar, How to Write & Sell Your First Novel, Writer's Digest Press, Cincinnati, 1990.
37. Baum, Frank, The Wonderful Wizard of Oz, HarperCollins; 100th Anniversary edition, 1990 (Originally published in 1900).

38. Dickens, Charles, A Tale of Two Cities, Signet Classics; Reissue edition, New York, 1998 (Originally published in 1859).
39. Burns, Michael R., Some thoughts on Deus ex Machina, Colorado Springs Fiction Writing Group, http://www.csfwg.org/archives.htm, 2004.
40. Irving, John, The World According to Garp, Ballantine Books; Reissue edition, 1990 (Originally published in 1978).

Chapter 10

Scene and Sequel

A *scene* is a unit of conflict. A *sequel* is the transition period that links two scenes. Whereas scenes are the "showing" part of a novel, sequels are the "telling part." The usual basic structure of a novel consists of a scene followed by a sequel, with the pattern being repeated a number of times until the final scene. Each scene and sequel supports the other, before and after. Your construction and handling of the scenes and sequels are the keys to a strong plot.

A sequel doesn't always have to follow a scene, but too many scenes with back to back action will tire your reader; so make sure to put sequels in at appropriate places. It's probably a good idea when you write your first draft to follow the scene-sequel-scene pattern. Then on rewrite if your story is more suited to occasionally altering that pattern, possibly by leaving out a sequel now and then, that's the time to do it.

Conflict provides the action of each scene; it grabs the reader's attention and keeps him interested. Your protagonist should leave most scenes in worse shape than he was when he went into them.[1,2]

SCENE

Alicia Rasley defines a scene as *a unit of action and interaction taking place in more or less in real-time and centering on some event of plot development.* Scenes are where the action takes place, where conflict occurs, and where the excitement and danger is. They are the places where the protagonist is pitted against other characters, machines, the environment, or any number of other opponents. A scene raises a question to snare your reader; will the protagonist achieve his goal for the scene or will he fail to do so? Conflict in scenes is always external. Thus, scenes are built on dialogue and action. Internal conflict belongs in sequels.

Every scene should center on something that is happening in the here and now—not a dream, not a flashback, not a flash forward, and not introspection. A scene should consist of a fight, either physical or verbal. The goals in scenes are short term ones. If the protagonist is successful in achieving his short-term goal, he moves closer to achieving his long-term goal. If he is unsuccessful, he moves further away from it. To attain the long-term goal, he must first accomplish a number of short term goals. Once he achieves his long-term goal, the story is over.

Scenes should vary in intensity to keep the reader from getting either bored or emotionally drained. Intensity level is determined by the importance of winning the conflict and the risks involved. Generally, scenes near the climax of the novel should be more intense than the ones in the middle.

A scene should evolve from everything that has happened up to that point in the story. All scenes should end in disaster except the final one.[1,3,4]

Questions to Answer

Dwight Swain says that there are five questions you should answer before you start writing each scene: (1) where does the scene take place, (2) who is involved, (3) what goes wrong, (4) how does the scene unfold, and (5) why do you need the scene in the first place?[5]

Where Does the Scene Take Place? What is the setting of the scene? Is it a scorching mid-day in the Mojave Desert in the present day, a frigid midnight in the Alps in 1860, or the bottom of the sea in 2037? Does the action take place in a barroom, on a large lake, in a bedroom, or in a department store?

Think of ways you can strengthen your setting? For example, a face-to-face confrontation in a crowd is stronger than a telephone conversation in an isolated telephone booth. An encounter in the middle of the state fair during a roaring storm is more powerful than one in a nice restaurant on a beautiful day.[4,5]

Who is Involved? Who will be the viewpoint character in the scene—the character who has the most to lose, the character who has the most to gain, the character who initiates the action, or the character who is just along for the ride? In most scenes, the viewpoint character should be the aggressor—the one who's active, dynamic, and always driving forward. Therefore, the viewpoint character in a scene could be the protagonist, the antagonist, or any other important character. And as we have seen, the viewpoint character in most modern-day genre novels may vary from scene to scene and chapter to chapter.

As a rule, most of the time each scene should involve only two characters so you can alert the reader to a change of speaker simply by starting a new paragraph without a lot of identification tags. If you need to have more than two characters in a scene, give each a distinctive way of speaking (stutter, accent, formal language, slang, and so forth) so readers can tell who is speaking without a lot of identification tags. Remember, even a debate in Congress isn't going to involve every last Representative.[4,5-7]

What goes Wrong? What goes wrong with your characters plan? What happens that he fails to anticipate? Why does his plan fell despite his anticipation of developments? And don't forget Murphy's Law. Think of ways you can use it. Think of a scene as building toward some surprise in the end, something the viewpoint character and the reader don't expect.[4,5]

How does the Scene Unfold? You should choose your writing style and the words you use to match the action of the scene. If the scene is a mad dash through enemy territory at night with bombs falling all around, the writing style and the words you use should be different than those for a scene describing a character getting home at two o'clock in the morning and trying to sneak into bed without waking his wife.

How will the world of the story be different when the scene is over? For example, in a romance novel how will the events of the scene affect the relationship? In a thriller novel, if two characters are allies at the beginning of a scene, what events might cause them to become enemies by the end of the scene?[4,5,7]

Why Is the Scene Needed? The purpose of every scene is to maintain the story's momentum and to keep the story on track, moving toward the resolution of the story question. So the scene should somehow tie into the larger purpose of the story. The scene should either assist or obstruct the character's pursuit of his ultimate goal.[4,5,7]

Cause and Effect

A story follows the basic pattern of *cause and effect*; that is, the story question in the beginning of the novel leads to the answer of the question at the end of the novel. Similarly, much of plotting from chapter to chapter deals with one thing leading to another. And the scene question at the beginning of a scene leads to the answer at the end of the scene.

Any plot development must have a logical cause and effect, and subunits within a scene also follow the cause and effect pattern—what Dwight Swain calls interlocking *motivation-reaction units* (M-R units). You write M-R units by alternating between what your point-of-view character sees or hears (the motivation) and what he does (the reaction). Motivation-reaction units strung together form the basis for writing scenes.

A *motivation* stimulus is anything outside your character to which he reacts. It may be an alarm clock going off, someone throwing a punch, or a bomb exploding. A *reaction* is anything the character does in response to the motivation stimulus, such as bolting upright when the alarm sounds, ducking when someone throws a punch, or diving for cover when a bomb explodes. The simplest M-R Unit is two sentences—a motivation and a reaction.[1,5]

- *Motivation.* The thump of a pair of heavy shoes grew closer, then stopped behind her.
  Reaction. Reluctantly, she turned and faced him.

The reaction can be divided into *feeling, action,* and *speech,* always in that order.

- **Motivation.** The thump of a pair of heavy shoes grew closer, then stopped behind her.
  Reaction:
    Feeling. Her pulse quickened and she gasped for breath.
    Action. Reluctantly, she turned and faced him.
    Speech. "Zeke, I didn't expect to see you here."

When you put it all together, it sounds like:

- The thump of a pair of heavy shoes grew closer, then stopped behind her. Her pulse quickened and she gasped for breath. Reluctantly, she turned and faced him. "Zeke, I didn't expect to see you here."[5]

Scene Stages

Swain divides a scene into three stages: (1) Goal, (2) conflict, and (3) disaster. The only scene that should not end in disaster is the final one of the novel.[7]

Stage 1: Goal

Your character should enter the scene wanting something specific and concrete; that is, a goal. So what is your character's immediate goal? Is it to escape from the Mafia hit man, to get out of a burning building, or to steal the secret files from his powerful opponent's office?

What has to happen in the scene for the character to realize his short-term goal? What obstacles must he overcome (the more obstacles and the bigger they are the better)? What will be the consequences if the character fails to achieve his short-term goal? Will the antagonist obtain possession of the hidden treasure or will the protagonist lose his true love, his honor, or his self respect? What would be the best ways for the character to overcome the obstacles that are placed in his path?

Make sure the stated scene goal is clearly relevant to the

overall story question. Also, make sure the opposing character's goal, which is opposite the protagonist's goal, is important and clearly spelled out.

The scene goal is primarily a springboard to plunge your character into conflict. So the more quickly you establish the scene goal, the more quickly you can move on to action and unanticipated events. Therefore, the scene goal should be stated within the first half page of a scene.

The establishment of a scene goal causes the reader to ask the *scene question* "Will the protagonist accomplish whatever it is he set's out to do?" The scene question gives the reader something to worry about. You must end each scene with an answer to the scene question (Will the character achieve his short-term goal?). Possible answers are:

- *Yes.* Sam gets the best of Bart and rescues Sarah.
- *No (They Have to Try Something Else).* Sam tries to rescue Sarah, but fails. He decides to talk to a relative of Bart's and see if she has any idea where Bart might go to hide.
- *Yes, But (Something Unanticipated Happens).* Sam rescues Sarah, but one of Bart's henchmen appears suddenly and pulls a gun on Sam.
- *No, and Furthermore (Something Even Worse Happens).* Sam is unable to rescue Sarah. The one person, other than Bart, who might know where to find her turns up murdered.

Of the four offered answers, only the last three are options for a scene ending in the middle portion of the story. If the answer is yes, the story is prematurely over.[3-5,7,8]

Stage 2: Conflict

Conflict is two forces striving to achieve mutually incompatible goals (Sam wants to get Sarah back. Bart wants to keep her.). However, conflict for conflict's sake isn't enough. It's meaningless. There must be a plausible explanation for the conflict.

What is the central event (the conflict) of the scene? Is it a verbal confrontation or a physical fight about money, a woman, a man, or honor? How does your choice of the central event affect the overall plot?

Conflict can be external or internal. What external obstacles (complications) does your character encounter in trying to obtain his goal? Think of obstacles you can place in the scene by the antagonist or his allies—a car that won't start, a jimmied gas line in the house and a lit cigarette, a gun that won't fire. These obstacles test your protagonist's resolve and resourcefulness.

How does the overall external conflict manifest itself in the scene? For example, if the overall conflict is about the murder of blonde prostitutes, the short-term goal might be trying to catch him in a trap by using a police woman posing as blonde prostitute.

Where does the character start out emotionally? Is he nervous but hopeful, scared but determined, anxious but resolved? How does this manifest in his actions? Does he repeatedly glance at his watch, pace the floor, tremble, clench his teeth, or snap at friends? At the end of the scene, how does he differ emotionally than at the beginning of the scene?

Throw in twists and turns. Make it tough for your character by bringing in additional obstacles related to the situation. In other words, make it more difficult for your character to obtain his goal.

One way to make it more difficult for your character is to stress the strength of the opposition. Make sure he has a formidable opponent. If your antagonist is weak, there's not much of a conflict and, therefore, not much of a story.

For almost the entire story the protagonist and the antagonist should appear equally matched, although not necessarily in the same way and not necessarily in individual scenes. One may be much stronger than the other, but not quiet as smart so that it all balances out.

Whatever you do, avoid the easy way out. Your characters should be challenged, pushed to the wall, forced to improvise, and draw on inner resources and possibly physical strength

A conflict may be as simple as one man fighting another man, but the fight must have a reason for occurring. [4,5,8]

- Sam Hero tracks down Bart Villain and they get into a fist fight as Sam tries to rescue Sarah from Bart's evil clutches.

Stage 3: Disaster

A *disaster* is a logical but unexpected action or new information that leaves the character at a loss, creating a calamity. More simply put, it's a failure of your character to achieve his scene goal. Most, if not all, of your intermediate scenes should end in disasters, with matters apparently much worse than before. The protagonist should be defeated, although not utterly, creating tension and suspense that builds toward the final scene.[3,5,8]

- The battle has been going on for some time. Sam Hero seems to be getting the best of Bart Villain. Unexpectedly, Bart reaches into his boot and pulls out a small pistol. He shoots Sam in the leg and escapes with Sarah in tow.

A disaster serves as a hook to keep the reader reading by causing him to ask "Oh what will Sam Hero do now?" Disaster is also known as *complication* and *scene reversal*.

Scene Length

A scene can be a few sentences or several pages or anything in between. The important thing is for it to be long enough to get the job done. The average number of pages in a scene in a modern-day novel tends to run about six. In general, the length of a scene should be directly proportional to its importance in the overall story; that is, the greater the importance, the longer the scene and the lesser the importance, the shorter the scene.[5,8,9]

SEQUEL

Sequels are passive times. If scenes are the mountains, then sequels are the valleys. They are places to insert emotions, logic, and internal conflicts. They also are the places to convert your characters disaster from the prior scene into a goal for the next scene. They are the places where the character tries to gain control of his feelings and logically resolve conflicts in his mind. It is the place where he considers his options and decides on his next action.

The sequel is where you present necessary information to the reader that can't be presented in a scene because it would slow the action down too much. Since the sequel is the decision making area, it is where the reader finds out everything the character is thinking and agonizing over. It is the place for flashbacks or flash forwards as they pertain to the dilemma facing the character.

Sequels provide logic and plausibility to your story. They let readers know why a character is doing what he's doing and the thought processes behind his upcoming actions. You also can use sequels to set up your character's personality and give background information.

Long scenes equal big interest and long sequels indicate strong plausibility. So, in writing, you must decide which element is most important to you at each given point. If your story tends to drag or grow boring, strengthen and enlarge the scenes and build up the conflict. If an air of improbability pervades your story, lengthen your sequels by giving more explanation.

At some point, you'll end the cycle of scene-sequel-scene with the final scene. You'll give your character either ultimate victory or ultimate defeat, and that will be the end of the novel. But until you get there, the alternating pattern of scene and sequel is usually followed.[4,8,10-12]

Purposes of a Sequel

Swain states that the purposes of a sequel are threefold: (1) to translate disaster into a goal, (2) to telescope reality, and (3) to control tempo.[5]

Translate Disaster into Goal

A sequel sets forth your focal character's reaction to the scene just completed and provides him with motivation for the scene next to come. Thus sequel is the aftermath of the scene—the state of affairs and state of mind that shapes your character's behavior.

A sequel translates disaster into a goal by providing a bridge that gives your character a plausible reason for striking out in a particular new direction that will bring him into further conflict.

Despite the fact that there are always a number of options to choose from, he must decide on only one. He has to ponder the benefits and disadvantages of each option before coming to a decision. Only when he reaches a decision as to which road to take can your story precede logically.[5]

Telescope Reality

In a sequel you can skip or compress time rather than laying out action blow-by-blow. For instance, making a decision may take time and it may demand movement from one locale to another. Often it requires the introduction of new and non-dramatic material to help your character arrive at a decision. Hours, days, or months may pass before he can make up his mind what he wants to do. So what do you do? You telescope reality. You summarize the emotionally non-significant or non-pertinent material. You tell rather than show, or you use a combination of both.[5] Consider Swain's example of telescoping:

- *Fog and smog and soot-streaked snow. Steaming summer nights in New Orleans; the parched miles going across Wyoming. He knew them all, in the months that followed; knew them, and ignored them, because there was no room in him for anything but hate.*[5]

A transition, rather than a sequel, can serve as a link between two scenes. Let's say we are dealing with the feeling of anger, at first in New York and later in San Francisco. How do we handle the travel without using up too much space in our manuscript?

- In New York, sleep was too slow to come as he tossed and turned in bed. He hated Darryl and couldn't get him out of his mind. Then thankfully, sleep finally came—a fretful sleep with terrible nightmares in which he and Darryl slowly and brutally chopped each other to bits with machetes. He was still overwhelmed with anger when he stepped off the plane in San Francisco, but now fear had entered the picture.

Although emotion is used in this example, almost any subject can be used to create a transition. Transitions were covered in Chapter 7.

Control Tempo

In a novel it becomes necessary to speed up here and slow down there; that is, to control the tempo. Since a story is a series of peaks (scenes) and valleys (sequels), you can control tempo by varying the heights of the peaks and the depths of the valleys.[5]

Sequel Stages

Swain divides sequels into four stages: (1) Emotion, (2) dilemma, (3) decision, and (4) action.[5]

Stage 1: Emotion

The *emotion* stage of a scene is the place to show your character's state of mind after the disaster of the previous scene. Does he experience despair, anxiety, embarrassment, anger, bitterness, or grim determination? Or does he experience mixed emotions, such as fear mixed with resentment, bitterness mixed with disappointment, or suspicion mixed with confusion?

The only thing that counts in this stage is your character's preoccupation with the disaster. The reaction is dictated by the character's history and psychological makeup that you should have already developed. When something awful happens, the character staggers for awhile—off balance and out of kilter. So show him reacting viscerally to his disaster. Show him hurting. The emotion stage also is known as the *reaction* stage.[1,5,13]

There are three ways to show the emotional state of your character: (1) Describe it, (2) demonstrate it by his actions, and (3) have him discuss his feelings with someone else.

Describe It. Describing emotion is doing just that. You imagine how your character must feel, and you use words to describe those feelings.

- Sam had recovered from being shot, except for paralysis in one leg from the waist down. At first Sam denied his situation—that he would never walk again without crutches; then he bargained with God that if He would heal him he would go to church every time the door opened. When healing didn't happen, he became angry, only to have the anger transform itself into depression. With time, he gained acceptance. He would never walk normally again, and he knew it. But what good was acceptance to him now? Sarah was gone.

Demonstrate It. How does your character react to the disaster? Does he pace the floor or toss and turn in a sleepless state (anxiety)? Does he slam his fist through a wall or throw a telephone (anger)? Does he run away, hide, or tremble (fear)? Does he dab his wet eyes, blow his nose, or sit motionless with his head down (sadness). Does he walk aimlessly or forget an important appointment (confusion)? But most of all, does he accept defeat or decide to try again to achieve his goal?[1,5,13]

- Sam slumped in his chair and sat there motionless, his head held down. He had never felt so worthless in his entire life. He let out a long sigh. He was a failure and he knew it.

Discuss It. Here we set up a situation in which your character has a conversation with someone else—a friend, a lover, a partner—about what he's feeling. The other person might start the conversation by saying something as simple as "You look terrible. What's going on?" Your character may experience new emotions as a result of the conversation. The interaction, although a sequel, almost appears to be a scene, with dialogue, movement, and gestures.

Other characters also may have feelings about your character's defeat. Are they supportive or critical? Do they feel he's really a loser or have faith that he can rebound? The answers to these questions can be shown by narrative or by dialogue between your main scene character and other characters. Your character also may talk about earlier parts of the story or even his life.[5,14] In the example below, Robert is Sam's best friend.

- "Sam, I've about had it with you," Robert said. "I don't understand why you're behaving so irrationally—so irritable and moody. Before the injury, you always functioned on such an even keel. Self pity only goes so far, and then you have to get off your pity pot and get back into the stream of life— crippled or not. So do it, damn it."

Stage 2: Dilemma

So now your character is faced with a dilemma. He should manage to get a grip, to take stock, and to consider his options. He should move out of the blind feeling state into a thinking state. The problem is, there aren't very many options, and the ones available aren't very good.

The key to successful dilemmas is to present the character's toughest options, tighten the screws of tension by forcing a decision between the two worst ones, and make them apparent to the reader. Let your character agonize as he works through the choices.

He may learn new information in this stage that helps him toward arriving at a decision.[10,11,13]

- Word gets to John that Bart is holed up somewhere in a town only ten miles away, and that he is still holding Sarah prisoner.

Perhaps your character asks friends for advice about what he should do, or recalls something someone (father, mother, uncle, school teacher) once said to him that influences his decision. The point is, he doesn't have to try to reach a decision in total isolation. Others can be involved. The *dilemma stage* is also known as the *thought stage*.

Dilemma can be subdivided into three consecutive stages: (1) Review, (2) analysis, and (3) planning.[9,10]

Review. Your character looks back at the scene that has just passed. He mulls over the disaster and thinks about what it means in terms his story goal and why his story goal is important. He thinks back to earlier aspects of the story. For instance, in a mystery the detective may review earlier clues. In a romance, the heroine might recall earlier dates with her lover.[1]

- If only he had considered the prospect that Bart might have a hidden pistol. Somewhere in the past he had heard that Bart carried a small gun in his boot. Why had he forgotten it? Could he have avoided the bullet if he had just moved more quickly? Was he distracted by Sarah, tied up and crying in the corner? Obviously his judgment had been blunted temporarily. He still wants to pursue Bart and rescue Sarah, but how can he in such a handicapped state?

Analysis. Your character then moves into the analysis stage in which he tries to figure out the meaning of everything that's happened. He analyses the options available to him and painstakingly tries to arrive at a decision. This stage serves to further characterize your character because it shows how he thinks and what kind of person he is.[1]

- Is there anyway in his condition that he can go after Bart— someway he can trick him so he wouldn't have to be in a physical battle with him? Someway to get a jump on him? Even so, he would have to find him first. He had learned that Bart was in a town 10 miles away, but where was his exact location in the town. He could ask around. Bart had relatives nearby. Maybe they knew where he was. If they did, would they tell him? If not, should he threaten them with a gun? If he knew where to look, he would have to take a taxi there, since he was not yet able to drive. Then he could walk the rest of the way on his crutches and surprise Bart. He would have to shoot Bart before he could respond to his presence. No good. What if he had to climb a set of stairs to get to Bart? And even if there weren't any stairs to climb he was too unstable on crutches to hold a gun, aim it, and fire accurately. Too damn risky, but he had to do something. But what?

Planning. Taking into account all the pertinent factors he can think of, your character tries to come up with a new plan so he can move forward toward the story goal. He considers options, weighs them, discards some, rank orders others.[10]

- Okay, he would have to find Bart's location in the town first. Sam felt certain Bart's cousin John knew where Bart was. Sam and John had been friends all their lives. And John and Bart had fallen out recently. He could ask John if he knew where Bart might be hiding.

Stage 3: Decision

The final stage of sequel is *decision*. The character has reviewed what has happened to him and analyzed it in trying to determine the best path to follow. The decision process can be short or prolonged as the character collects more data. However, prolonged decision episodes run the risk of slowing the pace too much. So make your character decide on a new short-term goal, but make it risky. Give him a chance of succeeding, but only a chance. Having done so, the reader will be eager to turn the page, because now the character has a new goal, and the action is ready to begin all over again. But even after deciding on a goal, your character may still be nagged by doubts, scared, and confused.[1,10,11,13]

• Sure enough, Bart's cousin John had known where Bart was and he had been willing to share the information. Now, knowing Bart's location, Sam would ask Sarah's brother, Robert, to help him rescue Sarah. Robert was a big man and strong as an ox. Surely these strengths would compensate for Sam's weakness. The two of them could do it together, couldn't they?

Stage 4: Action

Your character gets back into action—making a telephone call, buying a gun, purchasing an airplane ticket, or doing whatever it takes to start him on his way to the time and place where he stands face to face with the same or a new opponent. This action sets up the next scene, which gives rise to further conflict. The new goal serves as a hook to keep your reader turning the pages.[1]

• Sam calls Robert and tells him he has decided to make another attempt to track down Bart and rescue Sarah. He asks for Robert's help. Robert agrees, so they decide on a plan to go after Bart.

So in the next scene the action will show Sam and Robert attempting to rescue Sarah from Bart and how Bart responds with resistance.[5,14]

Sequel Length

Sequel length will determine the overall mood of your story. Short sequels make the story fast-paced, longer Sequels make it introspective. You should choose sequel lengths accordingly.[5]

VARIATION OF SCENE-SEQUEL STRUCTURE

While not a hard-and-fast rule, most well-paced stories use the scene structure of Goal-Conflict-Disaster followed by sequel structure of Emotion-Dilemma-Decision-Action because it provides a method to move the plot and character development forward. If you have good reasons for varying from the classic scene pattern or sequel pattern, you may do so. However, if you do decide to vary from the classic pattern, you need to be absolutely sure it makes sense in the overall story. Don't chose to write a scene structure variation just for the challenge of doing so. If it doesn't improve your plot, stick with the classic scene and sequel pattern.[1]

Scene Structure Variation

Bickham gives a number of ways you can vary your scene structure, including (1) starting your scene somewhere other than at the classic entering point of stating the scene goal, (2) ending somewhere short of a full-fledged disaster, (3) interrupting the scene anywhere by having other action intervene, (4) interrupting the conflict by having the viewpoint character's internalization develop into a sequel in the middle of things, and (5) presenting the Goal-Conflict-Disaster stages out of order.[1]

Sequel Structure Variation

Bickham also gives a number of ways you can vary your sequel structure, including (1) skipping one or more parts of the classic pattern of Emotion-Dilemma-Decision-Action, (2) presenting one or more stages in a few words, (3) amplifying any given portion out of proportion to the others, (4) mixing up the normal presentation order of the four stages, (5) interrupting a sequel with the unexpected onset of a new scene, and (6) inserting a flashbacks within the Dilemma stage.[1]

WAYS TO KEEP THE READER WORRIED

Bickham presents a number of ways you can play with the content of scenes and sequels to add to the reader's worry and keep him turning the pages.[10]

Scene Ways

Faulty Information. Show new information in the scene which makes it clear that your viewpoint character had faulty information coming in and, therefore, assumed something that was not true. This puts him at a big disadvantage, requiring him to work harder to attain his goal.

Hidden Agenda. Have your character think about or even orally hint at the fact that he has more of an agenda than the reader is fully aware of.

Higher Stakes than Expected. Show that the stakes are higher than your character had realized.

Reveal Something. Have the antagonist reveal something that the protagonist didn't know when the scene started. This puts the protagonist at a decided disadvantage.

Ticking Clock. Have the antagonist set a ticking clock on the duration of the scene, such as the bomb is set to explode in an hour.

Unknown to the Protagonist. Drop a hint about something the antagonist seems to know but the protagonist doesn't. This raises an ancillary issue for the reader to worry about.[10]

Sequel Ways

Hold Out. After your character arrives at a decision, hold out on what it is. Keep it from the reader until later. The reader will worry about whether your character has made the right decision or not.

Insufficient Thought. Have the antagonist's emotional reaction overwhelm him, so that he plunges back into the battle having insufficiently completed the thought process.

Interruption. Stage an interruption by an outside stimulus which forces the character to stop in the midst of a sequel and meet the new threat not completely prepared.

New Dimensions. In the dilemma segment, have your character realize whole new dimensions of the previous disaster and of his present plight that he hadn't thought of before.

Roadblock. Insert a "roadblock" scene in the action stage of the sequel so that the viewpoint character must do battle of some kind before finding his way back to the next scene, which normally would have followed the completed action stage.

Ticking Clock. Have the antagonist or the protagonist himself set a ticking clock so that the protagonist only has so many minutes to reach a decision before something bad happens.[10]

PACING

Pacing is the rhythm of a novel—the speed at which events in the novel occur and unfold. Sometimes the pace is quick, sometimes it's slow, but it is always flowing toward the end of the novel. It is making specific choices of structure to tap the emotions of the readers so that they feel what you want them to feel at any given time during the story.

Through your handling of scenes and sequels you can control the pace. Since conflict makes up the bulk of typical scenes, scenes are swift and exciting. Sequels slow things down as the character rehashes what has happened to him and considers his options. Heavy dramatic scenes should be followed by something lighter. [1,5,15-17]

The following table lists some things you can do to keep the story moving quickly or to slow the pace. In general, reversing those things that increase the pace serves to slow the pace.

To Speed Up the Pace	To Slow Down the Pace
• Use active-voice grammatical constructions	• Use blocks of narrative or description
• Use crisp, sharp verbs	• Extend the length of existing sequels
• Decrease the use of adjectives and adverbs	
• Eliminate excessive scene verbiage	• Use flashbacks (sparingly)
• Use dialogue action sequences	• Use long flowing sentences
• Use shorter sequels between scenes or eliminate the sequel between two scenes	• Use long paragraphs
	• Use non-action-related narration and description,
• Increase the intensity of the conflict	• Use non-tension factors (eating, sleeping, shopping, polite conversation)
• Increase urgency (rattlesnake in bed with you)	• Use passive-voice grammatical constructions,
• Link two scenes with a transition instead of a sequel	• Use soft-sounding verbs
• Use minimum switching to subplots that don't directly further the main plot	• Switch back and forth among subplots that don't directly further the main plot
	• Convert a scene to a sequel
• Don't waste words	• Enter a scene with a sequel in middle of things
• Use short paragraphs and sentences.	• Have your character internalize during a scene
• Use sentence fragments	• Increase physical time of sequel (days instead of hours)
• Add a more exciting scene and make disasters more disastrous	• Expand sequel length
• Shorten physical time between scenes (hours instead of days)	• Make scenes slower and duller to read (if all else fails) [1,15,16]

The type of novel you've chosen to write determines the pace. In a action-adventure story the emphasis is on action. You want a swift pace with pressurized disasters so that the main character doesn't have much time to think before acting. Thus, the scenes are generally long and the sequels are generally short. In a romance novel, however, you might devote many pages to the dilemma stage of the sequel as your heroine goes over and over her emotional reactions to the disaster that just affected the course of her romance. And in a spy story, the decision section might be greatly expanded as your spy starts carefully working his way toward his next goal—setting up false leads and sending out confusing signals.[10]

References

1. Bickham, Jack, Scene and Sequel: Two Keys to a Strong Plot, In The Writer's Digest Handbook of Novel Writing, Ed. By Tom Clark, William, Writer's Digest Books, Cincinnati, 1992.
2. Snider, Hollie, How to Create Realistic Scenes - Part 2: Scene Versus Sequel, http://www.csfwg.org/archive/2002-01_article-how_to_create_realistic_scenes2-scene_versus_sequel.pdf, 2002.
3. Dibell, Ansen, Plot, Writer's Digest Books, Cincinnati, 1999.
4. Rasley, Alicia, Scenes on Fire! 15 tips to fire up your scenes, http://www.sff.net/people/alicia/artscenesonfire.htm, 2001.
5. Swain, Dwight V., Techniques of the Selling Writer, University of Oklahoma Press, Norman, 1973.
6. Grafton, Sue (Ed.), Writing Mysteries: A Handbook by the Mystery Writers of America, Writer's Digest Books, Cincinnati, 1992.
7. Watson, Mary, Writing action scenes, http://members.aol.com/lynnturner/action.htm, 1995.
8. Scene and sequel: scene, Writing.com, http://www.writing.com/ main/ books/entry_id/320559/action/view, 2005.
9. Bickham, Jack, The 38 Most Common Fiction Writing Mistakes, Writer's Digest Books, Cincinnati, 1992.
10. Bickham, Jack, Scene and Structure, Writer's Digest Books, Cincinnati, 1993.
11. Ingermanson, Randall, Writing the perfect scene, http://www.rsingermanson.com/html/perfect_scene.html.
12. Kilian, Crawford, Constructing a scene, The Fiction Writer's Page, http://www.capcollege.bc.ca/dept/cmns/scene.html.
13. Kay, Patricia, Scene and Sequel, Writing Articles, http://www.patriciakay.com/article.php?articleid=004
14. Scenes: The building blocks of novels, Suite 101.com, http://www.suite101.com/article.cfm/novel_writing/14516/2.
15. Hamper, Rich, Controlling your story's pace, http://home.comcast.net/~rthamper/html/body pacecontrol.htm, 1998.
16. Hinze, Vicki, Pacing, Fiction Factor, The Online Magazine for Fiction Writers, http://www.fictionfactor.com/guests/pacing.html, 2003.
17. Kelman, Judith, How to write a publishable novel, http://www.kelman.com/fiction/index.html#pacing.

Chapter 11

Characterization

*C*haracterization is the creation of imaginary people (*characters*) who appear to be real and believable to the reader. In most stories, characters and their interactions drive the plot and create the suspense and tension. Characters are usually human, but can be animals, aliens, robots, or anything you want them to be. Characters have names, physical appearances, and personalities. They often wear certain kinds of clothes, speak using slang or jargon, and sometimes have accents. They communicate with each other verbally and nonverbally.[1]

CHARACTER CLASSIFICATION

Characters are classified as either major or minor. However, some character types may be either major or minor, depending on the magnitudes of their roles in the story. Bishop classifies characters as cumulative, immediate, or cumulative and immediate. *Cumulative characters* grow or progress to a higher level of understanding in the course of the story until at the end of the novel they are fully complete. Because of this, they also are referred to as *dynamic* characters. *Immediate characters* (family butler, traffic cop, waitress, local minister) play only one role.

Whenever they appear, they are always the same. Secondary characters can be *immediate and cumulative.* They have specific roles which support the major characters, yet have independent stories of their own. Their development over the course of the story occurs in proportion to their contribution to the major characters' stories.[2,3]

Major Characters

Major characters, also known as *round characters*, are three dimensional figures. The three dimensions are physiological, psychological, and sociological. The *physiological dimension* is the height, weight, age, sex, body type, and so forth. Physiological data is important because it impacts how characters view themselves and thus how they act. Within the *psychological dimension* are phobias, fears, inhibitions, patterns of guilt, longing, fantasies, and so forth. The *sociological dimension* refers to the character's social class, the kind of neighborhood he grew up in, how he fit in with classmates in school, his current social class, his politics, and so forth. Knowing his roots will help you understand how that character will react today.

The goals, ambitions, and values of major characters should change as a result of what happens to them in the progression of the story. Like real people, they should have particular fears and aspirations, strengths, weaknesses, secrets, and sensitivities. They are not all good or all bad.

A major character may have inner contradictions; that is, simultaneous attraction toward and repulsion from an object, person, or action. Inner contradictions give a character a great potential for unpredictability. While the character is deeply involved in one pursuit or feeling, the reader doesn't know if the character will suddenly shift into a different pursuit or change his feelings.[4] For example, consider the following example from Leonard Bishop:

- *A surgeon is operating on a patient who, in a drunken spree, killed the surgeon's father. He has a chance to kill the patient without being discovered, yet while operating he is reciting his oath to preserve life. What will he do?*[2]

The two *major characters* in fiction are the protagonist (hero, heroine) and the antagonist (villain). The antagonist is the character or force that opposes the protagonist. Every major character should have his own look, pattern of speech, personality, mannerisms, strengths, weaknesses, fears, hopes, goals, and motivations. The *main character* may be the protagonist, another character, or a narrator. In rare occasions it may be the antagonist.[4]

Protagonist

The *protagonist* is the character who dominates the story. He is the prime mover of the plot. He should be someone the reader cares about, and as a result has a strong desire for him to achieve his story goal.

Attributes

The protagonist is a complex character who should have three attributes: (1) A need or want, (2) a strong point, and (3) a character flaw.

A Need or a Want. The protagonist has a need or want that translates into a story goal. He should want to attain the goal badly enough that he's willing to fight for it, and sometimes even die for it. The goal can be wanting to:

- *Gain Possession of Something.* A girl, a sum of money, a better job, the Holy Grail
- *Get Relief from Something.* Domination, fear, blackmail, captivity, oppression
- *Prevent Something.* A murder, a robbery, a kidnapping, a terrorist attack, destruction of the world
- *Get Revenge for Something.* A betrayal, a murder, an embarrassment, a rape

A Strong Point. The protagonist should possess a strong point, such as courage, wisdom, persistence, or kindness which confers on him the potential for triumph.

A Character Flaw. The protagonist also should possess a character flaw, such as alcoholism, prejudice, greed, gullibility, fear of heights, or fear of authority that unless overcome may lead to his downfall.[3,4]

Things to Attempt

To make your protagonist interesting you should have him attempt:

The Impossible. Of course it only appears by all logic to be impossible. But somehow your protagonist figures out how to get around the rules of the game, the rules of nature, or the rules of physics to accomplish his goal.

The Unobtainable. The unobtainable is something we can't have, for whatever reason. It's the short, ugly, shy college student who marries the homecoming queen. It's obtaining the golden chalice despite the fact that it is guarded by giants and dragons and witches and whatever.

The Forbidden. Tell some people they can't have something or can't do something and they'll lie awake at night figuring out how to get it or do it. Your protagonist is one of these people. Just like Eve in the Garden of Eden, tell him he can't partake of the fruit of the apple tree and he won't sleep until he's taken a bite.

The disastrous. Readers love characters who attempt the disastrous and who flirt with calamity. That's why escape artists like Harry Houdini were so successful. Would he or wouldn't he survive the locked chest with the chains around it at the bottom of the river?[3,4]

Main Character

The *main character* is the person the audience views the story through. Most of the time the main character is the protagonist; at other times the main character is a narrator; and at other times it is a secondary character. Each gives valuable insights into the protagonist from an outside prospective.

In Anne Rice's *Interview with the Vampire* (1973), Louis, the vampire who is giving the interview and thus telling the story, is clearly the Main character in the book. But he is not the protagonist. He simply recounts the happenings in the story. Lestat, the vampire about whom the story is centralized around, is actually the protagonist. Lestat is the driving force for the plotline.

He is the prime mover of events toward a goal in which the other characters are persuaded also to seek.[5]

Antagonist

The *antagonist* is any character that opposes the efforts of the protagonist. He's the bad guy. There wouldn't be much conflict for your protagonist to overcome without the antagonist to throw up roadblocks. Many stories have only a single antagonist or one main one, while longer works, especially novels, may have more than one. It is often said that the strength of your story is only as good as the strength of your antagonist.

The primary characteristic of the antagonist is ruthlessness. He is determined to have his way regardless of other peoples' feelings, needs, and well-being. He is uncompromising in this determination to get what he wants.

An antagonist need not be unattractive. He may well be quite handsome and charming. And he is unlikely to be ruthless in every aspect of his life. His dastardly behavior may be limited to a single area or situation, such as a Mafia hit man who is a loving father and a member of the PTA or a murderous dictator who has a soft spot in his heart for homeless animals.

Like the protagonist, the antagonist needs to be a three-dimensional character. The reader must be able to get inside his head and learn what drives him to act the way he does. Remember, no one sees himself as mean or evil or insane. Your antagonist won't either. To him, his actions and his logic are perfectly justifiable.

Although you should portray your antagonist as being an intelligent, logical, complex person who does what he does because his reasons are sound to him, you should also show his devious, misguided nature.[3,4,6-8]

Thomas Harris's evil genius, Hannibal Lector, in *The Silence of the Lambs* (1989) is a gifted psychopath whose nickname is "The Cannibal" because he likes to eat parts of his victims. Isolated from all uncontrolled physical contact with the human race, he plays a manipulative game of "clue" with young and vulnerable FBI trainee, Clarice Starling, providing her with snippets of data that, if she is smart enough, will lead her to the identity of the psychotic serial killer she seeks. Lector's interest in her increases the reader's fear that something bad is going to happen to her.[9]

Minor Characters

Minor characters, also know as *flat characters*, are almost always one or two-dimensional characters. They have only one or two striking qualities, and are usually all good or all bad. Minor characters are sometimes referred to as *static* characters because they don't change in the course of the story.[3,4,8]

Minor characters include (1) bit players, (2) stock characters, and (3) sacrificial characters

Bit Players

Bit players are the walk-ons—cab drivers, incidental friends, waiters, clerks, doormen, bellhops coworkers, neighbors, waitresses, maintenance people, and so forth. They are flat characters who rarely have more than one or two distinguishing characteristics (tall red-headed woman, short fat man, skinny old lady). The reader is not meant to remember them and they are not assumed to have any significant degree of importance in the story. However, the more important ones can be given some quirk or bit of color that lifts them somewhat above the masses (a maintenance man who spits snuff into a paper cup, a waitress who always wears black lipstick, a doorman who always appears to be intoxicated).[4]

Stock Characters

A *stock character* is a stereotyped character, such as a mad scientist, the absent-minded professor, the cruel mother-in-law, or the ditzy blonde. In general these characters should be avoided, unless you have a really good reason for using them.[6]

Sacrificial Characters

Sacrificial characters usually are subservient characters (chauffeurs, double agents, crooked policemen, mistresses, and so forth). They are killed for various reasons, including to keep them from revealing information. The protagonist may kill one or more skilled killers to demonstrate his prowess. When an assassin is killed, the reader should be made aware of his training to be an assassin and given information about the murders he has committed.

Sacrificial characters can be given some status, such as a skilled heart surgeon, wealthy lawyer, or a benevolent benefactor of the down trodden, to make their deaths seem more significant.

The protagonist tracking down a sacrificial character to get information adds to the suspense of the plot. If he gets the information, the plot turns in one direction. If the antagonist kills the sacrificial character before he gives up the information, the plot shifts in another direction.[4]

Major or Minor Characters

Characters that can be either major or minor, depending on their roles in the story, include (1) foil characters, (2) off-beat characters, (3) memorable characters, and (4) phobic characters.

Foil Characters

A foil is a piece of shiny metal put under gemstones to increase their brightness. *Foil characters* are closely associated with the character for whom they serve as a foil, usually a friend or lover in whom he can confide and thus disclose his innermost thoughts. The purpose of the foil, through comparison and contrast, is to bring out the brilliance of the protagonist. In the Sherlock Holmes stories, Dr. Watson's perceptiveness serves to highlight Holmes' genius. The foil can be a supporter of any of the characters, not just the Protagonist. He even can be a supporter of the antagonist.

Some foil characters are included for comedy relief. Others are included to reinforce the goal or the beliefs of the character they support. Still others are introduced to provide contrast for the antagonist. Foil characters are also known as *confidants, sidekicks, or faithful followers.*[3,10]

Off-beat Characters

Eccentrics. *Eccentrics* are oddballs. They follow their own rules of behavior. They know their belief or behavior is right and everyone else's is wrong. An eccentric might avoid spending money like the plague despite being a multimillionaire, arrange bills by serial number in his wallet, believe the world is flat, or wear earmuffs in August.[4]

In the movie *Fly Away Home* (1996), a 13-year-old girl, Amy Alden (Anna Paquin), goes to live with her estranged father, Tom Alden (Jeff Daniels), following the death of her mother. He's an eccentric Canadian living in the country and doing his own thing—working on multiple sculptures and experimenting with flying machines. At first Amy is withdrawn and reclusive, but finds renewed happiness when she adopts an orphaned flock of baby geese and later teaches them to migrate using an ultra light airplane designed and built by her father.

Psychos. The *psycho* character, on the surface, often appears normal, but the reader is aware that he is not. In fact, the psycho may be normal in all aspects but one, and that one is strange and bizarre, often hidden from the public. For instance, he might appear to be a mild mannered accountant during the day, but wander through neighborhoods at night killing cats. Or worse, he might brutally murder women who look like the old girlfriend who rejected him. Whatever the psychiatric abnormality of your psycho character, get the facts before you start writing. If you want him to be a paranoid schizophrenic, or have any other psychiatric disorder, pick up a psychiatric textbook or go to a psychiatric site on the Internet and read about the signs and symptoms of the disorder.[4]

Norman Bates (Anthony Perkins) in the movie *Psycho* (1960) is the classic psycho character. In the story, Phoenix, Arizona office worker, Marion Crane (Janet Leigh), is fed up with the way life has treated her. She and her lover Sam cannot get married because Sam has to pay most of his money as alimony. One Friday, Marion is trusted by her employer to bank $40,000. She takes the money and leaves town, headed toward California. Tired after a long drive and caught in a storm, she gets off the main highway and pulls into The Bates Motel. The motel is managed by a quiet young man who seems to be dominated by his mother. The shower scene is remembered for its stark brutality—and yet the camera never shows the knife stabbing into Bates's victim, nor does the camera even show a wound. It's all in the viewer's mind.

Memorable Character

The *memorable character* is one who is strikingly different. He may have an extraordinary height or weight, wear wildly colored clothes, be an oddball priest who grows pot in the church's rectory, or be a lovable idiot savant. To create a memorable character, select some unique aspect of body, mind, or personality. Exaggerate it and make it striking and colorful (Nero Wolfe's weight, Mr. Spoke's lack of emotion, Silas's albinism in Dan Brown's *The Da Vinci Code*).[4]

Phobic Character

A *phobia* is a persistent, abnormal, and irrational fear of a specific thing or situation that compels one to avoid it, despite knowing that it is not dangerous. Symptoms can be breathlessness, dizziness, excessive sweating, nausea, dry mouth, feeling sick, shaking, heart palpitations, inability to speak or think clearly, a fear of dying, a sensation of detachment from reality, or a full blown anxiety attack. Individuals with phobias make interesting characters.

Erskine Caldwell's *Tobacco Road* (1932) is a tale of violence and sex among rural poor in the American South. It is the story of Georgia sharecropper, Jeeter Lester, and his family who are trapped by the bleak economic conditions of the Depression, as well as by their own limited intelligence and destructive sexuality. Jeeter has an abnormal fear of rats, stemming from as a child having seen his father virtually eaten alive by a pack of them.[11] And who can forget Indiana Jones's phobia, ophidiophobia, in *Raiders of the Lost Ark.* Oh, ophidiophobia is an abnormal fear of snakes.

The following is a list of common or interesting phobias. Think of how you could use some of them to generate interesting characters:

Selected Phobias

Ablutophobia - washing, bathing, or cleaning
Achluophobia - darkness or the dark
Acousticophobia - noise or sound
Acrophobia - heights or high levels
Agateophobia - insanity or becoming insane
Agliophobia - pain
Agoraphobia - open spaces, leaving a safe place, or crowded public places
Agyrophobia - streets or crossing the street
Ailurophobia - cats
Amathophobia - riding in cars
Apiphobia - bees
Apotemnophobia - persons with amputations
Arachnephobia - spiders
Arsonphobia - fire or flames
Astraphobia - thunder and lightning
Automysophobia - being dirty
Aviophobia - flying high buildings
Bathmophobia - stairs or steep slopes
Bufonophobia - toads
Bacillophobia - microbes
Bacteriophobia - bacteria
Batophobia - heights or being close to high buildings
Claustrophobia - confined or small spaces
Climacophobia - stairs, climbing stairs, or falling down stairs
Coimetrophobia - cemeteries
Cynophobia - dogs, canines, or rabies
Demophobia - crowds
Dentophobia - dentists

Dermatopathophobia - skin disease or skin lesions
Driving Phobia - driving a motorized vehicle
Earthquakophobia - earthquakes
Eisoptrophobia - mirrors or of seeing oneself in a mirror
Entomophobia - insects or bugs
Equinophobia - horses
Gephydrophobia - crossing bridges
Glossophobia - speaking in public or trying to speak
Helminthophobia - being infested with worms
Hemaphobia - blood
Herpetophobia - reptiles or creepy, crawly things
Hobophobia - bums or beggars
Homichlophobia - fog
Hoplophobia - firearms
Iatrophobia - doctors or going to the doctor
Ichthyophobia - fish
Kenophobia - voids or empty spaces
Ligyrophobia - loud noises
Lilapsophobia - tornado or hurricanes
Maniaphobia - insanity
Meningitophobia - brain disease
Microbiophobia - microbes
Misophobia - being contaminated with dirt or germs
Murophobia - mice
Necrophobia - death or dead things
Nosocomephobia - hospitals
Nosophobia -becoming ill
Obesophobia - gaining weight
Ochlophobia - crowds or mobs

Ombrophobia – rain, rained on
Ornithophobia - birds
Ophidiophobia – snakes
Parasitophobia - parasites
Pediculophobia - lice
Pediophobia - dolls
Peladophobia - bald people
Peniaphobia - poverty
Phalacrophobia - becoming bald
Pogonophobia - beards
Pteromerhanophobia - flying
Ranidaphobia - frogs
Rhytiphobia - getting wrinkles
Rupophobia - dirt
Scoleciphobia - worms
Siderodromophobia - trains, railroads, or train travel

Social Phobia - social situations
Spectrophobia - specters or ghosts
Spheksophobia - wasps
Tachophobia - speed
Verminophobia - germs
Virginitiphobia - rape
Wiccaphobia – witches, witchcraft
Taeniophobia - tapeworms
Taphephobia - being buried alive or cemeteries
Toxicophobia - poison or being accidentally poisoned
Xenophobia - strangers or foreigners
Zoophobia - animals[12,13]

CHARACTER DESCRIPTION

Dwight Swain gives an excellent discussion of character description, which he divides into (1) dominant characteristics, (2) tags, (3) uniqueness, (4) involvement, (5) desires and goals, (6) compensation, and (7) self image.[4] The following discussion is adapted primarily from Swain.

Dominant Characteristics

Characters, like people, are primarily defined by four dominant characteristics: (1) Their sex, (2) their age, (3) their vocation, and (4) their manner.

Sex. He, she, man, woman, male, female

Age. Little girl, little boy, old man, young woman, teenager, adolescent, child, 17-year-old

Vocation. Doctor, lawyer, chef, housewife, bum, bag lady, mechanic, waitress, policeman, druggist, nurse, undertaker, professor, preacher, prostitute

Manner. Loud, pushy, timid, shy, whiny, grouchy, sloppy, surely, friendly, worried, long-faced, stupid, pompous, hypocritical, pious

Vocation and manner can be combined—pushy doctor, timid lawyer, shy chef, whiny housewife, grouchy bum, sloppy professor, surely mechanic, pious preacher, stupid undertaker, or long-faced nurse.[4]

Tags

A tag is a label used so the reader can tell one character from another.

Categories

According to Swain, most tags fall into four categories: (1) Appearance, (2) speech, (3) mannerism, and (4) attitude.[4]

Appearance. Some people are tall, others are short; some are handsome, others are ugly; some are blue-eyed, others are brown-eyed; some are well-groomed, others are sloppy. They may be old or young, fat or thin, muscular or frail. They may be fastidiously dressed or markedly sloppy in their appearance. They may have a drooping eyelid, a missing earlobe, or a crooked nose. Kojak's lollipop was a tag, as was Colombo's wrinkled raincoat, Long John Silver's hook, and Alex Cross's piano playing in Tom Patterson's series of detective novels.[4]

Speech. College professors talk differently than most truck drivers. Preachers' wives speak differently than most prostitutes. The content and manner of a character's speech helps to evoke personality; that is, give an indication of whether he is shy and reticent, aggressive and frank, coy, or humorous.

One's use of language reflects background, education, experience, occupation, social status, psychology, and a host of other things. A character may habitually refer to every man as "sir" or "dude" or say a word or expression frequently, such as "you know what I mean" or "really now." A character may stutter or speak with an accent; people from Brooklyn certainly speak differently than those from Mississippi or California. And people from Germany speak English differently than those from Russia or France. And some flavor their speech with jargon or slang.[4]

Mannerisms. Some men tend to scowl and some women tend to smile, it seems like all the time. Some people are hand-rubbers, knuckle crackers, ear-lobe tuggers, doodlers, nail cleaners, or seat squirmers. Others are nail bitters, chin rubbers, lip biters, nose pickers, or constant frowners. Yet others have an eye tic, raucous laugh, or are constantly flipping a coin.[4]

Attitudes. Does your character tend to be easy-going, deceitful, sullen, flamboyant, bitter, or withdrawn? Some people are habitually apologetic, fearful, irritable, vain, arrogant, or shy. Others are cynical, lazy, rude, eternal optimists, racists, sexists, suspicious, or discontent. Yet others are worriers, freeloaders, hypocrites, selfish, or dishonest. And others are incapable of loving, revere their parents, or hate children.[2,4]

Purpose

Since the purpose of tags is to separate one character from another, it stands to reason that you shouldn't duplicate tags between characters. Tags also characterize, so if a man is timid let it show in his handshake and speech. If a woman is a floozy, show her flirting with a married man or two.

So how many tags should you give a character? Minor characters need only one or two—a grossly overweight redheaded woman, a skinny old man. But for a major character, constantly making note of one or two tags pretty soon gets tiresome to the reader. The solution is to give them more tags. You may want to give them tags from all four categories—a burley truck driver who stutters, tugs at his ear, and is painfully shy.

Use tags in action—"His dark eyes glinted coldly" is a whole lot better than "He had dark eyes." And use tags often. Don't assume the reader will remember them if they are only used once or twice. If a woman has long blond hair, have her run her fingers through it, brush it, comment on how much trouble it is, get it cut or permed, have it blow in the wind, and let it become wet and stringy in the rain.[2,4]

Uniqueness

What makes a character unique? According to Swain it's (1) the body he possesses, (2) his mental ability, (3) the environment he lives in, (4) the experiences he has had over the years, (5) his motivation, and (6) the ideas he has about various things.[4]

Body. Because a man's body is different from a woman's, society has different expectations of the two sexes. Many expect a woman to stay home and raise the children (A woman's place is in the home. Keep them barefoot and pregnant.). We speak of the glass ceiling, above which historically women have been unable to rise above in the corporate world. In one woman's mind she may simply feel it's not worth the effort and simply give up. Another woman may be determined and, despite the odds, rise to be the president of the company.

A small man may be intensely aware that he lacks the physical size and strength of a rival (the high school quarterback). The rival gets the girl of his dreams (the cheerleader). The small man can sulk off with his head hung low and spend the rest of his life feeling sorry for himself, or he can raise his head high and compensate for his diminutive size by working hard and becoming a success at what ever he chooses. His old rival (the ex-football player) and his wife (the ex-cheerleader) then will have to look up to him and wish they too could belong to the country club, live in a wealthy neighborhood, and send their kids to the same fancy private school.

Heredity plays a big part here. Our ancestors, to a large degree, determine our height; that is whether we are a dwarf or a giant or any height in between; have a big head, short neck, wide hips, or narrow shoulders; or have various diseases, such as diabetes, high blood pressure, or sickle cell anemia.[4]

Mind. Some people are scholarly, others are illiterate; some are curious and others are indifferent to learning. There is the character of normal intelligence, the idiot, the genius, and the idiot savant. The genius may be a failure because of lack of motivation and the person with lower intelligence may be a success because of his hard work.[4]

Environment. The big city slum boy and the country boy aren't the same. Neither are the residents of a small southern college town and a large northern town with a big university. Similarly, the Louisiana Cajun, the West Virginia mountaineer, and the Pennsylvania Amish man all have their differences because of their environment.[4]

Experience. The experiences of a salesman are different than those of a cowboy and the experiences of a factory worker are different than those of a neurosurgeon. Similarly, the experiences of a preacher's wife are different than those of a prostitute.

Experience to a large extent is the reason we act like we do. Insult one man and he explodes in foul-mouthed language; insult another and he walks away apologizing for making you angry; insult another and he punches you in the nose without so much as saying a word. Still another will smile and plan behind your back what he is going to do to get even.[4]

Ideas. We all have ideas about certain things, and so should your characters. We are Republicans or Democrats because we have ideas that agree more with one of political party than the other. Some people in the world firmly believe in the free-market system, while others are staunch socialists. Some are fervently religious, while others are atheists. Each can clearly express the ideas that make him who he is.[2,4]

Involvement

People, as well as story characters, are involved in (1) love, (2) work, and (3) society.[4]

Love. Is your character married, divorced, or single? Is he heterosexual or homosexual? If married, how is the relationship? Does he love his wife as much as when they got married, or more? Do they have children? If so, how does he get along with them? How do the children feel about him? Is he divorced? If so, why? How does he get along with his ex? If single, does he have a girlfriend or boyfriend, play the field, or not date at all? If he's in a relationship, what attracts them to each other?

Work. To many people, especially men, work is who they are. One of the first questions we ask a new acquaintance is "What do you do?" Meaning what kind of work do you do? We don't even have to state what we mean when we ask the question. People know automatically.

Employee and employer view the world from separate viewpoints. Similarly, cowboy and banker and lawyer and farmer and office worker operate in different frames of reference.[4]

Society. What are your character's friends like? Are his friends on the same level as he in terms of financial, social, and educational status? Does he have Caucasian, African-American,

Mexican-American, Arab-American, or oriental friends? What do he and his friends do together—play pickup basketball games, go to nightclubs to pick up women, watch football games on TV, or drink at happy hours? Does he go to church? If so, what denomination is he, and how does his religion show in his every day behavior?[4]

Desires and Goals

Every character in a story desires things to varying degrees and has personal goals. Whatever these desires and goals are they form the basis for your characters' motivations to act. The plot should show how your characters, with particular strengths and values, react under stress or when they are pursuing their goals.

A great source of difficulty for a character is when he has goals and desires that are mutually exclusive—two things that are equally important to him, but he can't have them both. Which one will he chose? You can imagine the anguish he goes through trying to come to grips with the situation. The reader will be in a constant state of tension as your character tries to make the decision.

The more characters you have, the less well the reader will get to know each of them, and the less the reader will care about their desires and goals. Readers need to make a connection with the characters, and it's easier to make a connection with fewer characters. So limit your characters to a realistic number.[14]

Compensation

Everyone, including story characters, has strengths and weaknesses. What gives him his strength, his drive, and his motivation? How does your character compensate for his weaknesses? What price does he pay for making up for his weaknesses? In other words, when faced with a catastrophe, does your character fight or flee? Is he the small man who makes up for his diminutive size by developing such drive and ambition that he amasses a fortune, or is she the woman who tries to forget her fading beauty in a bottle?[4]

Self-image

Self-image is how we feel about ourselves. We see ourselves as attractive or ugly, smart or dumb, dashing or dull. We react as if this subjective image is an accurate picture and try to live up to the role in which we see ourselves. The characters in your story also will have self concepts. This doesn't always bear any similarity to reality. A repulsive man may see himself as suave or an aging woman may think of herself as the cute chick she once was. Self-confidence does affect outcome. In my experience, the guy who gets the most desirable girl is not the best looking male but the one with the most self-confidence.[4]

CHARACTER DEVELOPMENT

You should develop a character only to the limited degree that he needs to be developed to fulfill his function in the story. You give an impression and approximation of his life, rather than attempting to duplicate his life itself. Characters should come into being gradually. Initially they may be no more than an impression—little girl, weakling, old man, athlete, coward, and the like. Then, a little at a time, you add more and more detail.

Characters have specific homes, habits, possessions, medical histories, tastes in clothes, and political opinions. Does your character abstain from drinking or go to sleep every night with a bottle in his hand? Was he once an alcoholic or drug addict and is now in recovery, or is he still drinking or using? Is he a womanizer, constantly trying to pick up women in bars, or is he shy and seldom goes out on a date?

Each new example of behavior should be consistent with what we already know of the character, yet it should reveal some new aspect of personality. Behavior under different forms of stress should be especially revealing.

The characters should have good and sufficient reasons for their actions, and should carry those actions out with plausible skills. If readers don't believe the characters would do what you say they are doing, the story fails.[4]

229

Methods of Creating Characters

Characters are created in a number of ways, including from (1) their actions, (2) their thoughts and feelings, (3) the narrator's description, (4) what other characters say about them, and (5) what other characters think about them.

- ***Character's actions.*** When no one was looking, Marshall sneaked a peak at himself in the mirror.
- ***Character's Thoughts and Feelings.*** "God, my mother hates me," Ann thought. "I don't believe her dropping me on my head when I was a baby was an accident."
- ***Narrator's Description.*** He was a big man with arms and legs that appeared too long for his body. He had small, dark eyes and equally dark hair. His nose tilted slightly to the left, the result of too many fights in his youth. His chin appeared too long for the rest of his face. His faded, blue overalls hung loosely on his gangly frame.
- ***What Other Characters Say about Them.*** "You can't trust Bill," Jennifer said. "He's been a dishonest bastard ever since he stole an apple from the grocery store when he was five years old."
- ***What Other Characters Think about Them.*** "I can't stand Jack," Melissa thought. "He's such a pompous ass."[1,2,15-19]

Character Change

As characters seek to carry out their agendas, they run into conflicts, fail or succeed, and confront new problems. As a result, they should change over the course of your novel. If a character seems unchanged at the end of the story, the reader should be aware of whatever factors kept him from growing and developing. Character change should not be stated; it must be shown. There are three phases to a believable change in a character.

- *A Shocking Awareness of a Character Fault.* In *Caduceus Awry* (2000) Dr. Mark Valentine becomes painfully aware of the fact that he's an alcoholic, but he has no desire to quit drinking.

- *A Strong Desire to Change.* When Mark's teenaged daughter is kidnapped by a Mafia crime boss who threatens to kill her, Mark finally finds the necessary desire to quit.
- *An Action that Proves Change Has Occurred.* Mark attends his first AA meeting since being discharged from an alcohol treatment program months earlier. [1,2,15-19]

NAMES

Names are identifiers. As such, they also are tags. Two people are called Sam and Edna to tell them apart. However, most people know two or more people with the same name. There's Sam who goes to our church and Sam who fixes the car, and Edna the sister-in-law and Edna the florist. If telling people apart in real life is confusing, how much more confusing is it going to be in your novel if you don't identify your characters clearly?

A character's name can say a lot about him. Whether you choose a name with symbolic meaning or just one that has a good sound, the name should fit the character. You wouldn't want to name a 98-pound weakling Sampson, unless it was done intentionally to be ironic. If you want to portray a charming, sunny, ordinary girl, you wouldn't call her Witchina. If you want to convey that your male protagonist is "all man," you wouldn't call him Bruce, unless you do so to be humorous. Similarly, if you're writing historical fiction, your names should be historically accurate. Some names that are popular today didn't exist in the past, and some names in the past don't exist today.

Also, the name should be one that the reader can pronounce. A name that was particularly awkward for me to pronounce was Inspector Dalgliesh in P. D. James's *Death in Holy Orders* (2001). Throughout the novel I never became comfortable trying to pronounce it, but maybe that was just me.

Groups use special names that you must be aware of. African-Americans, for instance, favor both traditional names, such as Washington, William and Alice and also newly-created ones, such as DeeVine. They also favor African ones such as Rajarshi. They are fully aware of the significance of these names, and so should you as a writer.

Don't start too many characters' names with the same letter

(Janice, Jane, Jamie). The reader will have trouble remembering which is which. Also, names that sound too much alike (Ed, Jed, Fred) can be a problem. In addition, Anne and Patty and Janet all share an identical vowel. This makes them flat and repetitive. Instead, contrast your sounds. For instance, if you have a few names with "a" sounds, like Anne, Patty and Alice, create contrast with some "u," "i," and "oo" sounds, such as Lucy or Kim, or Tootsie.

It also helps to use different rhythm patterns. In other words, you shouldn't name five guys in a car pool "Ted, Ed, Sam, Rod, Ham." Name them something like "Sam, Jacques, Everett, Oscar, Pasquale."[20,21]

The Internet is a great source for character names. Websites also can be found for names of dogs, cats, horses, and other animals. Some possible names for human characters can be found at:

- *African-American.* http://www.swagga.com/mname.htm
- *Arabic.* http://www.babynameworld.com/arabic.asp
  baby- names.html
- *Chinese.* http://www.weddingvendors.com/baby-names/
  origin/chinese/
- *French.* http://www.babynamebox.com/french-baby-
  names.html
- *German.* http://www.babynamebox.com/german-baby-
  names.html
- *Hindu.*
  http://www.saranam.com/Astrology/hindubabynames.asp
- *Irish.* http://www.babynamebox.com/irish-baby-names.html
- *Italian.* http://www.babynamebox.com/italian-baby-
  names.html
- *Japanese.* http://www.babynamebox.com/japanese-baby-
  names.html
- *Russian.* http://www.babynamebox.com/russian-baby-
  names.html
- *Spanish.* http://www.babynamebox.com/spanish-baby-
  names.html
- *Yiddish.* http://www.babynamebox.com/yiddish-baby-
  names.html

If you wish to use names from groups other than the ones above, simply do a search of the Internet for that group using one of the search engines, such as Google (www.google.com) or Yahoo (www.yahoo.com).

PERSONALITY COMPONENTS

Personality components are those emotional and psychological attributes people (and characters) possess. The following table, from Sandy Tritt, gives a list of personality components.[22] Each major character should possess several of these attributes to be well-rounded.

Abrasive	Articulate	Conceited
Absent-minded	Artistic	Condescending
Abusive	Assertive	Confident
Accident-prone	Audacious	Confused
Accommodating	Authoritative	Congenial
Accomplished	Belligerent	Conscientious
Adaptable	Bewildered	Conservative
Adventurous	Bewitching	Considerate
Affectionate	Boisterous	Consistent
Aggressive	Bored	Content
Agnostic	Bossy	Contrite
Agreeable	Brave	Controlling
Alone	Brazen	Conventional
Aloof	Calculating	Cooperative
Ambitious	Callous	Cowardly
Amusing	Carefree	Crafty
Angry	Careful	Cranky
Annoying	Charismatic	Creative
Antisocial	Charming	Critical
Anxious	Chaste	Crude
Apathetic	Cheerful	Cruel
Apologetic	Classy	Cultured
Appreciative	Clumsy	Cunning
Apprehensive	Cocky	Curious
Approachable	Compassionate	Cynical
Argumentative	Compliant	Daffy
Aristocratic	Composed	Dainty
Arrogant	Compulsive	Debonair

Deceitful	Finicky	Impeccable
Decent	Flamboyant	Impudent
Defiant	Flippant	Impulsive
Delicate	Flirtatious	Incoherent
Despicable	Flustered	Incompetent
Detached	Focused	Inconsiderate
Determined	Forgiving	Indecisive
Dignified	Fragile	Indifferent
Direct	Frank	Indiscreet
Disciplined	Friendly	Inept
Disgusting	Frigid	Infantile
Dishonest	Frugal	Informed
Disorganized	Frustrated	Inhibited
Distant	Fun-loving	Inhumane
Distraught	**G**audy	Innocent
Dogmatic	Gentle	Inquisitive
Domineering	Glamorous	Insecure
Dowdy	Gloomy	Insensitive
Downtrodden	Good-natured	Insightful
Dramatic	Graceful	Insouciant
Dull	Gracious	Insulting
Dumb	Grandiose	Intellectual
Easy-going	Greedy	Intelligent
Eccentric	Gregarious	Intelligent
Educated	Grotesque	Intimidating
Egocentric	Grumpy	Intolerant
Egotistic	**H**aggard	Introspective
Elusive	Hateful	Introverted
Embittered	Heartbroken	Intuitive
Emotional	Hesitant	Inventive
Empathetic	Holy	Irresponsible
Energetic	Honest	Irreverent
Enigmatic	Honorable	Irritable
Enthusiastic	Hopeful	**J**ealous
Excessive	Hospitable	Judgmental
Excitable	Humble	**K**ind
Exotic	Hypocritical	Knowledgeable
Extravagant	Hysterical	**L**ascivious
Exuberant	**I**diosyncratic	Lazy
Faithful	Ignorant	Lethargic
Fanatical	Imaginative	Lewd
Fatalistic	Immature	Liberal
Fearless	Immodest	Logical
Feisty	Impatient	Lonely

Loving	Perceptive	Sarcastic
Macho	Persistent	Sassy
Maniacal	Persuasive	Savvy
Manipulative	Pert	Self-absorbed
Masochistic	Perverted	Self-conscious
Materialistic	Pessimistic	Self-effacing
Mature	Petty	Selfish
Mean	Philanthropic	Selfless
Melodramatic	Pious	Self-righteous
Merciful	Plain	Senile
Messy	Polite	Sentimental
Meticulous	Pompous	Serene
Miserly	Practical	Serious
Modest	Presumptuous	Sensitive
Moody	Pretentious	Sensual
Naïve	Prim	Shallow
Nasty	Private	Sheepish
Neurotic	Profane	Shy
Noble	Promiscuous	Silent
Noisy	Prosaic	Silly
Nonchalant	Proud	Simple
Non-committing	Psychopathic	Sincere
Nostalgic	Psychotic	Sleazy
Obedient	Pushy	Sloppy
Obnoxious	Quiet	Sluggish
Obscene	Quirky	Smart
Observant	Rational	Sneaky
Obsessive	Rebellious	Snobby
Open-minded	Reclusive	Soft-spoken
Opinionated	Reliable	Spiritual
Opportunistic	Religious	Spiteful
Optimistic	Remorseful	Squeamish
Organized	Remote	Stern
Ornery	Resentful	Stingy
Outgoing	Reserved	Stoical
Outspoken	Resilient	Straight-laced
Overbearing	Respectful	Strict
Paranoid	Righteous	Stubborn
Paranoid	Romantic	Submissive
Passionate	Rowdy	Subtle
Passionate	Rude	Supportive
Passive	Ruthless	Surly
Passive Patient	Sadistic	Suspicious
Patient Perceptive	Saintly	Sweet

235

Sympathetic	Tyrannical	Verbose
Tactful	Unapproachable	Vindictive
Talkative	Unassuming	Virtuous
Temperamental	Unclean	Vivacious
Tense	Uncommunicative	Vulgar
Tentative	Unconventional	Vulnerable
Thoughtful	Uneasy	Well-groomed
Thrifty	Uninhibited	Wholesome
Timid	Unmotivated	Wicked
Tireless	Unreasonable	Withdrawn
Tolerant Tough	Unscrupulous	Worldly
Traitorous	Vain	Zany
Trusting	Vengeful	Zealous

EXAMPLES OF CHARACTER ATTRIBUTES

The character attributes given below are taken from a number of novels I have read over the years. I have divided them into six categories: (1) General appearance, (2 physical attributes, (3) skin, (4) disposition, and (5) apparel.

General Appearance

- *Air of confidence, blocky white man, hideously deformed*

Physical Attributes

Head/Neck

- **Head.** *Big head on a scrawny neck, birthmark on forehead, too-big head, broad forehead*
- **Hair.** *Black as tar, blue-tinted white, sprayed stiff, slicked-back, dyed so blond it was almost white, flopping everywhere, wind blown, wild*
- **Voice.** *Cold tone, funeral voice, high tinny voice, honey-smooth voice, guttural and savage snarl, high pitched, resonant, scratchy, whiny*
- **Face.** *Bird face, bulldog face, freckles across nose and forehead, haggard, pale, fleshy, movie idol, ruddy, scrubbed looking, sour*

- **Eyes.** *Accusing, close-set, penetrating black, cold watchful, cold black, empty, sad, fear filled, deep set, mournful, penetrating*
- **Nose.** *Large, misshapen, prominent aristocratic, stub, beak of a no*se
- **Ears.** *Small ears for her size, cauliflower ears, missing earlobe*
- **Mouth/teeth/lips.** *Down-turned mouth, crooked teeth, full lips, teeth wrapped in silver braces, chapped lips, thick lips, tiny mouth*
- **Smile/laugh.** *Boozy grin, pouting smile, mocking laugh, saucy grin, amiable smile, crafty smile, goofy grin, ugly smirk, wry smile*
- **Mustache/beard.** *Bird's-nest goatee, drooping mustache, scraggly beard, salt and pepper goatee, beard littered with crumbs*
- **Neck.** *Bull neck, sizeable Adam's apple, graceful delicate neck, veins standing out, short neck, slender throat*

Extremities and Torso

- **Arms/hands.** *Arms pitifully thin and wrinkled, meaty hand, fingernails painted pink, effeminate hands, beefy hands, one arm, stubby fingers*
- **Legs/feet.** *Fat ankles, soft thick thighs, toenails painted pink, bony knees, spidery legs, stick legs, trim ankles*
- **Shoulders.** *Massive, narrow, slight droop, rounded, square, thin*
- **Torso.** *Chunky, heavy bottom, pear shaped, angular, generous gut, barrel chest, delicately built, thick in the middle, thin waist*

Skin

- *Deeply tanned, wine-colored birthmark, flawless complexion, unhealthy gray tint to his skin, coarse, perpetually tanned, unhealthy*

Disposition

- *Businesslike, cool detachment, hard-nosed, timid quiet man, gregarious, obnoxious, reclusive, laid back, gentle demeanor, bossy*

Apparel

- **Glasses.** *Aviator specs, coke-bottled glasses, rimless glasses, tiny old-fashioned glasses with round steel rims, bug-eyed glasses, glasses with a chain*
- **Jewelry.** *Gold stud in left ear, gold chain around neck, four earrings in left ear*
- **Clothes.** *Baggy trousers, blue blouse the color of her eyes, crumpled suit, soiled and tattered overalls, elbow-patched sweater*
- **Shoes.** *Sturdy hiking boots, Gucci shoes, sandals with two-inch cork heals, sensible old-lady shoes, high-top shoes, dusty shoes, ostrich-skin boots*

HOW TO BRING IN A CHARACTER

Now that you have created your characters how do you bring them into your story? There are four ways: (1) Describe them, (2) have them do some action, (3) have them speak, or (4) have them reflect on something.

Description. Edgar's body was what I noticed first. It was huge and misshapen. His left arm and leg were shorter than the right ones and his head was to small for his bulk.

Action. Sam rolled over, pulled the Derringer from his boot, and fired off a shot. A small trickle of blood appeared between Bart's eyes.

Dialogue. "You didn't think I would find out, did you?" Inspector Arkin said. "It never occurred to you that fingerprints could be lifted from Angela's neck."

Thought. "God, I hate her," Adam thought, forcing a smile. "If I could wring her neck and get away with it I'd do it."[1,6]

CHARACTER CHART

One useful way to "learn" more about your characters is to fill out a character chart for each of them—at least for the more important ones. It's a great deal more information than you will actually use in your novel, but it will help you as a writer to understand your characters more fully as people. With experience, you will be able to selectively fill out only those portions of the chart you feel will be pertinent to your character.

Name	
Full name?	Nickname?
Reason for nickname?	
Physical Appearance	
Age?	How old does look?
Height?	Weight?
Type of body build?	Eye Color?
Glasses or contact lens?	Hair Color?
Wears hair how?	Balding?
Shape of face?	Distinguishing Marks?
Predominant features?	Right or left handed?
Favorites	
Favorite color?	Favorite food?
Favorite music?	Favorite book?
Favorite clothes (work, leisure, formal)?	Favorite movies?
Habits	
Smokes?	What brand?
When smokes?	How much he smokes?
Drinks?	What brand?
When drinks?	How much he drinks?

Other vices (sweets, chocolate, swearing, over spending, gambling)?	
Hobbies/leisure activities	
What are his hobbies?	Recreation?
How often participates?	With whom?
Background	
Hometown?	Type of childhood?
Race/Ethnic background?	Education?
Most important childhood events that still affect character?	Past relationships? How did they end?
Financial status growing up?	Degree of activity in his religion?
Family	
Married/divorced/ children?	If divorced does he pay child support?
Mother's name?	Relationship with mother?
Type of work mother did/does?	Father's name?
Relationship with father?	Type of work father did/does?
Siblings?	Relationships with siblings?
Aunts/Uncles/grandparents/nieces/nephews?	Relationship with them?
Attitude	
When most at ease?	When most ill at ease?
Priorities?	Philosophy of life?
Desires?	Thankful for?
How he feels about himself?	How he feels about others in his life?
Past failure he would be most embarrassed to have people know?	Manners/social graces?
Personality	

Greatest source of strength in character's personality (whether he recognizes it as such or not)?	Greatest source of weakness in character's personality (whether he recognizes it as such or not)?
Soft spot?	How does he react to adversity?
How does he act when angry?	What regrets does he have?
Sense of humor (dry, weird, earthy)?	

Traits	
Optimist/pessimist?	Introvert/extravert?
Drives and motivation?	Talents?
Positive characteristics?	Flaws?
Mannerisms?	Peculiarities?
Biggest regrets?	Biggest accomplishments?
Darkest secret?	

Self-perception	
How he would describe himself?	What does he consider his best physical characteristic?
What does he consider his worst physical characteristic?	Is his assessment of these physical characteristics realistic?
How does he think others perceive him?	What would he change about himself (physical or mental)?

Relationship with Others	
How does he relate to others?	How is he perceived by strangers, friends, family members, fellow workers, lover?
What do friends/family like most about him?	What do friends/family like least about him?
Most important person in his life before books starts?	Most important person in his life after book starts?

Goals	
Immediate personal and professional goals?	Long-range personal and professional goals?

How does he plan to accomplish these goals?	
Problems/Crises	
How does he face problems?	How does he react in a crisis?
What kind of problems does he usually have?	How does he handle change?
Personal	
Favorite kind of clothes?	Least favorite clothes?
Does he wear jewelry? What?	Where he would like to live. Why?
Spending habits (frugal, spendthrift)?	Religion? Degree of participation?
Who does he secretly admire? Why?	Person is/was most influenced by. Why?
Most prized possession?	How did he spend the week before the book starts?
Have pet(s)? What? Names?	Method of transportation? If car or motorcycle, what make and model?
Home (house, apartment, own, rent)?	Profession/Income?
Talents (piano player, juggler, poetry writer)?	Special skills (Carpentry, race car driving, marksman)?
Medical problems?	Hangs out where?
Nervous habits?	Sexual orientation?[22-24]
Typical daily schedule?	

References

1. Silvester, Niko, Creative Writing for Teens, http://teenwriting.about.com/library/weekly/aa111102a.htm.
2. Bishop, Leonard, Dare to be a Great Writer, Writer's Digest Books, Cincinnati, 1992.
3. Bokesch, Laura, Literary terms, Literary elements, Academy of the Arts, http://www.orangeusd.k12.ca.us/yorba/literary_elements.htm.
4. Swain, Dwight V., Techniques of the Selling Author, The University

of Oklahoma Press, Norman, 1974.
5. Rice, Anne, Interview with the Vampire, Knopf, New York, 1973.
6. Characterization, Suite 101.com,
http://www.suite101.com/article.cfm/novel_writing/15433.
7. Collins, Tess, Villains readers love to hate, The Writer Magazine, February 2001.
8. Kittredge, Mary, Hot to Plot! A Plotting "System" That Works, In The Writer's Digest Handbook of Novel Writing, Ed. By Clark, Tom, William Brohaugh, Bruce Woods, Bill Strickland, and Peter Blocksom, Writer's Digest Press, Cincinnati, 1992.
9. Harris, Thomas, The Silence of the Lambs, St. Martin's Press, New York, 1989.
10. Masterson, Lee, Casting your characters, Fiction Factor, http://www.fictionfactor.com/articles/casting.html.
11. Caldwell, Erskine, Tobacco Road, University of Georgia Press; Reprint edition, Athens, 1995 (Originally published in 1932).
12. The Phobia List, The Phobia Clinic, http://www.changethatsrightnow.com/phobia_list_of_all_phobias.asp?SDID=6542:1944.
13. Rose, Elizabeth, Creating characters with phobias, http://www.scribesworld.com/writersniche/articles/characterswphobias.html.
14. Swiniarski, Steven, Sci Fi Editor, http://www.scifieditor.com/Swiniarski.htm.
15. Elements of fiction, English, http://www.newton.mec.edu/brown/ENGLISH/eng_elements_of_fiction.html#character.
16. Elements of fiction, VirtuaLit : Interactive Fiction Tutorial, http://bcs.bedfordstmartins.com/virtualit/fiction/elements.asp.
17. Kilian, Crawford, Advice on Novel Writing, http://www.steampunk.com/sfch/writing/ckilian/#13.
18. Milhorn, H. T., Caduceus Awry, Writers Showcase, San Jose, 2000.
19. Strever, Jan, Elements of fiction, http://ol.scc.spokane.edu/jstrever/lit/lit131/fiction.htm.
20. Clarke, Caro, Margaret, Maggie, Marge and Meg: Problems with names and how to avoid them, Writing Advice 4, http://www.mallet.dircon.co.uk/nadvice4.html, 1998.
21. Morrell, Jessica Page, Biography Info for Main Characters, The Writing Life, http://www.writing-life.com/fiction/biography.html.
22. Tritt, Sandy, Character trait chart and personality components, Elements of craft, Inspiration for Writers, http://www.inspirationforwriters.com/tip8.html, 2001.
23. McCleod, Carol, Character Chart, http://www.simegen.com/romance/charchart.html.

24. Schnelbach, Susan D. and Christopher Scott Wyatt, and, Tameri Guide for Writers, http://www.tameri.com.

Chapter 12

Dialogue

People communicate with each other using two forms of language: *verbal* (the spoken word) and *nonverbal* (body language). Verbal communication (*dialogue*) is discussed in this Chapter and nonverbal communication in Chapter 14. Dialogue generally refers to anything spoken by a character, even if the character is not actually speaking to anyone.

- "What do you mean Vito's disappeared with the money?" Angelo asked.

Sometimes the term is broadened to include the thoughts of a character.

- "If I tell him the truth he'll kill me," Pasquale thought.

CONVERSATION VERSUS DIALOGUE

Conversation, the way we speak to one another in daily living, isn't dialogue. Whether conversation in real life is dull or interesting has little bearing. The opposite is true of dialogue; it has to be interesting. Dialogue is said to be a special kind of conversation; that is, conversation with drama.

Most people don't speak precisely or concisely enough for fictional characters. With dialogue you need to create the illusion of real conversation, but pare it down to as few lines as possible to convey the necessary information. Don't waste words as people do in normal conversation. Consider the following:

- "Hello, how are you?"
- "I'm fine?"
- "Glad to hear it."

This is conversation, not dialogue. It's boring, offers no drama, and it doesn't advance the story.[1-5]

DIRECT AND INDIRECT DIALOGUE

In a story, we are told what a character says either *directly* or *indirectly*. The direct statements of characters are indicated by the use of quotation marks. Indirect quotations report what the reader says, and do not require quotation marks.[1-5]

- *Direct.* Bill said, "My head hurts."
- *Indirect.* Bill said his head hurts.

USES OF DIALOGUE

Dialogue can be used for a number of things, including to: (1) Advance the plot, (2) build suspense, (3) convey a sense of place and time, (4) convey character, (5) present information, (6) create a hook, (7) develop conflict, (8) foreshadow, (9) inject humor, (10) show an emotional state, (11) show a relationship, and (12) show an attitude.

Advance the Plot. Sometimes a plot requires that a piece of information be passed from one character to another. Dialogue is a logical means of achieving this. For instance, suppose your plot needs a character to find a particular item, but the character doesn't know where to look. Talking to another character might help him find the answer.[4]

- "It's the statue, John. Look inside the statue."

Build suspense. Dialogue can set up the reader's expectation that something bad may happen.

- *"We'll drill right through the tunnel."*
  "Yeah? I remember the boss telling about the time he tried that. He was the only survivor."
  "The boss hasn't been on the job as long as I have. And I say we can drill through the tunnel."[6]

Convey a Sense of Place and Time. Accent, syntax, vocabulary, slang, and other details of voice can reveal location in place and time. An American Southerner might refer to a group of people as "y'all," a Northerner as "you guys," an Englishman as "chaps," and an Australian as "mates."[4,7,8]

Convey Character. Two ways that a person's character is most strongly revealed are through the things they do and the things they say. The things they say can be written as dialogue.[4,6-8]

- "Trust me. They'll never know we took it."

Convey Information. Rather than putting in a big block of explanatory text, tell readers through the conversations of the characters what they need to know to make sense of the story.[4,6]

- "John, you don't understand. $E=mc^2$ is not just the basis for the atomic bomb, it's the foundation for all nuclear reactions."

Create a Hook. A line of dialogue can hook the reader faster than any other way.[9] For example, in Laura Renken's *My Lord Pirate* (2001) she starts out with:

- *"Draw no blood, men. Remember, this is to be a wedding party."*[10]

The reader wonders who is speaking? Why would he even have to mention drawing blood, whose wedding party is it, and what are the men planning to do?

Develop Conflict. Show how some people use language to dominate others, or fail to do so.[6-8]

- "Are you telling me we have to go tomorrow night?" Arlene asked.
  "That's right," Martin replied.
  "I wouldn't be caught dead at that party!"
  "You'll go if I say so."
  "Go screw yourself. I'm not going."

Foreshadow

- "Watch out for Edwina. Rumor has it she's man crazy, and I hear you are high on her list."[6]

Inject Humor. Humor is a great way to show the playfulness or personality of a lighthearted character. Or perhaps even a normally dark character who has a spirited side to him.[9]

- "Did you hear about the blonde who wanted to become a nuclear physicist? She dyed her hair brunette to increase her IQ."

Show an Emotional State

- "What the hell's going on? We were just at the hospital last month when he fell and hit his head. And before that it was a sprained ankle. Now damn it he's gone and cut his arm. Something's wrong with that boy."[6]

Show a Relationship. Since dialogue usually takes place between two people, you can use it to indicate that relationships are beginning, deepening, being confirmed, continuing, being reaffirmed, or being concluded.

- *Beginning.* "I couldn't help but notice you from across the room. You're the most beautiful woman I've ever seen."
- *Deepening.* "I love you more now than ever."
- *Confirming.* "I love you as much as I love life itself."
- *Continuing.* "Now that we have both graduated from college it's time to get married and start a family."
- *Reaffirming.* "After all these years I still love you."

- *Concluding.* "Darlene, I've had it up to here. I'm leaving you."[11]

Show Attitude. Attitudes are usually defined as a disposition or tendency to respond positively or negatively towards a certain idea, object, person, or situation.[12]

- "If people would just listen to me I could save them a lot of strife."

TYPES OF DIALOGUE

Tom Chiarella describes four types of dialogue: (1) Directed, (2) interpolated, (3) misdirected, and (4) modulated. These types are not mutually exclusive and can be combined to create a variety of dialogue techniques.[13]

Directed Dialogue

With *directed dialogue,* one character leads the discussion and the other follows. Description is kept to a minimum. Directed dialogue may begin with a general statement by one character, which leads to a description or overview by the other character. For example, the first character might say "What's up?" prompting the second character to launch into a description of his current situation.

With directed dialogue, movement shifts from one character to the other. As an example of this type of dialogue, consider a radio talk show in which listeners call in and the host leads the conversation.[7,13]

- "Line 6. Sam in San Diego. What's on your mind, Sam?"
Silence
"Sam! Are you there?"
"Hello."
"Yes Sam. Go ahead. You're on the air."
"Can you hear me?"
"What's your question, Sam?"

"Sorry. I'm nervous. First-time caller."

"That's okay. Take a deep breath and spit it out. What's on your mind."

"It's about the Chargers. I think they should get rid of Coach Schmidt. He's a bum."

"What makes you say that? He has a winning record up till last year."

"You're only as good as your last season," Sam said.

"That's pretty naïve. Life is never that simple, and neither is football. The Chargers had a lot of injuries. Don't you think you should take that into consideration?"

Interpolated Dialogue

With *interpolated dialogue*, the focus is solely on one character. The dialogue is placed within a narrative, breaking it up into smaller blocks. Interpolated dialogue is primarily used when the character has something important or particularly revealing to say. Often a single line of dialogue is interpolated into a far larger moment in the scope of the story.[7,13] Consider the following example of interpolated dialogue from Chiarella's book.

* *Then I said, "No, I won't have it ready. Not when you want it." That's what I told him. My life is a mess. I'm behind in everything, the reports pile up faster than I can get them out and I just hate the new payroll system. I hold everything in, too. I mean I really bury it. I hate it all. I look at everything on my desk and I just want to start fresh.*[13]

Misdirected Dialogue

With *Misdirected dialogue*, the movement shifts between characters at random. It is characterized by rapid subject changes and the characters are generally focused on different topics. People don't answer each other, subjects change without warning, and characters respond to stray thoughts. Answers come late or don't come at all. Questions are answered with what sounds like answers, but aren't quite answers. Characters speak to themselves, and more than one conversation can be carried on at the same time.[7,13]

Consider the following conversation among three men at the halftime of a televised NFL football game:

1st Person	2nd Person	3rd Person
"Anyone want a pizza?"		
	"I saw Peyton Manning the other day."	
"What about that pizza?"		
		"Where did you see him?"
	"At the mall."	
		"No kidding."
	"Would I lie to you?"	
"Probably."		
	"I'd like some pizza?"	
"Have you ever seen him?"		
		"Not in person, but I've seen him play."
"I'm eating. I'm starved"		
	"Me too, let's get a pizza."	
"Did you talk to him?"		
	"Who?"	

"Peyton Manning."		
	"I couldn't get close to him."	
		"Come on guys. What about the pizza?"

Modulated Dialogue

Modulated dialogue uses narrative and scenic detail to extend the complexity of expression. Each piece of dialogue becomes a point of entry for the writer to move toward other details. The narrator can comment on the words in the dialogue or launch into a description of something that stems from the dialogue. In addition, a character's words can call up a forgotten moment or lead to a flashback at the end of which the dialogue picks up again.[7,13]

In the following example, Sarah's best friend, Anna, has dropped by to visit her. They sit in the den across from the fireplace. The following scene ensues:

- Sarah looked down at the floor, trying to hide the tears that began trickling down her cheek. "God, what am I doing? I must be out of my mind," she thought.

  "Are you okay?" Anna asked.

  Sarah glanced at the picture of her and Bernard on the mantle. It had been taken during their honeymoon ten years before. He was tall and handsome in blue jeans and a Duke University T-shirt. She was wearing shorts and a halter top that showed off the best features of her figure. A fellow tourist had taken the picture. Niagara Falls in all its splendor was in the background. "What would Anna do if she found out I'm sleeping with her husband," she wondered.

  "I've got to tell you something," Anna said, controlled anger in her voice "It's driving me crazy. Edward's having an affair. I hired a private detective. He called me just before I came."

  Sarah felt like she'd just been hit in the stomach with a

baseball bat. "Has he found out who the other woman is?" she
blurted out. She hoped Anna hadn't noticed the anxiety in her
voice.

"He's coming by in an hour to tell me her name. He said
I'd better be prepared for a shock."

DIALOGUE TECHNIQUES

Individual techniques used by writers to create dialogue
include (1) detail; (2) echo; (3) idioms; (4) hesitation, interruption,
and tailing off; (5) reversal; (6) shift in pace and tone; (7) silence;
and (8) blending with narrative

Detail. Detail is the describing of a person, place, or thing. It
may be brief or more detailed.[13]

* "The team is like the stadium beer—flat and not much punch."

Echo. Echoing is repetition. One character repeats what has
just been said, or part of what has just been said, by another
character.[13]

* "If you think the Saints are going to win more than half of
  their games, you're setting yourself up for a season of
  disappointment."
  "Disappointment?"
  "Yeah, like they ain't going to do it."

Idioms. *Idiom* can refer to a particular grammatical
construction, mode of expression, or unique quality peculiar to a
specific person, group of people, or language. It often refers to a
phrase or expression that cannot be understood by knowing what
the individual words in the phrase mean. For example, to "roll out
the red carpet" means to extravagantly welcome a guest; no red
carpet is needed. To "let the cat out of the bag" means to reveal a
secret. The phrases are misunderstood when interpreted in a literal
fashion.[13,14]

Hesitation, Interruption, and Trailing Off. Much real dialog
goes unfinished. When a character is interrupted or hesitates, end

the dialog with an em-dash (--), which is typed in the manuscript as two hyphens. When a character trails off without completing the thought, end the dialog with ellipsis points (...), which is three periods.

- *Interruption.* "I know what disappointment means."
  "Do you? Then you must be -- "
  "A Saints fan. Yes, I'm a Saints fan."
- *Hesitation.* "Dan, I -- I can't." Mary looked away.
- *Trailing Off.* "I knew I was doing wrong, but I ..."[13,15]

Reversal. A reversal involves moving from one type of dialogue to another, such as moving from sarcasm to challenging to chiding.[13]

- *Sarcasm.* "I believe in luck; how else can you explain the success of people like Sam?"
  Challenging. "What the hell does that mean?"
  Chiding. "If you are as smart as you think you are, figure it out for yourself."

Shift in Pace and Tone. With *shift in pace* the dialogue starts slow (not much action) and picks up (increasing action) or starts fast and slows down. *Shift in tone* involves moving from one tone to another, such as from glib to grim.[13]

- *Glib.* "Hey man. How's it hanging?"
  Grim. "Not good. I just found out I have penile cancer."

Silence. This is exactly what it says—silence. One character says something; the other one doesn't respond. Silence is most often indicated by starting a new paragraph and simply writing "Silence" to indicate that no one is speaking. It may heighten tension, provide resolution, or signal agreement or a parting of the ways.[13]

- "I saw you with Jane last night. You didn't think I knew, did you?"

Silence
"No need to deny it, I saw you with my own eyes."

Blend with Narrative. Blending dialogue with narration, including described speech, creates a flow from one character to another. The impression that two characters are together and talking to each other is achieved.[2]

- I entered the waiting area, wiped the sweat from my brow, and approached the lady behind the glass. "I'm here for my test results."
  She pointed at a chair and told me to take a seat.
  Minutes later, a young, overweight nurse stuck her head through a door, beckoned to me to come, and then showed me to an examination room.
  After what seemed like an eternity, but couldn't have been more than 20 to 30 minutes, Dr. Smith came in. "Mr. Jones, I'm afraid the news is not good."

DIALOGUE CONVENTIONS

Dialogue conventions are the usual way writers use dialogue. Several examples follow:

Men Talking to Men

Men talk differently when there are no women present than when there are. They are more apt to curse, talk vulgarly about sex, tell dirty jokes, and use words and phrases that sound macho. And women talk differently when there are no men present. They're more apt to talk about their children, who's having an affair with whom, who's getting a divorce, and what the latest style is in clothes. They also talk about sex and tell dirty jokes, but as a rule they tend not to be as vulgar about it as men. Also, people talk differently when talking to their peers than to someone who makes them nervous or on guard, such as a boss or a parent.[5]

Bits and Pieces versus Chunks

It helps if information comes in bits and pieces, rather than large chunks. Compare the two parts of an example from Dwight Swain. Both are pure dialogue. The first one presents the same information as the second one, but comes in a chunk of dialogue. The second example presents the dialogue in bits and peaces.

- *"There are lots of bars in town, but probably she's gone to one of the ones down on Denton Street. That's Eddy's turf. The only trouble is, Heimlich's moving in there too. And if he gets hold of her—well, we'd better move fast."*

- *"Where could she have gone?"*
  "The bar, probably."
  "Thanks a lot. I doubt there's more than a hundred bars in town."
  "Not on Denton Street."
  "Denton Street! My God, she couldn't have gone there."
  "It's Eddy's turf."
  "Heimlich's too! And if he gets hold of her ..."
  "Oh, Lord, I read you! We've got to move."
  "Like fast."
  They hit the door running.[5]

It's plain to see which is the more interesting of the two to read and which of the two builds emotion best.

Situational Dialogue

Situations influence the speech pattern. Urgent moments loaded with action and tension tend to be characterized by short words, short sentences, and short dialogue. Episodes in which characters reflect, debate, try to decide what to do, or review past incidents move more slowly and require longer, more thoughtful speech patterns.[5]

Individuality

If readers can't tell which character is speaking without being told, as a writer you have a problem. Give each character his favorite words and expressions and each a different cadence. Remember, you can use dialects, slang, and jargon to set off characters. Also remember that minor differences go a long way in differentiating characters.[16]

Internal Dialogue

There are various ways to indicate internal dialogue; that is, when your character talks to himself in his head. The most common is *italics*. Another way is to treat the thought as spoken language, complete with quotation marks and dialogue tab. Still another way is to paraphrase the thought.

- **Italics.** *Now what do I do? I never expected Jim to spill his guts to the cops.*
- **As Spoken Language.** "Now what do I do?" Jonathan wondered. "I never expected Jim to spill his guts to the cops."
- **Paraphrase.** Jonathan wondered what he would do now. He never expected Jim to spill his guts to the cops.[17]

Emphasis

If you wish to emphasize a word in a sentence, put it in italics. If you wish to emphasize a word in a line of italics, use regular type

- Isn't she *ever* satisfied?
- *Isn't she* ever *satisfied?*[8]

Sounds

As a rule, don't sound out sound effects. Simply state something like, "The gun shot echoed through the house," instead of "bang!" Or "The church bell rang twice" instead of "clang, clang."

Speeches

If one of your characters gives a speech to an audience as part of the story, you certainly don't want to present the entire speech word for word. Instead, you can present a few lines of the beginning to establish that someone is giving a speech and a few lines at the end to indicate when the speech is over. During the middle portion you can work in the speaker's thoughts, activity within the audience, and narrative, including description of the speech. Consider a speech by a character who is running for Senator of the state of Mississippi:

- "Ladies and gentlemen, I stand before you, clearly the best candidate for this office. I intend to outline all I have done for this state and what I intend to do when I'm re-elected. This is not the time to change horses ..."
   Dozens of nameless faces were blurred in his vision. *This speech has got to be a winner. Damn it! Anderson's ahead of me. I can't let him win.* He heard a whisper behind him. His campaign manager was telling him to speak louder and to stop mumbling. *Maybe I shouldn't have had those martinis with lunch. It's affecting my thinking.*
   "...and you know how much industry I have brought to this state. Hundreds of our citizens now have meaningful, well-paying jobs."
   A woman in the back yelled "The hell you say," and waved a hand-lettered placard that said **Enough is Enough! Elect Anderson.** An elderly man five feet away from her slipped a bottle from his overalls pocket and took a sip.
   God, I could use a drink. He raised his voice and waved his fist in the air. "My opponent knows nothing about politics in Washington. He'll be lost and ineffective. What this state needs is experience, and I'm the candidate who has it," he said, pounding the lectern with his fist. Now he was feeling better. *Somebody get that bitch with the placard out of here.*

Continue this pattern until the end of the speech is presented and the audience responds. The scene can be used not only to present the speech but to explore the speaker's character and describe the audience—those for him and those against him, including a would-be assassin if one is present.[1]

Cursing

Let's face it, in real life some people curse. It's part of their personality. The same is true of fictional characters. Some of them you would just expect to curse. If so, then by all means have them do so now and then. You simply can't worry about what your mother will think of your fiction.

Pete Marino is a character you would expect to curse and are not surprised when he does. Marino is the overweight, chain smoking, hard drinking, grumpy, slovenly police captain in Patricia Cornwell's Kay Scarpetta series. In *Point of Origin* (1998) Marino opens a freezer door in a garage and discovers its ghastly contents.

- *Bolt cutters suddenly snapped loudly through steel, and the freezer door sucked open. "Jesus fucking Christ," Marino shouted. "Fuck," he cried."*[18]

Without an occasional curse word, Marino just wouldn't be Marino.

Once you've decided to let a character in your novel curse, don't overdo it. Cursing should be used sparingly and for emphasis as in the example above. The ghastliness of the find is emphasized by Marino's verbal response to it. You might want to avoid cursing altogether if you are writing a Christian or a young adult novel.

RULES FOR GOOD DIALOGUE

According to Alicia Rasley, good dialogue is active, dynamic, meaningful, short, and simple.[19]

Active. Watch for static conflict where you let characters argue about the same thing over and over. Pick out the best exchange that shows that conflict best, and then at the end of that exchange start something new.

Dynamic. The conversation should change the plot in some way. A character reveals something he didn't mean to, two characters figure something out together, a character makes an enemy by saying the wrong thing, and so forth.

Meaningful. Start conversations in a provocative way, like "Where the hell have you been?" or "I should have known I'd find you here."

Short. After three to four lines of dialogue insert an action, change speakers, or switch to a quick thought.

Simple. Use adverbs sparingly, although they can be useful in small doses—"she snarled viciously," "he added casually."[8,19]

DIALOGUE TAGS

Dialogue tags come in two forms: Speech tags and action tags.

Speech Tags

Speech tags indicate who is speaking (he said, she asked, Bill said, Jane asked). However, use them only when you must do so to avoid confusion about who's speaking. You can signal increasing tension by moving from "he said" to "he snapped" or "he snarled" and so on, but as a rule the dialogue itself should convey that changing mood and make such speech tags needless.

Most dialogue is "said"—not "muttered," "sighed," "screamed," or "exclaimed." Occasionally, you may use "he asked" or "he replied." In general, only when the tone of voice is not obvious should a tag other than these be used, such as:

- "Great!" she muttered upon hearing her daughter had wrecked the family car.

Using "said" in the above instance would fail to convey the mother's displeasure and the fact that "Great" is used as an expression of sarcasm.

Get your speech tags in as early as possible. There's nothing more frustrating than not knowing which character is speaking.

Keep your tags either interspersed with action and description or at the end of the statement. A tag at the beginning, although occasionally okay, tends to make the writing more passive. Consider which of the following two statements carries the most power:

- He said, "Help me. I need help."
- "Help me. I need help," he said.

I hope you chose the second example. In general, put the tag after the first completed clause in the sentence or at the end of the sentence.

- "You know," Jane said, "when Ed and I first got married things were wonderful."
- "You know, when Ed and I first got married things were wonderful," Jane said.

And when alternating lines of dialog, make sure you identify speakers at least every five or six exchanges.[15,20,21]

Action Tags

Action tags use character action to define who is speaking. Look for something meaningful, especially if it conveys something more than what the speaker says aloud.[19]

- Allen looked at her with a smirk on his face. "We'll never know unless we try."
- Jack kissed her on the forehead. "I've missed you."
- Mary wiped the tears from her eyes. "Leave me alone."

Creative Dialogue Tag Syndrome

With *creative Dialogue Tag Syndrome* the writer relies on creative tags (pouted, shouted, groaned, screamed, pleaded, replied, snarled, sobbed, and so forth) in an attempt to help the reader interpret the dialogue. The following is an example of this:

- "You don't really love me," she pouted.
"Oh, do we have to go through that again," he groaned.
"I was right, you really don't love me," she whined.
"Give me a break," he snarled. "Didn't I just buy you that 500 dollar bracelet you wanted?"
"Here," she sobbed, throwing it at him.

The problem is that the reader must interpret the tag and evaluate to see if the dialogue agrees with the tag. At best, the tags disrupt the flow. At worst, the reader decides the spoken word and the action tag are contradictory, and the writer loses credibility. Using creative dialogue tags is telling the reader how the words are said instead of showing it. If the dialogue is well written and the accompanying action is well chosen, a tag is redundant.[21]

Excessive Direct Address

Excessive direct address is naming the person spoken to with each statement, question, or exclamation. It's overkill.[8]

- "What did you do last night, Bill?"
"I stayed home and watched TV, Jane."
"Then why didn't you answer the phone when I called, Bill?"
"Jane, it's none of your business!"

OVERUSE OF MODIFIERS

Similar to creative dialogue tag syndrome is the overuse of modifiers.

- "Have you done your assignment yet?" he asked, standing by the door.
"Not yet," she said, slumping onto the couch.
"I'm going to do mine later tonight." He rubbed his nose.
"Maybe I'll do the same." She leaned back and stretched.

It is okay to use modifiers now and then to enhance your story, but don't overdo it.[2,21]

DIALECT, SLANG, AND JARGON

Dialect

Dialect can reveal the area of the world (England, Russia, Egypt), as well as the time frame of the story (1600, 2000). However, take it easy on dialect. When readers are required to sound out words most of them tire of it quickly. You don't want readers concentrating on how something is said, as opposed to what is said. Notice how the following example from Crawford Kilian distracts from the thought that is meant to be conveyed:

- *"Lawsy, Miz Scahlut, us's wuhkin' jes' as fas' as us kin."*[8]

Instead of excessive dialect, use the grammar and rhythm of the character to insinuate the dialect, or tag it with an explanation. Use as few misspelled words as possible:

- ***Grammar and Rhythm.*** "Lordy, Miss Scarlet, we is working just as fast as us can."
- ***Explanation.*** "Lordy, Miss Scarlet, we're working just as fast as we can," she said, her Southern accent thick as molasses.

Other examples of explanation are: "she said in her heavy German accent," "he spoke in a thick Polish accent," and "a slight shadow of a Swedish accent remained."

When using alternative spellings and uncommon contractions, keep it as close to the correct spelling as possible, avoiding things such as tripling vowels to create a drawl. Only a few words of dialect are usually needed. For example, the phrase "G'day mate" indicates an Australian speaker without using distracting spelling in the entire dialogue. Once it is shown that the speaker is Australian, the dialogue can proceed normally, with only a few quick words of reminder sprinkled throughout. Readers will continue the accent in their head, without you having to write every word in dialect.[7,8,16]

Slang

Slang is the non-standard use of words in a language of a particular social group, and sometimes the creation of new words or importation of words from another language. Slang excludes certain people from the conversation because they cannot understand the conversation. It functions as a way to recognize members of the same group and to differentiate that group from the society at large. Slang terms are often particular to a certain subculture, such as drug users, skateboarders, and musicians. The following are a few examples of street-gang slang:

- *8-ball.* A quantity of cocaine.
- *Double Deuce.* A 22-caliber handgun.
- *Home Boy.* Fellow gang member from the same neighborhood.
- *Durag* (Pronounced doo-rag). Handkerchief or bandana wrapped around a gang member's head.
- *My Bad.* It's my fault; my mistake.

Jargon

Jargon, the technical vocabulary of a particular profession, is distinguished from slang as jargon is not used intentionally to exclude non-group members from the conversation. It deals with technical peculiarities of a given field, which require a specialized language. Whereas slang generally implies informal speech, jargon often is used in formal speech when talking to other technical people.[22]

The following are a few examples of jargon used by people who are into computers:

- *FAT (File Allocation Table).* The table your operating system, such as Windows XP, uses to keep track of where each file is located on your hard disk or floppy.
- *Hacker.* Someone who breaks into someone else's computer.

- *Java.* Programming language created specifically for the Internet.
- *SWIM.* Chat room acronym for "See What I Mean."
- *WYSIWYG.* Stands for "What You See Is What You Get," referring to the fact that what appears on the monitor screen is the way it actually is.

Slang and Jargon Websites

Many sites on the Internet give examples of slang and jargon. Some are listed below. You can find others by using one of the available search engines.

- *American Slang.* http://www.manythings.org/slang/.
- *Aussie Slang.* http://dictionary-thesaurus.com/wordlists/ AussieSlangWords+Definit(368).txt.
- *British Slang.* http://www.peevish.co.uk/slang/b.htm.
- *Gangster Terms.* http://dictionary-Thesaurus.com/wordlists/GangsterTerms+Definit(405).txt.
- *Gay Slang.* http://www.hurricane.net/~wizard/19a.html.
- *Internet/web Jargon.* http://www.lib.berkeley.edu/TeachingLib/ Guides/Internet/Glossary.html.
- *Police Terms, Slang, and Codes.* http://www.hodrw.com/ cop1.htm, http://sinai.critter.net/mutant/dawn/slang.htm.
- *Prison Slang.* http://dictionary.prisonwall.org/.

PUNCTUATING DIALOGUE

Statements, Questions, and Exclamations

Commas and *periods* always go inside quotation marks. If a question mark or exclamation point is part of the quotation, it goes inside the quotation mark. A question mark follows the quotation mark if it applies to the entire sentence and not to a quotation within the sentence.

- *Statement.* Jack said he was "ready to fly solo," but his instructor disagreed.

- **Question.** John asked, "When's dinner?"
- **Question.** What did she mean by saying "You'll find out when the time is right."?
- **Exclamation.** I heard Fred shout, "Look out for the truck!"[15,17,23-26]

New Speaker

Each new speaker requires a new paragraph, properly indented and set off by quotation marks.[8,26]

- "What do you think about Bill and Janet getting together again?" Wanda asked.
  "Pretty strange couple, if you ask me," Jack responded.

More than One Paragraph of Dialogue

If a speaker goes on for more than one paragraph, do not close off the quotation marks at the end of the first paragraph. Simply place quotation marks at the beginning of the next paragraph and carry on to the end of the quotation where you place a quotation mark.[15,26] Consider the following two paragraphs spoken by the same character. Notice the lack of a quotation mark at the end of the first paragraph.

- "I couldn't believe he said such a thing to me. If I ever see that man again I'm going to give him a piece of my mind.
  "Oh, did I tell you about Bob. He has a new girlfriend. She's real pretty, but I got the impression after talking to her for only five minutes that she's probably a real bitch."

Nested Quotation Marks

If you need to have one character directly quoting another character, then use double quotes for your main dialogue and single quotes for the quote-within-a-quote in North America; in Europe and Australia use single quotes for the dialogue and double

266

quotes for the quote-within-a-quote.

- **North America.** "And then he said, 'Why should I do it?' The guys a jerk!" she said.
- **Europe and Australia.** 'And then he said, "Why should I do it?" The guys a jerk!' she said.[4,26]

References

1. Bishop, Leonard, Dare to be a Great Writer, Writer's Digest Books, Cincinnati, 1992.
2. Duncan, Apryl, Snappy Dialogue, FictionAddiction.net, http://fictionaddiction.net/articles/dialogue1.html.
3. Noble, William, Conflict, Action & Suspense, Writer's Digest Books, Cincinnati, 1994.
4. Silvester, Nicko, How to write successful dialogue, Creative Writing for Teens, About.com, http://teenwriting.about.com/cs/dialogue/ht/SuccessDialogue.htm.
5. Swain, Dwight V., The Things They Say, In The Writer's Digest Handbook of Novel Writing, Ed. by Tom Clark, William Brohaugh, Bruce Woods, Bill Strickland, and Peter Blocksom, Writer's Digest Books, Cincinnati, 1992.
6. Lee, Linda Hope, series 2, tip sheet #5: dialogue – functions, Tips for Writers, http://www.lindahopelee.com/tip5.html, 2003.
7. Kay, Kim, To Speak or Not to Speak: Creating Dazzling Dialogue, Parts I and II, Suite101.com, http://www.suite101.com/article.cfm/novel_writing/16304, February 9, 1999.
8. Kilian, Crawford, Advice on novel writing, "Let's talk dialogue," he pontificated, http://www.steampunk.com/sfch/writing/ckilian/#foreword.
9. Rose, Elizabeth, Writing: Parts I and II. Dialogue, http://www.scribesworld.com/writersniche/articles/WritingDialogue1ER.html.
10. Renken, Laura, My Lord Pirate, Jove Books, New York, 2001.
11. Hamper, Rich, Effective dialogue – rules of thumb, http://home.comcast.net/~rthamper/html/body_dialogue.htm, September 3, 2003.
12. "Let's talk about dialogue," he pontificated, The Fiction Writer's Page, http://www.capcollege.bc.ca/dept/cmns/dialogue.html.
13. Chiarella, Tom, Writing Dialogue, Story Press, Cincinnati, 1998.
14. Erichsen, Gerald, "Idiom," Spanish Language, About.com,

http://spanish.about.com/cs/vocabulary/g/idiomgl.htm.
15. Sawyer, Robert J., Speaking of dialogue, On Writing, SFWriter.com, About.com, http://www.sfwriter.com/ow08.htm, 1996.
16. Collier, Oscar, How to Write & Sell Your First Novel, Writer's Digest Books, Cincinnati, 1990.
17. Dialogue, The Teddy Lady, http://www.skeeter63.org/~silvablu/HMG/07-dialog.htm#Characters/.
18. Cornwell, Patricia, Point of Origin, G. P. Putnam's Sons, New York, 1998.
19. Rasley, Alicia, Dazzling dialogue tips, Article of the Month, http://www.sff.net/people/alicia/artdialogue.htm, 2001.
20. Schnelbach, S. and C. S. Wyatt, Tameri Guide for Writers. http://www.tameri.com http://www.tameri.com/write/dialogue.html, June 15, 2005.
21. Tritt, Sandy, Avoid creative dialogue tag syndrome, Elements of Craft, Inspiration for Writers, http://tritt.wirefire.com/tip4.html.
22. Slang, DictionaryLaborLaw.com, http://dictionary.laborlawtalk.com/.
23. Common grammatical errors, http://www.sunysuffolk.edu/Web/Selden/OWL/grammaticalerrors.htm
24. Common grammatical errors and how to fix them, Academic Resource Center, Sweet Briar College, http://www.arc.sbc.edu/grammar.html.
25. Quotation marks, http://www.wsu.edu/~brians/errors/quotation_marks.html.
26. Silvester, Niko, In Quotations: Formatting Dialog, About.com, http://teenwriting.about.com/library/weekly/aa010603a.htm.

Chapter 13

Emotions

Emotion refers to a feeling state (happiness, sadness, anger, fear, anxiety) involving (1) thoughts, (2) physiological changes (blood pressure, heart rate, sweating), and (3) an outward expression or behavior (body language).

CHARACTERISTICS OF EMOTIONS

Emotions are seldom simple. They can be mixed, have a wide range, and occur at different levels. And they are seldom something we have full control over. To a large extent, the success of your novel will depend on how well you portray the emotions of your characters; the stronger the emotions the more the readers feel the need to keep on reading.

Etiology of Emotions

An *emotion* is a mental state that arises spontaneously, rather than through conscious effort. It often is accompanied by physiological changes arising from the limbic system's control of the autonomic nervous system. The limbic system is the old, deep portion of the brain responsible for the fight or flight response. The most prominent physiological signs occur for excitement, fear, hate, and anger, and consist of increased pulse rate, pounding in the temples from increased blood pressure, tremor, sweating, decreased digestive secretions (dry mouth), muscle tightness, goose bumps, dilated pupils, and hypervigilance.[1,2,3]

Mixed Emotions

Emotions are not always one dimensional. They may be mixed and complex—anger mixed with confusion, anxiety mixed with fear, sadness mixed with suspiciousness, disappointment mixed with resentment, bitterness mixed with jealousy, and so forth. A bride on her wedding day, for instance, may experience happiness, anxiety, excitement, and apprehension.[1,2,3]

Range of Emotions

Not only may a character's emotions be mixed and complex, he may experience a wide rage of emotions. For instance, a character that begins the story in a state of despair may move to hope as the story progresses, and finally to happiness when in the end everything works out well. Similarly, a character may start out with anger, and then move in order through lust, jealousy, humiliation, fear, and understanding or any other emotions.[1,2,3]

Levels of Emotion

If the task of writing about emotions seems daunting so far, consider the fact that there are several levels for each emotion. Anger, for instance, can range all the way from being irritated (you discover your credit card is missing from your purse) to absolute rage (you discover your teenage son stole the credit card and used it buy several hundred dollars worth of merchandise— lingerie for his 15-year-old girlfriend).[1,2,3]

EMOTIONS AND BODY LANGUAGE

Emotions can be displayed by the power of suggestion and by the character's actions. For instance, the suggestion of sadness can be shown by crumpled tissues in a woman's hand, an open picture album on a bedside table, and mascara smears under the eyes. Similarly, a character who chops wood furiously, curses, clinches his fists, throws things, and rams a fist through a wall clearly is angry. And a character who strikes his forehead with his palm, walks aimlessly, forgets an important appointment, and has trouble following a conversation is obviously confused.[1,2,3] Body language is covered in the Chapter 14.

TABLE OF EMOTIONS

There are numerous emotions. Ann Hood, in her book *Creating Emotions* (1977) describes the various emotions and gives both bad and good examples of how to write about them.[2] The following table describes 34 of the more common emotions.

Emotion	Description
Anger	A feeling of strong displeasure in response to an injury or assumed injury. Related terms are (1) *annoyance,* which is a feeling of irritation, milder or more fleeting than anger; (2) *resentment,* which is subdued anger caused by a sense of unfair treatment and a powerlessness to remedy it; (3) *indignation,* which is anger based on a condemnation of something considered wrong or unfair; (4) *fury,* which is an intense form of anger that suggests lack of control and potential to do violence; (5) *rage,* which is violent anger, more intense than fury; and (6) *wrath,* which is a term for strong anger, often with overtones of a desire for revenge
Anxiety	Worry in the extreme, often about something that is going to happen, either real or imagined. Manifested physiologically as increased heart rate, sweating,

	trembling, weakness, and stomach or intestinal discomfort. It can be acute or chronic. Panic attacks may sometimes be a part of anxiety symptoms. A *panic attack* is a period of intense fear, typically with an abrupt onset and usually lasting no more than 30 minutes. Symptoms include trembling, shortness of breath and sensations of choking or smothering. Panic attacks appear to be unprovoked, and are often disabling. Most sufferers report a fear of dying, going crazy, or losing control of their emotions or behavior. They experience a strong urge to flee the place where the attack begins, and when associated with chest pain or shortness of breath they often seek aid from a hospital emergency room
Apathy	Impassivity, disinterest, indifference, unconcern, lack of feeling. A non-emotion. It is not cruelty or boredom.
Confusion	Bewildered, frustrated, befuddled. Trying to assemble stimuli or information without any sense of order.
Contentment	Everything is right with the world. The birds sing, the sun shines, a gentle breeze blows, the dog snoozes in your lap, your wife loves you. You can look at the past, present, and future with a feeling of satisfaction.
Curiosity	Desire to learn something new. Not nosy or snoopy, which is curiosity gone bad. Part of curiosity is discovery. A child learns by asking questions. Older children and adults learn by reading the newspaper, cruising the Internet, or reading a book.
Desire	A passion or craving for something. Can be sexual or nonsexual (desire for a woman or for a better life). Not a need to have what another has. That is envy or jealousy. A boy may desire a gun, a girl a Barbie doll.
Despair	Utter loss of hope, sense of futility or defeat. Not self-pity. Seen best when compared with a time of happiness.
Excitement	Sense of electricity crackling through one's body. A thrill, kick, bang, rush, or charge.

Fear	Deep concern for one's safety, real or imagined. Go to bed with lights on. Cover head with blanket. Afraid to close eyes. Grip tightens or holds even tighter.
Fondness	Feeling of comfort, warmness, affection, attachment, or devotion. His favorite pair of old jeans. Her favorite aunt. Should not be confused with love.
Forgiveness	Act of coming to grips with the fact that we are like other people: "I could have made the same mistake." Usually a sign of strength. Forgiveness shouldn't come too easily. It should be a struggle. What causes the character to forgive?
Gratitude	Thankfulness. Grateful to someone for something (an apple pie, a hug, a kind word).
Grief	Feeling we get when we lose something or someone we care deeply about. It can be very emotional (throws self on coffin) or repressed (sits stoically in chair).
Guilt	Feeling of responsibility for something bad that happened (death of child, car wreck that injured best friend). Character feels remorse. Associated with shame for the act. Tends to keep feelings to self. May eventually try to unburden self by telling someone.
Happiness	State of well being and contentment. Makes character jump, squeal, shout, skip, hum a tune, or cry. Shown best if character has experienced sadness or despair.
Hate	A feeling of intense dislike, anger, hostility, or animosity toward someone. Usually associated with a desire to do harm or wish harm to someone.
Hope	To desire with expectation of fulfillment. To long for with expectation of obtaining. Not necessarily based on logic (I hope I get the raise. I hope she feels the same toward me as I do her.).
Hostility	Feeling antagonistic. Sees someone or something as the enemy (If that SOB crosses me again he'll pay for it).

Irritation	Feeling of annoyance or exasperation. Irritations frustrate you, disturb you, and make you uncomfortable (Someone reading over your shoulder, talking behind you in a movie, running out of hot water in the middle of a shower). A slow build up of irritation can lead to anger.
Jealousy	Wanting something that someone else has. More than envy. May involve some hostility. Can consume us and make us do irrational things that destroy friendships and ruin loving relationships. Secretive (People are hesitant to admit they want their friend's job, wife, house, car, and so forth).
Loneliness	Not the same as being alone. Many people are happy reading, writing, watching TV, and so forth all by themselves. Loneliness is being alone and not liking it. Longing for companionship. Some people can be lonely in a crowd if they don't know the other individuals or if they are not skilled in social interaction. Loneliness especially occurs on birthdays, holidays, and anniversaries.
Longing	Persistent desire or yearning that cannot be fulfilled. Has inherent in it a sadness. We long for love, for a happier time, or for people who are far away. It is a little like desire except with desire we often can obtain the object of our desire. A husband may long for a time when he and his wife were in love, which is not obtainable.
Love	**Parent-child.** Mixture of other emotions (tenderness, happiness, jealousy, confusion, disappointment). Parents worry about their children, they feel pained by them, and they experience happiness by the things they do. **Romantic.** A mixture of deep and often conflicting emotions (hope, sorrow, desire, lust, hate, fear). Symptoms may be feeling twittery, not eating, lying awake, and moping in corners. Being away from the one we love can be painful. Sound of loved one's voice can make one's heart pound.
Passion	Passion consumes us. It takes over. It is all

	encompassing, reckless, and wonderful. Makes us feel like nothing exists but the object of our passion. Everyone remembers the passion of Burt Lancaster and Deborah Kerr lying on the beach entwined in each other and kissing while a wave washes over them in *From Here to Eternity*.
Resignation	Accepting what you were born with, or given, or came across in life, although you were initially in denial or unwilling to accept it. It does not carry with it regret or sadness. It is often at the end of a process (Wife in coma, never to wake up. Her husband grapples with despair, then hope, and then anger on his way to resignation of her state.
Restlessness	Restlessness is kinetic; that is, it has motion with it (tapping foot, drumming fingers, getting up and sitting down and repeating the process). At its root is discontentment, waiting or hoping for something to happen.
Revenge	Directed at those who have hurt us, betrayed us, or done us wrong (actual or perceived). Spend hours thinking about and planning how to get even. Next step is an action.
Sadness	Not about death or other major loss. Deeper than mere unhappiness from missing a telephone call or burning dinner. May not have an identifiable cause.
Shame	Comes from guilt, unworthiness, or disgrace. Disappointed in ourselves or the lives we are leading (taking government handout, having affair with sister-in-law). Based on a comparison of our circumstances with our concept of what our circumstances should be. Do not want other people to find out so they won't think as low of us as we already do.
Surprise	Emotion we feel when we are caught unaware (gun suddenly in back, mouse skittering across floor, dear John letter, body hanging in our closet).
Suspicion	Distrust without proof or evidence (wife doesn't come

	home until late at night, so she must be having an affair).
Sympathy	Sharing the feelings of another. If one woman is ashamed of her body (thin shoulders and heavy bottom, another person shares and identifies with her feelings ("Who among us is perfect?").
Tenderness	A gentle emotion (the way a mother handles her newborn child or the way a long-married couple hold hands as they walk from their car to the movie theater).
Worry	Much less than fear. A nagging feeling in one's gut that something may be wrong (midnight and your 17-year-old daughter is an hour late getting home. You hope she's okay, but you don't start calling hospitals).[2,4-8]

EXAMPLES OF EMOTIONS

Descriptive Phrases

The following are examples that describe emotion. They are from genre novels I have read.

- *Anger. Blood hammered in his temples, blood roared in his ears, chin thrust forward ready to fight, clenched and unclenched his fists, cords of his neck tightened, eyes blazed, eyes were black pools of festering hatred, face hardened and eyes narrowed, face was crimson with rage, flinty silence, nostrils flared, stalked through the door*
- *Anxiety. Air was heavy with tension, current of anxiety buzzed through him, eyes darted nervously behind thick glasses, belly quivered so badly she thought she was going to vomit, palms wet with nervous perspiration, roamed about the large room like a tiger in a cage, sweat began to trickle down her brow, tightness in her chest and throat, voice was uncertain and crackling, wrapped her arms around herself and began pacing*
- *Fear. Bitter taste of stomach acid rose in his throat, black silence draped the room, breath caught in her throat, bright*

knife of terror plunged into her heart, every once of blood drained from his face, felt a long slow shudder work through him, felt an icicle go through his chest, minute sliver of fear edged its way up his spine, scream caught in her throat, tremor reverberated in her voice

- **Happiness.** *Current of intense pleasure ran through him, felt a smile creep across his face, giggling like school children, humming a little tune, quite exuberance flowed through her, smile swelled into a grin, thought made her warm and tingly, warmed her heart, whistled a little tune.*

- **Pain.** *Bolts of pain shot through his forehead, face contorted in pain, face twisted with agony, felt the onslaught of a headache behind her eyes, pain screeched through her ankle, pain surged through his head, throat felt like raw meat and her lungs burned with each breath as if she were inhaling fire, pain tore through her shoulder*

Emotional Situations

Now considers some emotional situations from the literature. Clearly they go far beyond saying "He was anxious" or "he said angrily."

Anger. A woman comes home to find her boyfriend in a compromising position.[6]

- *There was no silent second of shock, no delay of any kind. She ran instantly into the bathroom and yanked Matt up by his hair. "Get out!" she screamed. "Get the hell out of my house!" She dug her fingers into Matt's upper arm and shoved him as hard as she could into the hall, picking his clothes up from the floor next to the tub and throwing them after him. She did not touch the woman but continued screaming all the while, anguished, angry invectives that included both of them.* (*The House*, 1999, by Bentley Little).[9]

Anxiety. The narrator is waiting for her teenage son to come home.[2]

- *At two, Zack's expected arrival time, he wasn't home. I decided to read. At two-thirty, he wasn't home. At three, he wasn't home. At three-fifteen, the phone rang once, then stopped. At three-thirty, I heard Bibi's car slowly approaching, coasting in; she was driving with admirable care and they were almost home. But they weren't. The car paused, then moved on. When I went to look out, it was gone. Empty street, in quiet darkness. (Poltergeists, 1993, by Jane Shapiro).*[10]

Confusion. A mother thinks about her 19-year-old daughter and her relationship to her by reflecting on different times in the girl's life.[2]

- *There was a boy she loved painfully through two school semesters. Months later she told me how she had taken pennies from my purse to buy him candy. "Licorice was his favorite and I brought him some every day, but he still liked Jennifer better'n me. Why Mommy?" The kind of question for which there is no answer. (I Stand Here Ironing, 1961, by Tillie Olsen).*[11]

Desire. A story about a 15-year-old boy struggling for manhood and independence against the sharecropping system in the deep South of the 1930s. He expresses his desire for a gun.[2]

- *He poured his plate full of molasses and sopped it up slowly with a chunk of cornbread. When his father and brother had left the kitchen, he still sat and looked again at the guns in the catalogue, longing to muster courage enough to present his case to his mother. Lawd, ef Ah only had the pretty one! He could almost feel the slickness of the weapon with his fingers. If he had a gun like that he would polish it and keep it shining so it would never rust. N Ah'd keep it loaded, by Gawd! (Almos' a Man, 1940, by Richard Wright).*[12]

Fear. Anna finds her youngest daughter, Molly, terrified at having awakened alone in the car.[2]

- *"Molly," I whispered, and pulled her to me as I clamber*

in. Her body began to shape itself to mine, to cling to me, even before she really woke up. "Molly," I said. "Molly." And then she started to cry, screaming in sharp pain like a child who's just fallen, who's bitten her tongue, who's put her hand on a hot kettle, who's lost.

"Mommy!" she screamed. She cried and held me tighter even than I held her. "Mommy! Mommy!" she shrieked as she would over and over in my memory of this moment. (The Good Mother, 1994, by Sue Miller).[13]

Irritation. A boy and his stepfather are irritated with each other.[2]

* *My stepfather developed this new habit of referring to me as him and never talking directly to me or even looking at me except when he thought I didn't notice or when he was drunk. He'd like say to my mother, Ask him where he's going tonight. Tell him to take out the goddam trash Ask him why he goes around with torn clothes and wearing earrings in his ears like a goddam girl and in his nose for chrissake, he'd say with me watching TV right there in front of him. (Rule of the Bone, 1996, by Russell Banks).*[14]

Love. The main character sums up one kiss full of absolute meaning.[7]

* *He leaned down, this rough cowboy of hers. His lips touched hers with a tenderness so sweet her heart swelled to near bursting. It was a promise, a melding of spirits. (The Perfect Family, 2001, by Patricia Potter)*[15]

Revenge. Bernice is the provincial cousin visiting the glamorous Marjorie. After taking Marjorie's advice on how to be popular, Bernice becomes so popular her cousin schemes to get her to bob her hair, an act that ruins Bernice's hair. Bernice acts on her vengeful feelings at the end.[2]

* *She was by the bedside now, very deliberate and calm. She acted swiftly. Bending over she found one of the braids of Marjorie's hair, followed it up with her hand to the point*

nearest the head, and then holding it a little slack so that the sleeper would feel no pull, she reached down with the shears and severed it. With the pigtail in her hand she held her breath. Marjorie had muttered something in her sleep., Bernice deftly amputated the other braid, paused for a moment, and then flitted swiftly and silently back to her own room. (Bernice Bobs Her Hair, 1922, by F. Scott Fitzgerald).[16]

Suspicion. Nat becomes concerned when one of his fellow shop owners doesn't show up to open his store.[5]

- *When Nat Small noted that Abdul Parki's souvenir shop still hadn't opened at noon on Wednesday, he became concerned. ... Nat, a wiry fifty-year-old with a narrow face, hooded eyes, and a troubled past, could smell trouble just as distinctly as anyone who got near him could smell the combination or stale cigars and liquor that was his personal scent. (You Belong to Me, 1998, by Mary Higgins Clark)*[17]

Worry. Gripped by worry, Neil waits for his male lover to arrive at Neil's mother's house.[2]

- *He stands, and the dogs circle him, looking up at his face expectantly. He feels renewed terror at the thought that Wayne will be here soon: Will they sleep in the same room? Will they make love? He has never had sex in his parent's house. How can he be expected to be a lover here, in this place of his childhood, of his earliest shame, in this household of mothers and dogs? (Territory, 1997, by Neal Leavitt).*[18]

References

1. Bickham, Jack, Scene & Structure, Writer's Digest Books, Cincinnati, 1993.
2. Hood, Ann, Creating Character Emotions, Story Press, Cincinnati, 1997.
3. Noble, William, Conflict, Action & Suspense, Writer's Digest Books, Cincinnati, 1994.
4. Dictionary.com, http://dictionary.reference.com/.
5. Duncan, Apryl, Emotional rollercoaster: Writing suspicion,

WritersBreak.com,
http://www.writersbreak.com/Fiction/articles/article_fiction_suspicio
n_1.htm.

6. Duncan, Apryl, Emotional rollercoaster: Writing Anger,
   WritersBreak.com,
   http://www.writersbreak.com/Fiction/articles/article_fiction_anger_1
   .htm.

7. Duncan, Apryl, Emotional rollercoaster: Writing Love,
   WritersBreak.com,
   http://www.writersbreak.com/Fiction/articles/article_fiction_love_1.
   htm.

8. MedTerms Medical Dictionary, MedicineNet.com,
   http://www.medterms.com/script/main/hp.asp.

9. Little, Bentley, The House, Signet Books, New York, 1999.

10. Shapiro, Jane, Poltergeists, In Erdrich, Louise and Katrina Kenison,
    The Best American Short Stories 1993: Selected from U.S. and
    Canadian Magazines, Houghton Mifflin, New York, 1993.

11. Olsen, Tillie, I Stand Here Ironing, In Tell Me a Riddle, Delta;
    Reissue edition, 1971 (originally published in 1961).

12. Wright, Richard, Almos' a Man, Harper's Bazaar, New York, 1940.

13. Miller, Sue, The Good Mother, Delta Trade Paperbacks, New York,
    1994.

14. Banks, Russell, Rule of the Bone, Vintage Canada, Toronto, 1996.

15. Potter, Patricia, The Perfect Family, Berkley Publishing Group, New
    York, 2001.

16. Fitzgerald, F. Scott, Bernice Bobs Her Hair, In Flappers and
    Philosophers, Scribners, New York, 1922.

17. Clark, Mary Higgins, You Belong to Me, Simon & Schuster, New
    York, 1998.

18. Leavitt, Neal, Territory, In Family Dancing: Stories, Mariner Books,
    New York, 1997.

Chapter 14

Body Language

*B*ody language *(nonverbal communication)* is the unspoken communication that goes on in every face-to-face encounter with another human being. While speaking, a character may nervously tug his ear, clear his throat, or shift from foot to foot. Using body language in your writing keeps the reader visualizing the scene and contributes to its rhythm.

Usually body language occurs subconsciously; yet the body language we use decides to a large extent the quality of our communication. Animals (cats, dogs, rabbits, horses, iguanas) also have their own body language.

Body language is just as much dialogue as the written word. In writing, it can be used to amplify the words a character speaks and to give flow to the scene. Body language is especially helpful in complimenting dialogue in regard to emotions or feelings.

The following example illustrates the use of body language in combination with dialogue.

- "Well Edna, are you going to sell me your share of the company?" A muscle in his jaw twitched as he waited for her answer.

    She slumped in her chair. "Yes Robert, I've decided to sell."

Both characters are emotional, a fact you could not get from the verbal dialogue alone. The twitch in Robert's jaw muscle gives him away. He's tense and perhaps angry. Edna slumps in her chair, clearly feeling defeated.

If we don't like someone, it's often difficult to say that directly to the person; however, we may make it clear, either intentionally or unintentionally, through body language. The opposite is also true; we may say that we are angry through words yet our body language may be saying loud and clear that we are not. This is usually described as giving out double messages—one message in words and an opposite message in body language. Whenever there's a conflict between the words that a character says and his body signals and movements, the reader almost always will believe the body. For example, a character says, "You idiot!" Without body language, the reader doesn't know what the emotional value of this statement is.[1,2]

- "You idiot!" Bill said, waving his fist in the air.
- "You idiot!" Bill said, laughing and slapping his knee.

TYPES OF BODY LANGUAGE

Lisa Hood points out four types of body language: (1) facial expression, (2) gestures, (3) posture, and (4) spatial relationship. Therefore, your characters' face, hands, posture, and spatial orientation express what is going on inside of them, regardless of what they say.[3]

Facial Expression

Some *facial expressions*, such as smiling and frowning, are natural and universal, while others, such as eye contact, are learned and have different meaning from culture to culture. In some countries, direct eye contact is considered insulting or challenging. In the United States, it is often considered a sign of trustworthiness. So, if your character is Anglo-Saxon, regular, attentive eye contact would convey honesty, straight forwardness, and approachability. However, a hard, unblinking stare sends a much different message. It implies intensity. It may also mean romantic interest, aggression, or fear. Making very little eye contact can either convey shyness or submissiveness. The middle ground of a gaze says that you are interested, secure, and at ease.

- Her hard stare burned a hole through me. "Where the hell is my necklace," she demanded through clenched teeth.

However, body language is not always reliable. For instance, one group that excels at making eye contact that appears very sincere is pathological liars.[3,4,5]

Gestures

Gestures break up the spoken dialogue and inject a change of pace in the story. Gestures also highlight suspense and other emotions by adding another dimension. The character is doing something (offering a cigarette, shifting his eyes, running a hand through his hair, tapping his fingers on a table, waving for a waiter). [3,4,6]

Three useful types of gestures in writing fiction are (1) general gestures, (2) particular gestures, and (3) incidental gestures.

General Gestures

General gestures are those gestures in a society that have meaning and apply to almost everyone. For instance, in the United States fidgeting shows boredom and restlessness. Pressing the fingers together to form a steeple shows interest, assertiveness, and determination. Touching the nose or rubbing the eyes may indicate dishonesty. A hand to the back of the neck may indicate withdrawal from a conversation. Other gestures particular to our society are habitually shifting weight from one foot to another when anxious or chewing gum side to side in a rapid manner when angry. [3,4,6]

Particular Gestures

A *particular gesture* is a movement or action unique to an

individual—a woman who always touches the top button of her blouse before she speaks, a man who droops one shoulder when he lies, and a card player who always wraps his fingers around the cards when he holds a good hand.[7]

• Walking up to the line, the quarterback licked his fingers, and then placed his hands under the center.
  "It's going to be a pass," the middle linebacker shouted.

Incidental Gestures

The incidental gesture is something someone does that has no particular inward meaning, but may lend reality to the situation: The grave robber bats the gnats from his face as he scratches the dirt off the top of the coffin or the little boy sticks his fingers in his ears as the fire truck goes by.

Other incidental gestures are the kind that might take place in a group of people, say at a bar: The football game flickers on TV, the door to the street (and daylight) flops open and then closed, and a man lifts his hands so the bartender can pass through with his rag as he wipes the counter.[7]

• "Damn horseflies," Jack said, swatting at the air.

Posture

The way people hold themselves gives important information. For instance, body *posture* can be closed or open. Interested people pay attention and lean forward. Leaning backwards demonstrates aloofness or rejection. A firm handshake gives the impression of assertiveness or honesty; too firm a handshake can indicate arrogance or a challenge. Folding the arms across the chest or body gives the impression of a character who is closed, guarded, and defensive. People with their arms folded, legs crossed, and bodies turned away indicate that they are rejecting the message. People showing open hands and both feet planted on the ground are indicating acceptance. A head held straight up signals a neutral attitude. A head tilted to the side indicates interest. A head down indicates someone is negative and judgmental.

When a character is feeling low in confidence he can hunch his shoulders and keep his head down. When he feels aggressive or is trying to defend his space, he can "puff" himself up by standing straight and placing his hands on his hips.[3,4]

- He sat there staring blankly at me as I continued my presentation. Then he folded his arms across his chest and turned his body toward his partner.
  "Oh shit, I've lost him," I thought.

Spatial Relationships

Body Zones

There are four distinct zones in which most people operate: (1) Public zone, (2) social zone, (3) personal zone, and (4) intimate zone. How we guard our zones is an integral part of how we relate to other people. Knowing their significance will allow you to use them effectively as you writing fiction.[8]

Public Zone. The *public zone* is generally over 12 feet; that is, when we are walking around town we try to keep at least 12 feet between us and other people. Of course there are many times when we can't do this. We tend to notice other people who are within this radius. The closer they get to us, the more we become aware of them and ready ourselves for appropriate action.

When we are distant from another person, we feel a degree of safety from them. A person at a distance cannot suddenly attack us. If they do seem to threaten, we will have time to dodge, run, or prepare for battle.[8]

Social Zone. The *social zone* is four to 12 feet. Within this zone, we start to feel a connection with other people. We can talk with them without having to shout, but still keep them at a safe distance. This is a comfortable distance for people who are standing in a group, but maybe not talking directly with one another. People sitting in chairs also tend to like this distance.[8]

Personal Zone. The *personal zone* is two to four feet. In this zone, conversation gets more direct. Two to four feet is a good distance for two people who are talking in earnest about something.[8]

Intimate Zone. The *intimate zone* is less than two feet (within arms reach). When a person is in the intimate zone, we can touch him in intimate ways. We can also see more detail of his body language and look him in the eyes. He also blots out other people so all we can see is him. Romance occurs in this space.

Entering the intimate zone of another person can be very threatening, unless invited in. Invading this zone is sometimes done deliberately to give a non-verbal signal that the other person is powerful enough to invade your territory whenever he chooses.[8]

Body Orientation

The orientation of speakers and listeners (face to face, side to side, or back to back) can send powerful non-verbal messages. In a group situation, when the leader faces the group and turns toward the one in the group who is speaking, he conveys strong attention. When two people are communicating, competitors are more likely to sit facing each other, while collaborators are more likely to sit more to the side. If one person stands while the other is sitting, the standing person may be sending a dominance signal, which can stifle free exchange of ideas.[3]

- Halfway through our discussion John stood up, his six-foot-six frame towering over me. "You're right," I babbled. I should have listened to you in the first place."

GROUPS

Body language may be even more important in group communications than in one-to-one communication. In a group, each person has an open body language channel to all other people in the group, while speaking is typically limited to one person at a time. The larger the group, the more body language starts to dominate.[9]

TABLE OF BODY LANGUAGE

The following is a table of body language for various emotions. Think of ways you can use some of them in combinations with dialogue and narrative.

To Convey	Use
Anger/ aggression	*Making the body big* (hands on hips with elbows wide, standing upright and erect with the chin up and the chest thrust out, legs may be placed apart), *facial signals* (disapproving frowns, pursed lips, sneers, snarls, jaws clenched, staring and holding the gaze for a long period, squinting with constricted pupils, nostrils flared, curled lips), *gestures* (shaking fists, whole arm sweeps, pointing finger, exaggerated movements, slamming closed hand on table, handling objects roughly, fists clinched)
Anticipation	Rubbing hands, licking lips.
Apprehension, anxiety, nervousness	Locked ankles, pacing, clearing of throat, exhaling audibly, fidgeting, jiggling money or keys, tugging ear, wringing hands, adjusting tie, clutching object tightly, pacing, scratching, rubbing arms.
Boredom, lack of interest	*Distraction* (looking anywhere but at the person who is talking. Doodling, talking with others, staring around the room, playing with objects on desk), *repetition* (tapping toes, swinging feet, drumming fingers, repeatedly looking at watch or wall clock, picking at clothes), *tiredness* (yawning, whole body sagging as individual slouches down in seat or leans against a wall, face appears blank, head resting in hand, eyes downcast, sitting with legs crossed and foot kicking slightly).
Close minded, non-receptive	*Arms or legs* (arms folded, legs crossed in 11 position, when legs are crossed but arms are not, it can show deliberate attempts to appear relaxed. This is particularly true when legs are hidden under a table.), *head* (looking away, head may be inclined away from the person and may be tucked down, frown).

Confidence, superiority	Sitting with hands clasped behind head, legs crossed; brisk, erect walk with head held high, good eye contact,
Deception, lying	A deceptive body is concerned about being found out, and this concern may show anxiety (sweating, sudden movements, minor twitches of muscles around mouth and eyes, fidgeting). To avoid being caught, there may be various signs of over-control, such as signs of attempted friendly body language (forced smile - mouth smiles but eyes do not, jerky movements, oscillation between open body language and deceptive body language), touches face, hand over mouth, pulls ear, eyes down, shifts in seat, looks down and to the left, avoids eye contact. Palms hidden.
Defiant	Standing with hands on hips, frowning, hard stare.
Dejection	Walking with hands in pockets, shoulders hunched, eyes downcast.
Disagreement	Turns body away, leans further back in chair, shakes head side to side.
Doubt, disbelief	Looking down, face turned away, rubbing eye, rolling eyes, touching or slightly rubbing nose.
Eagerness	**Sitting** (feet under chair, legs open), **Standing** (on toes).
Evaluation, thinking, making a decision	Hand to cheek, stroking chin, steepling hands, sucking glasses or pencil, looking up and to the right, index finger to lips, legs crossed in 4 position, slightly raised forehead with slight lines across it, pursed lips.
Exasperation	Eyes rolled up, frown
Happiness	Smiling, shoulders back, head held high, wink.
Impatience	Tapping or drumming fingers, shifting from one foot to the other.
Indecision	Pulling or tugging at ear or hair, cleaning glasses, biting lip, pacing, fingers to mouth.
Insecurity, lack of self	Biting nails, patting or fondling hair, adjusting tie, palm up handshake, minimum eye contact.

confidence	
Pain	Grimacing, flinching, drawing hand back.
Power, authority, dominance	*Handshake* (grabs palm firmly, palm down, pulls other character in and holds his elbow with left hand. Places hands behind back). *Touching.* Touching can be threatening and is used to demonstrate power (pats shoulders and back, guides people with a palm in the small of their back, greets them with a hand on the back, touches them on the elbow or other safe area). *Gesture* (beat with a finger, a palm, or even a fist when talking.) *Walking* (walks with exaggerated swinging of arms. Kinks elbows outward to make the body seem wider. Slight swagger. When walking with others, walks in front of them. When going through doors, if going to an audience, goes first. If going from an audience, goes last guiding others through door). *Other* (leaning back and placing both hands behind the neck, hands on hips, feet on desk, standing while other is sitting).
Readiness to leave	A ready body is poised for action. *Pointing* (any part of the body may be pointing at where the character is thinking about—another person or the door. The body part doing the pointing may be as subtle as a foot or as obvious as the whole body leaning. Eyes may also repeatedly flash in the intended direction.) *Tension* (body is tensed up and ready for action. If sitting, hands may hold onto armrests in readiness to get up, legs are tensed ready to lift the body. Things in the hands are gripped. Attention is away from everything except the intended direction.) *Movement* (movement is in preparation for further movement—legs uncross, hands grab bag, straightens clothing, buttons jacket. The whole body leans in the intended direction.)
Respect and interest	Maintains good eye contact, tilts head to one side or the other, nods, leans forward, high blink rate, open feet, arms behind back.
Readiness to agree	Closes papers, puts pen down, hands flat on table, nods head up and down.
Romantic	*Eyes* (Initially, from a distance, a person may look at

interest	the person of interest for slightly longer than normal, then look away, then look back again for a longer period.) *Preening* (What is basically being said is I am making myself look good for you—tossing of the head, brushing hair with hand, polishing spectacles, brushing or picking imaginary lint from clothes.) *Self-caressing* (stroking arms, leg, or face. This may either say "I would like to stroke you like this" or "I would like you to stroke me like this."). *Leaning* (Leaning the body toward another person says "I would like to be closer to you." It also tests to see whether the other person leans toward you or away from you. It can start with the head by a simple tilt. This may be coupled with listening intently to what the person is saying.) *Pointing* (A person who is interested in another person may subtly point at him with a foot, knee, arm, or head. It says "I would like to go in this direction."). *Other* (sensual or dramatic dancing, crotch display in which legs are held apart to show off genitalia area, faked interest in others to invoke envy or hurry a closer engagement, nodding gently as if to say "Yes, I do like you."). *Touching* (Touching may start with "accidental" brushing, followed by touching of "safe" parts of the body, such as arms or back. Caressing may start in the safer regions and then stray (especially when alone) to sexual regions.)
Sincerity, openness, relaxed	*Arms* (not crossed, person may be animated and moving in synchronization with what is being said. Palms held slightly up). *Legs* (not crossed, often are parallel. May even be stretched apart. Feet may point forward or to the side or at something or someone of interest). *Head* (may be directed solely towards the other person or may be looking around. Eye contact is likely to be relaxed and prolonged.). *Clothing* (jacket open).
Stunned	Wide-eyed, stone still, hand to chest with fingers spread, gaping jaw.
Submissiveness	*Body* (Hunching inward to reduce the size of the body, arms held in. Crouching position may be taken, with knees slightly bent). *Head* (head and chin down, avoids looking at other person). *Gestures* (hands out

	and palms up shows that no weapons are held, a common pleading gesture. When the submissive person must move small gestures are often made. These may be slow to avoid alarming the other person, although tension may make them jerky).
Surprise	Rapidly raised eyebrows
Tenderness	Stroking, touching, lips parted.
Unhappiness	Hunched shoulders, staring at floor, head hangs forward and down. When seated, body tends to slump. Walk is more of a shuffle. Arms hang limply by side. [10-13]

EXAMPLES OF BODY LANGUAGE

The following are some examples of body language from popular novels I have read:

- **Head.** *Head snapped to one side, let his head hang down with his chin against his chest, mopped his forehead with a handkerchief, nodded with a polite smile, rubbed her temples, tucked his head down, wiped sweat from his brow*
- **Hair.** *Brushed her long hair out of her eyes, plowed her hair with one hand, tossed her hair, twisted a strand of hair around her finger*
- **Face.** *Screwed up his face, rested chin on his hand, cradled her chin in her hands, face puckered sourly, face reddened, facial muscles slackened, not a muscle twitched in his drawn face, jaw dropped, scratched his mustache, stern look came over his face, stroked his shaggy gray beard*
- **Eyes.** *Averted her eyes, batted her lashes, blinked rapidly, clamped her eyelids tight, cocked her eyebrows seductively, eyes drifted to me, eyes slitted, eyes widened with surprise, gazed at the ceiling, lifted one eyelid, rolled his eyes wearily, stared down at her feet, wearily rubbed his eyes*
- **Mouth.** *Clicked her teeth together, licked her cracked lips, lips spread into a stringy smile, moistened her lips with her tongue, teeth rattled, touched the tip of his tongue to his top lip, wet his lips, wiped his hand across his mouth.*

- **Nose.** Blew his big nose, picked his nose, pinched the bridge of his nose, scratched his nose, scratched the side of his nose, touched the tip of her nose, wrinkled her nose
- **Neck/throat.** Adam's apple bobbed up and down, cleared his throat, coughed, craned his neck, loosened his tie, swallowed the phlegm, tore open his tight collar
- **Upper Extremities.** Brisk handshake, clutched her hand to her breasts, drummed his fingers on the table, eagerly pumped his hand, entwined his fingers, grip on his hand suddenly grew tight, hands locked on the steering wheel so tight they ached, hiked his shoulders, rubs his hands briskly, she put her shoulders back further to elevate her breasts as much as possible, snapped his fingers, twisted the ring on his finger
- **Body.** Dragged herself up, drifted down the stairs, edged forward, fell back into his chair as if he had been shot, managed to squirm to a sitting position, moved cat swift, rocked back and forth, rose slowly like a man with a bad back, slumped back in his chair, tottered like an old man, twisted violently, wiggled when she walked, wobbled out of the darkness, backed away as if the package had turned into a rattlesnake, crept cat silent, lumbered drunkenly down the steps, paced the small room in excitement, slinked out of the room, swaggered into the room.
- **Lower Extremities.** Crossed his legs, re-crossed his legs, sat cross-legged, shifted from foot to foot, tucked his size twelves under the chair, dragged his foot

References

1. Leabo, Karen, Dialogue, BooksForABuck.com, http://www.booksforabuck.com/writers/dialogue.html.
2. Van Marwijk, Frank, The importance of body language, SelfGrowth.com, http://www.selfgrowth.com/articles/Van_Marwijk.html.
3. Hood, Lisa, Using body language to create believable characters, Fiction Factor: The Online Magazine for Fiction Writers, http://www.fictionfactor.com/guests/bodylanguage.html.
4. Schaefer, Sherri, Everyday body language, SelfGrowth.com, http://www.selfgrowth.com/articles/Schaefer1.html.
5. When body language lies, Working Knowledge, Harvard Business

School,
http://hbswk.hbs.edu/item.jhtml?id=3123&t=career_effectiveness&noseek=one, September 30, 2002.
6. Noble, William, Conflict, Action & Suspense, Writer's Digest Books, Cincinnati, 1994.
7. Chiarella, Tom, Writing Dialogue, Story Press, Cincinnati, 1997.
8. Social distance, ChangingMinds.org,
http://changingminds.org/techniques/body/social_distance.htm.
9. Examples of body language in use, Body Language Training,
http://www.bodylanguagetraining.com/examples.html.
10. Examples of body language, Sparcs,
http://www.deltabravo.net/custody/body.htm, 1998.
11. Quilliam, Susan, Body Language, Ontario, Firefly Books, 2004.
12. Reading body language, Job-Employment-Guide.com,
http://www.job-employment-guide.com/reading-body-language.html.
13. Using body language, ChangingMinds.org,
http://changingminds.org/techniques/body/body_language.htm.

Chapter 15

Additional Information

COPYRIGHT AND PLAGIARISM

Copyright

Copyright for authors is the legal right granted to an author for the exclusive publication, production, sale, or distribution of a literary work. It is a form of protection provided by the laws of the United States (title 17) to the authors of "original works of authorship" This protection applies to both published and unpublished works. It is important to understand that you cannot copyright an idea, only a written work. For instance, if someone publishes a novel similar to a story you've been thinking about for years, you are out of luck. You should have gotten to work and written the novel.

The use of a copyright notice is no longer required under U.S. law, although it can be beneficial in a court of law. Original works are copyrighted and protected the moment they are written, whether they have a copyright notice or not.[1]

A copyright typically lasts for life of the author plus 70 years. The copyright for certain works, including those created for an employer, lasts 120 years from creation or 95 years from publication, whichever occurs first. Copyright law is mostly civil law, although new laws are moving copyright violation into the criminal realm. Copyright law is still violated whether you charged money or not; only damages are affected by charging money.[2,3]

Copyright Notice

The copyright notice should contain the following three elements:

- *A Copyright Indicator.* The Symbol ©, the abbreviation CR or Copr, or the word Copyright can be used.
- *The Year of First Publication of the Work.* In the case of compilations or derivative works incorporating previously published material, the year date of first publication of the compilation or derivative work is sufficient.
- *The Name of the Owner.* Either the owner's name, or an abbreviation by which the name can be recognized, or a generally known alternative designation of the owner can be used."[1]

The following are examples of copyright notices:

- © 2006 Tom Milhorn
- CR 2006 Tom Milhorn
- Copr. 2006 Tom Milhorn
- Copyright 2006 Tom Milhorn

Registration is accomplished through the U.S. Copyright Office (http://www.copyright.gov), which supplies the registrant with the appropriate application form. The registration fee is currently $30.[1]

Copyright Infringement Penalty

An individual found guilty of copyright infringement is liable for either (1) actual damages suffered by the copyright owner as a result of the infringement and any profits of the infringer that are attributable to the infringement or (2) instead of actual damages and profits, statutory damages of a sum of not less than $250 nor more than $10,000, as the court considers just.[4]

Plagiarism

Plagiarism is presenting someone else's words as though they are your own. It includes (1) quoting someone else's exact words without documenting the source, (2) modifying or summarizing someone else's words without documenting the source, and (3) failing to get permission to use someone else's work.

Information considered to be common knowledge does not need to have its source documented. Common knowledge is information generally known by everyone. For example, that George Bush was elected to a second term as president of the United States in 2004 is common knowledge.[5]

Famous Examples of Plagiarism

- *George Harrison.* Successfully sued for plagiarizing the Chiffons' *He's So Fine* for the melody of his own *My Sweet Lord.*[6]
- *Senator Joseph Biden.* Forced to withdraw from the 1988 Democrat presidential nominations when it was revealed that he had plagiarized several campaign speeches, notably those of British Labour leader Neil Kinnock and Senator Robert F. Kennedy.[6]
- *Alex Haley.* Settled out-of-court for a large sum of money after admitting he copied large passages of his novel *Roots* from *The African* by Harold Courlander.[6]
- *James Cameron.* Science fiction author Harlan Ellison sued and won in a case claiming that Cameron's film *The Terminator* plagiarized his episodes *Soldier* and *Demon With a Glass Hand* of the show *The Outer Limits.*[7]
- *Jan and Paul Crouch.* The Crouches settled the plagiarism lawsuit filed against them by West Virginia minister Sylvia Fleener, who alleged that the Crouches stole liberally from Fleener's 1997 doomsday novel *The Omega Syndrome* for

their successful 1999 film *The Omega Code.*[8]

Steps to Avoid Plagiarism

Krista Barrett gives a number of things you can do to avoid plagiarism.[9]

Include Quotation Marks and Source. If you are including word for word material from another source, you need to put quotes around it and then list the source, either in brackets at the end of the quoted material or as a superscripted numeral that refers the reader to a reference at the end of the chapter or book. For instance: "Joe Blow said that writers should be aware of the rules to prevent plagiarism" (Joe Blow, Writer's Weekly Magazine, 2006) or "Joe Blow said that writers should be aware of the rules to prevent plagiarism."[14] The superscripted 14 refers the reader to the list of references of which the Joe Blow source is the 14th in the list.

Internet Use. All information on the Internet is not free to use. If you use material from an article on the Internet you must treat it just as if you were using it from a printed source.

Obtain Permission. Permission must be obtained when using a substantial amount of material from any source. In the case of printed material it's not a bad idea to request permission from both the publisher and the author. You must wait until you receive confirmation of this permission before publishing your work. Having said this, does it mean that if you wish to use as little as a single sentence from a source you have to obtain permission? The answer is no. So how much material can you quote without getting permission? Most authorities agree that you can quote up to 300 words, as long as you put it in quotations and give the source credit.

Summarizing. What if you are merely summarizing material in your own words instead of quoting? Do you still have to get permission? The answer is no; however, you do have to give your source credit.[9]

GETTING IDEAS

If you pay attention to the world around you, you probably

will find more story ideas than you can use. The hard part is figuring out which ones will make the best stories.[10] For an idea to be worth writing about, it should meet three criteria:

- *It Must be Interesting.* A novel about the life and times of a typical American citizen—his birth, childhood, education, marriage, and children—won't hold anyone's attention for long.
- *It Must Have Appeal for a Large Number of People.* No matter how exciting a novel is if it only is of interest to people who belong to the Badger Watchers Association of Greater Seattle it's not going to sell many copies.
- *It Should Deal with a Specific Aspect of a Subject.* A novel about war is too broad. A novel about the effect of war on a 13-year-old Jewish girl and her family who are forced into hiding by the Nazis during World War II is a specific aspect of war.[11]

Sources for Ideas

So where do you get ideas? The answer is "from almost anywhere."[12] The following table gives places that various writers have said they get ideas:

A conversation	Relative	Psychiatry books
Advice columns	Family	Psychology books
A fascinating person	Friends	Radio programs
An experience	Internet	Songs and poems
A landscape	Life events	Stupid criminal books
An object	Magazines	The Bible
An building	Medical books	The classics
A sermon or lecture	Memory	True crime books
Conversations	Movies	TV commercials
Dreams	Newspapers	TV Guide/shows
Death of a friend or	Photographs	Yellow Pages

Brainstorming is a common way to come up with ideas. You simply start by writing down words or phrases that occur to you, no matter how unusable they might seem. You can start with a word, like banjo, and write everything that comes to your mind.

Then study what you've written to see what pops into your head.[13]

Record Your Ideas

It is essential to get your ideas recorded as soon as possible after you think of them. The longer you wait, the more the idea will fade, and the less likely you will be to remember it when you are ready to start planning your novel. This means you have to be able to take your ideas down wherever you are. There are a number of ways to do this:

- *Carry a handheld computer, PDA, or micro cassette recorder.*
- *Carry a small notepad in your purse, briefcase, or pocket.*
- *Keep a dashboard clipboard with a small notepad in your car.*
- *Keep a notebook on your bed stand.*[14]

MANUSCRIPT

Format

Over the years, publishers have developed certain standards to make their jobs easier. The standards are there for a reason. They are not arbitrary. The wrong format or font won't destroy your chances of getting your manuscript accepted; it may not even hurt them. It's a question of whether you're willing to take the chance that you're writing is good enough to overcome the difficulties creating by not following the proper guidelines.[15] Publishers have their own formatting guidelines, so be sure to get a copy and go by them. The following are typical guidelines:

- Use 8-1/2" x 11", 20lb white bond paper. If you can, laser print your manuscript. Inkjet is a second choice, as long as you use the highest quality print setting. Use black ink.
- Use margins at least 1 inch all around. This gives the editor somewhere to jot notes.
- There is a controversy about which font to use. Some recommend a font with serifs, such as Times New Roman,

since fonts with serifs let each letter flow into the next and are more pleasant for long reading. Non-serif fonts, like Arial, are said to tire the eyes when reading large blocks of text; however, they are considered good for headings. Others recommend a mono-space font like Courier for text because it makes it more accurate to estimate manuscript length from word count. So pay attention to the requested font in the guidelines from the publisher you plan on sending the manuscript to.

- Regardless of whether you use Times New Roman or Courier, use a 12-point font size. Editors have a lot to read each day, and their eyes get tired. Using 12-point ensures that they won't have to struggle to focus on your words.

- Do not indent the first line of the first paragraph. Also do not indent the first line after a section break, but do indent every other paragraph five spaces (1/2 inch).

- Indicate italics by underlining.

- Do not automatically hyphenate words (the publisher's typesetter will include the hyphens if needed).

- Double space between lines. This makes your work easier to read and gives a place for editors to mark on manuscripts after they have purchased them for publication, including edits, corrections, and instructions to the typesetter, Don't double space after periods or other punctuation marks.

- Use a pound sign (#) in the center of a line instead of a skipped line to denote a break between scenes. The publisher's typesetter will convert these into skipped lines or whatever he chooses to indicate a scene break in the published novel.

- Don't justify the right margin because doing so can create strange spacing between words within lines.

- Put your name and contact information (address, telephone number, e-mail address) in the top left-hand corner of the cover page. You may want to include the word count of your novel as well. Don't write "Approximately" by the word count. Editors know the word count is approximate. Round the word count off to the nearest 100.

- Type the title centered on the page a few spaces below your contact information on a over page. The title is usually set off in some way from the rest of the text, such as using all capitol letters. Put your byline two spaces under the title (by H. Thomas Milhorn).

- Don't put on a copyright notice. It's unnecessary
- Begin Chapter One on the page following the cover page, and start each new chapter on a new page.
- Add a right-justified header to every page except page one. It should include the page number as well as your last name. It may be a good idea to include the title, a short version of it, or some key words as well—31/Genre Fiction/Milhorn.
- Print on one side of the paper only.
- At the end of the manuscript skip a couple of lines and type the word "END."[15,16,17]

Revision

You've finally finished your manuscript. No matter how good your first draft is, you'll have to do some editing. So it's time to revise it. The hardest thing about revision is a writer's own resistance to it. You may struggle with, "But I love that paragraph," or "I spent three days writing that scene, so there's no way I'm going to delete it," and, "I've worked on this story long enough. If it's not good enough the way it is, then I just don't care." So, get over it. If it's needs to be cut, cut it. If it needs to be rewritten, rewrite it, and if it's worth writing it's worth revising.[18,19]

Types of Revision

Rachel Simon divides revision into three types: (1) Cosmetic changes, (2) surgical strikes, and (3) major overhaul.[19]

Cosmetic Changes. These are minor changes—the little things you change here and there, such as substituting one word for another. Maybe you decide the heroine should have blue eyes instead of green ones, so you make the change. Or maybe you realize you have two sentences making the same point. You eliminate one of them. Cosmetic changes are the easiest to make, and as a result they are what many novice writers mistakenly think is meant by revision. Fix a word here and there and the story is finished.[19]

Surgical Strikes. These are similar to cosmetic changes, except instead of working at the level of the word or sentence, they're on the level of the paragraph or section. Surgical strike, then, is a bit more challenging than a cosmetic change because it means giving up something substantial that was in your first draft, or putting in something substantial that was not there previously. Sometimes you have to trace the change throughout the entire manuscript.[19]

Major Overhaul. This is the most formidable level of revision. You come to realize you don't have a good story and that for you to get to one, you need to eliminate a major part of your first draft. With major overhaul, you rescue only those parts of the story that work and you rewrite those parts that don't. Hopefully your manuscript won't need a major overhaul, but if it does, dig in and go to work.[19]

Steps for Revising

Cynthia Sterling gives 15 steps for revising a manuscript.[19] I have added ten more.

1. Print a Copy. Words look different on a computer screen— so print out a hard copy of the complete manuscript. Next, find a comfortable chair and a colored pen or a stack of sticky notes.

As a step prior to printing a copy I increase the zoom on my word processor to 125-150 percent and do an initial proof reading on the screen in Print Layout view, making corrections as I go. The increased size makes it easier to identify minor errors. Then I print a hard copy.[20]

2. Read the Manuscript Out Loud. Listen to your words. Reading out loud is the best way to catch awkward phrasing, repetition, and stilted dialogue. Mark the errors you find with the colored pen or sticky note. If you get confused or bored or if your concentration tends to drift your reader will experience the same reaction. If you change a word, read that part out loud again. After your first read-through go back and fix all the areas you marked.

Reading one's own work objectively is an important skill that is very difficult to learn for most people, although you can get better at it with practice.[18-20]

3. Eliminate redundancy. Look for redundancies at the word level. For instance, instead of "now playing at a theater near you" say "playing at a theater near you." Instead of saying "passed the test successfully" say "passed the test." And instead of saying "nodded his head" say "nodded." The same goes for redundancy at the sentence, paragraph, or section level.[19]

4. Eliminate Inaccuracies. Now is the time to check your facts, whether historical or contemporary. Consult a Webster's ninth dictionary to verify words that are appropriate for your time period. Consult other sources to be sure your facts are correct. If you've got a Civil War battle taking place in 1860, you've got a problem.[20]

5. Take a Closer Look at Descriptions. Do you have long passages of narrative that could bog down the story? Or do you have the opposite problems—scenes and people so sketchily described the reader will have no sense of how anything or anyone looks? Have you made good use of senses in your descriptions? Judicious use of odors, sounds, and sensations will bring your story to life.[20] See Chapter 3 for a discussion of description and Chapter 6 for a discussion of the senses.

6. Study Your Transitions. Does the story move smoothly from scene to scene and chapter to chapter? Are point-of-view changes clear? See chapter 7 for a discussion of transitions and Chapter 5 for a discussion of point of view.[20]

7. Look at the Passage of Time. Have you used the passage of time appropriately? Do you provide enough clues so your readers know when scenes take place in relation to each other? Has enough time passed between events for them to realistically take place in your story? A visual timeline of the pivotal scenes may help you keep time sequences straight.[19] See Chapter 7 for a discussion of time.

8. Reread Your Chapter Endings. Do your chapter endings propel the reader on, urging him to read just one more chapter? Or do some of the chapters end with the resolution of a problem, making it easy for the reader to set the book aside for another time? If your chapter endings don't propel the reader onward, consider ending chapters on a suspenseful hook or an enticing question or even in the middle of a scene.[20]

9. Reread the Beginning of Each Chapter. Do your chapter beginnings hook the reader right away, pulling him into the story?

If not, revise them.

10. Clean Up Dialogue Tags. Can you eliminate some tags? Do you need to add others in order to help the reader know who is speaking? Replace awkward tags with a simple "he said." Try to eliminate descriptive adverbs that describe emotions, such as "he said angrily," "wearily," or "happily." Instead, use your character's actions, body language, or words themselves to convey emotion.[20] See Chapter 12 for a discussion of dialogue tags.

11. Reconsider Your Use of Character Names. Every time you use a character's name when you are writing in that character's point of view, you take the reader out of that person's head for a moment and remind him that he is reading a fictional story. When possible, replace character names with "he" and "she," as long as it's easy for the reader to keep track of who the pronouns represent. Likewise, in real life, people seldom use names in conversation, except for particular emphasis. Also, be sure the names you have chosen for your characters are significantly different from one another.[20] See Chapter 11 for a discussion of character names.

12. Eliminate or Replace Valueless Modifiers. Reading aloud, you may have noticed a tendency to use valueless modifiers, such as "rather," "perhaps," "slightly," "really," "basically," "virtually," and so forth. Cut them when possible. See Chapter 5 for a discussion of valueless modifiers. [19,20]

13. Replace Weak Verbs. When possible, replace weak verbs with strong ones. Instead of saying "The bank was robbed by Paul" say "Paul Robbed the bank." See Chapter 7 for a discussion of verb strength.

14. Delete Nonspecific Adjectives. Instead of describing a house as beautiful, say the place was an elegant mansion or that it rivaled Buckingham Palace. See Chapter 5 for a discussion of nonspecific adjectives.[20]

15. Vary Sentence Beginnings. Do too many of your sentences begin with he or she? If so, use a variation of sentence structures to add variety and improve the flow. For instance, instead of writing "He growled like a bear as he barreled through the door," you could write "Growling like a bear, he barreled through the door."[20]

16. Hone In on Emotions. Emotion is the heart of genre novels. Are your character's emotional reactions appropriate and believable for the situation?[19] See Chapter 13 for a discussion of emotions.

17. Check Your Backstory. Did you effectively weave backstory into your story or did you present it in chunks. Do you need to revise your approach to backstory. See Chapter 3 for a discussion of backstory.

18. Consider Body Language. Review your characters' body language. Have you made good use of body language? See Chapter 14 for a discussion of body language.

19. Review Your Setting. Do you make use of time, place, experience, and mood? Have you used senses and the weather effectively? See Chapter 6 for a discussion of setting.

20. Take a Look at Your Characters. Are your main characters adequately developed? If not, rework them. See Chapter 11 for a discussion of Character development.

21, Review Your Flashbacks. If you used a flashback, did you first establish your major characters and story line before doing so? See Chapter 3 for a discussion of flashbacks.

22. Evaluate Your Use of Imagery and Figurative Language. Have you used imagery and figurative language effectively? If not, consider how you can add more of these into your writing. See Chapter 4 for a discussion of imagery and figurative language.

23. Take a Look at Your Pacing. Review your scene-sequel patterns. Do you need to strengthen any scenes or lengthen any sequels to improve the pacing? Do any scenes or sequels need to be eliminated? Do you need to lengthen or shorten any sentences? Have you used sentence fragments effectively? See Chapter 10 for a discussion of pacing.

24. Make Use of a Friend. If possible, develop and make use of a trusted reader — someone whose critical opinion you value. You don't want a friend who thinks it's great simply because you wrote it. You want a friend who will be critical—someone who will push you further than you have already gone and assure that the story gets better and better.[19]

25. Do a Final Polish. Run a spell/grammar check and correct any remaining misspelled words, typos, and grammatical errors. If possible, set the manuscript aside for a week or two, then print out a fresh copy and do another read-through. Chances are this time you'll find only a few minor corrections.[18,20]

QUERY LETTER AND SYNOPSIS

Query Letter

A query letter can be the key to getting the attention of an editor, who is instrumental in getting your work published. The letter should be brief, well-written, and snappy. While a query letter should be brief, it should also be detailed enough to leave the editor eager to read your synopsis or see your complete manuscript.[21]

Parts

There are nine parts to a query letter: (1) Letterhead; (2) date; (3) editor's name and address, (4) salutation, (5) introductory statement; (6) novel description; (7) genre, word count, and market; (8) your credentials; and (9) and ending.

1. Letterhead. Place a personal letterhead at the top of the letter. It should include your name, address, telephone number, and e-mail address. You may want to use a different font, such as Arial, or put the letterhead in bold to set it off from the body of the letter. By all means, center it unless you have professionally designed stationary that has the letterhead in a different position.

2. Date. And don't forget to date your letter. You may center it or left align it.

3. Editor's Name and Address. Don't address the letter to "Dear Editor." Do your homework and address it to the right person in the correct department. If you don't know who that person is, call the company and ask.

4. Salutation. If the editor is a woman, find out if she is usually addressed as Ms., Mrs., or Miss.

5. Introductory Statement. This should be short and to the point—no wasted words (Proposed novel: Caduceus Awry).

6. Novel Description. Your book description should be as brief and compelling as you can possibly make it. Secondary plots and characters have no place here. You need to get to the meat of your story. What drives this manuscript?

7. Genre, Word Count, and Market. Have you written a medical thriller, a time travel science fiction, a gothic romance, or a police procedural novel? Genre and subgenre were discussed in Chapter 2.

Don't say something like "The word count is approximately 89,383 words. The editor or agent will know that it is an approximation. Round the word count off to the nearest hundred (89,400).

The market will be the market for the particular genre in which you have chosen to write your novel—romance, science fiction, thriller, mystery, and so forth.

8. Your Credentials. Keep it short and sweet. Don't list every award you have received, if you've received a bunch, but do be careful not to leave out something important.

9. Ending. End your letter by asking if you can send your entire manuscript for consideration. Thank the editor for his time and mention that you're looking forward to hearing from him at his earliest convenience. And don't forget to sign your letter.[21-23]

Format

A query letter is a formal business letter and should be written as such. Type your letter using 12-point Times New Roman font on 8-1/2 by 11 inch paper. Leave a 1-1/2 inch margin on the left and 1 inch margins on the other sides. Use good quality white paper, laser printed if possible. Single-space your paragraphs and double-space between paragraphs.

If at all possible, your query letter should be no longer than one page, and should always be professionally written, edited, and proofread. When your mail your query letter, be sure and include a stamped, self-addressed envelope so the publisher can reply to you. A few editors now accept query letters by e-mail. If you plan on sending your query by e-mail, be sure the editor is one of these.[22,23]

Sample Letter

The following is an example of a possible query letter for a novel.[24]

Sam Author
342 Fictitious Court
Jackson, Mississippi 39216
601 684-5398
jackson123@bellsouth.net

January 6, 2006

Sally Bookworm, Editor
Everyday Publishing Company
195 Parkway Drive
New York, NY, 10006

Dear Ms. Bookworm:

Proposed novel: Caduceus Awry

Divorced, depressed, stripped of his medical license, and struggling to overcome alcoholism, Dr. Mark Valentine must discover the identity of Charity Hospital's serial killer in order to save the life of the hospital director if he is to have any chance at all of getting his license to practice medicine reinstated.

Caduceus Awry is a medical thriller with a word count of 81,000 words. The market includes the broad market of readers interested in thriller novels and the more specific market of readers interested in medical thrillers in the mold of Robin Cook, Michael Crichton, and Michael Palmer.

I have 35 years writing experience in which I have produced six books, 12 chapters in books, and over a 100 articles. "Drug and Alcohol abuse: The Authoritative Guide for Parents, Teachers, and Counselors," published by Da Capo Press, made the Academic Top-20 Best-Seller List in 1994 and was named one of the Top-20 Best Read eBooks by Questia Media in 2002. Nicotine dependence was named as one of the top four articles written by a family physician in 1989. In 1997 "Caduceus Awry" was a finalist in the Eudora Welty Film and Fiction Festival novel contest. In 2005 I was inducted into the Lincoln Memorial University

Literary Hall of Fame. I have outlined the plots for two additional novels.

Please let me know if you are interested in reading "Caduceus Awry." Thank you for your time and consideration. I look forward to hearing from you at your earliest convenience.

Sincerely,

Sam Author

Sam Author

Synopsis

A synopsis is a narrative summary of a novel. Its purpose is to tell the editor what your book is about—not how things happen. You have to condense a 250 to 500 hundred page manuscript down to a few pages.

Your synopsis has to (1) make sense, (2) cover all the important points of the story, and (3) be interesting enough to catch the eye of an editor who probably reads thirty or forty synopses a week.

Secondary characters and sub-plots, although probably important to the story's outcome, are not important in the synopsis unless they are important to the resolution. So stay focused on the primary characters and major events.

The synopsis should be written in the style of the manuscript. For instance, a fast-paced novel requires a fast-paced synopsis. Use vivid verbs and specific nouns, and avoid modifiers.[25-28]

There are many different ways to approach a synopsis. The following is one of them.

What Is Needed

Before beginning the writing of your synopsis, you will need the following information from your novel:

- *Main Characters.* The goals, motivations and conflicts of the characters central to the plot
- *Setting.* A brief description
- *Plot.* Main and important subplots (if they are important to the outcome of your story)
- *Sequence of events.* How the story progresses
- *Theme.* If there is a theme, what is it?[25]

Synopsis Steps

Writing a synopsis can be broken down into four steps: (1) Start with a hook, (2) construct the body, (3) explain the crisis and resolution, and (4) revise the synopsis.

1. Start With a Hook. Having fretted over the perfect opening to your novel, now do the same for your synopsis. Remember, an editor has numerous submissions to go through every day. Make sure yours doesn't have an opening that reads something like: "Ed Smith was five-feet, eight inches tall and had red hair and green eyes." That won't grab the editor's interest. Begin your synopsis with an opening paragraph that presents a clear, brief view of your protagonist, his world, and the situation he is in when the novel opens. It should provide a hook— something to make the editor want to read the rest of the synopsis.[26,27,29] For example:

- Divorced, depressed, stripped of his medical license, and battling alcoholism, Dr. Mark Valentine, a 42-year-old ex plastic surgeon working on a limited institutional license in Atlanta's Charity Hospital, must discover the identity of the hospital's serial killer and prevent the murder of the hospital director if he is to have any hope at all of getting his license reinstated.

In that opening paragraph, I've briefly introduced you to my protagonist, Dr. Mark Valentine, his current state of affairs (divorced, depressed, ex plastic surgeon stripped of his medical license, struggling with alcoholism), his world (working on a limited institutional license in a charity hospital in Atlanta), the fact that he's trying to get his license reinstated, and that he is at the heart of solving a serial murder mystery in the hospital.[24]

The next paragraph of the synopsis is the place you present the element of change that triggers the main conflict.[25] For example

- Abducted at gun point from Charity Hospital emergency room, Mark is flown to Miami where he is forced to perform plastic surgery on a ruthless mobster who has been indicted by a federal grand jury and is certain to be sent to prison if the case goes to trial.[24]

The main conflict, being abducted at gun point, is the event that sets all of the other events of the novel in motion.

2. Construct the Body. The body of the synopsis should introduce the remainder of your main characters and their conflicts—all woven together in the narrative. Tell their motivations, conflicts, and goals, but stay away from detailed physical descriptions unless this information is pertinent to your story. Secondary characters, although they may be important to the story's outcome, are not important in a condensed version of your novel, unless they contribute an integral portion to the resolution. Type a character's name in all caps the first time he is introduced.

Write the high points of your story in chronological order. Each high point should have its own paragraph. Keep these paragraphs tight; don't give every little detail.

Don't try to write a summary of every chapter in the order they occur in the novel. Instead, select the most important elements of each chapter and present them in the order they make sense (A flashback has no place in a synopsis.). When possible, link these elements with simple transitions.

Remember, each scene should include action, reaction, and a decision. Omit secondary characters, sub-plots, minor events, and individual scenes. For example, if you have written 10 pages on an exciting battle scene, your synopsis should describe it very succinctly. You don't need to explain the battle in detail. A simple, active sentence or two will convey the right message.

Avoid using dialogue unless its essential to reveal character or plot or to provide a dramatic moment. If included, keep it brief. And don't ask empty questions in your synopsis (Will Claude survive the gun fight?). They serve no purpose. Your synopsis is a tool used to explain your story, so asking questions will mean that you must answer them too. This wastes precious space.[25-29]

3. Explain the Crisis and the Resolution. Next, explain the crisis and then the resolution of your novel—no cliffhangers or teasers. Editors want to know that you know how to successfully conclude your story. Keep this simple, but make sure you show your main characters' reactions. One or two paragraphs should suffice.[26,28,29]

4. Revise the Synopsis. Rewrite your synopsis until each sentence is polished to the point of perfection. Use strong adjectives and verbs, and always write in the present tense. Make every word count.

Don't rely on your computer's spell-checker and grammar-checker. Reread your own work thoroughly—several times. Keep your writing active; edit out any passive voice sentences. Delete any redundancies.

When you are as sure your synopsis is a tightly written condensation of what your novel is about, send it to a friend or another member of a critique workshop and ask one simple question—"would you be tempted to read the entire novel after reading this synopsis?" If the answer is no, rewrite it. If the answer is yes, move on to other aspects of your submission package.[26,29]

Format

- Regardless of which tense you have chosen to write your novel in, always write your synopsis in present tense. This gives the outline a sense of urgency and reminds the editor that he is reading a much-condensed version of something bigger. Also, it should be written in third-person point of view.
- Your synopsis should be typed in the same format you used for your novel manuscript. Use black type on clean white paper. Set your margins for one inch all around. Do not right-justify your text. Use a standard font, like Courier or Times New Roman.
- There is no specific rule about the length of a synopsis. Typically, a synopsis should be one to two pages single spaced or five to six pages double spaced. However, some books, such as historical novels or adventure/thriller novels, are too complicated or long to summarize with such a short synopsis. For these longer works, the rule is roughly one page per 25

pages of manuscript. Always check the publisher's guidelines to see if they contain any instruction for synopsis length.

- At the top left of the first page, type your contact information, single spaced. Also at the top left, type the genre type, word length, and the word "Synopsis," also single-spaced. If your synopsis is longer than a few pages, drop down about 1/3 page and type the title, centered and in all caps. Drop down four lines and begin the opening paragraph.

- After page one put a left header on every page. It should consist of your last name, the title of your novel or a few key words from the title, and the word "Synopsis"—for example: Milhorn/CADUCEUS AWRY/ Synopsis.

- Also, starting on the second page, place a page number at the top right.

- Print your synopsis, preferably on a laser printer. A good quality inkjet printer is an acceptable second choice.[26,27]

References

1. Copyright, United States Copyright Office, http://www.copyright.gov/, December 5, 2005.
2. Allan Chan & Associates, Frequently asked questions, What is copyright?, http://www.chanesq.com/faqs.html#18, 2005.
3. Templeton, Brad, Ten big myths about copyright explained, http://www.templetons.com/brad/copymyths.html, October 2004.
4. Writer's Encyclopedia, WritersMarket.com, http://www.writersmarket.com/encyc/c.asp.
5. What is plagiarism? Adam's State College, http://www2.adams.edu/library/plagiarism_definition/plagiarism_definition.php.
6. Plagiarism, Masterliness, The World Knowledge Library, http://www.masterliness.com/a/Plagiarism.htm.
7. Farlex, The Free Dictionary, Plagiarism, http://encyclopedia.thefreedictionary.com/plagiarism.
8. Sforza, Teri, Plagiarism suite, The Orange County Register, January 1, 2002.
9. Barrett, Krista, Plagiarism: What it is and how to avoid it, Writing101.com, http://www.write101.com/plag.htm, 2005.
10. Silvester, Niko, How to get ideas, Creative Writing for Teens, About.com, http://teenwriting.about.com/library/submissions/tips/blallideas.htm.

11. Banks, Michael A., Where do you get your ideas...? Writers Write: The Internet Writing Journal, http://www.writerswrite.com/journal/mar98/banks.htm.
12. Giles, Michelle, 25 unique places to find story ideas, http://www.writing-world.com/fiction/giles.shtml, 2002.
13. Dixon, Angie, The Idea's The Thing--Getting and Working with Novel Ideas, Novel Writing, Suite101.com, http://www.suite101.com/article.cfm/novel_writing/106007/2.
14. Miller, Sandra, Catching ideas, SandraMiller.com, http://www.pgtc.com/~slmiller/writing-tips-ideas.htm.
15. Rothman, Chuck, Manuscript format, http://www.sfwa.org/writing/format_rothman.htm, January 4, 2005.
16. Betancourt, John Gregory, Manuscript preparation, The obligatory manuscript format article, http://www.sfwa.org/writing/format_betancourt.htm, 1997.
17. Silvester, Niko, How to format a manuscript for publication, Creative Writing for Teens, About.com, http://teenwriting.about.com/cs/formatting/ht/FormatManu.htm.
18. How to write a query letter, ehow.com, http://www.ehow.com/how_3165_write-query-letter.html.
19. Collins, Nancy R., Writing a killer query can be simple, Fiction Factor, The Online Magazine for Writers of Fiction, http://www.fictionfactor.com/articles/killerquery.html.
20. Masterson, Lee, Writing the perfect query letter, Fiction Factor: The Online Magazine for Writers of Fiction, http://www.fictionfactor.com/articles/query.html.
21. Milhorn, H. Thomas, Caduceus Awry, Writers Showcase, New York, 2000.
22. Kelly, Sheila, Workshop: Writing the novel synopsis, Vision: A Resource for Writers, http://fmwriters.com/Visionback/Issue%2015/workshop.htm, 2003.
23. Masterson, Lee, Mastering the dreaded synopsis – condensing your novel, Absolute Write, http://www.absolutewrite.com/novels/dreaded_synopsis.htm.
24. Morrell, Jessica page, Tips for writing a synopsis, The Writing Life, http://www.writing-life.com/fiction/synopsis.html.
25. Writing a novel synopsis, Fiction Writer's Connection, http://www.fictionwriters.com/tips-synopsis.html.
26. Beck, Vivian, 5 steps to writing a synopsis, Vivian Beck Agency, http://www.vivianbeck.com/writing/5_steps_to_writing_a_synopsis.htm.
27. Silvester, Niko, Part 11: Reading and revision, Writing Fiction: A Beginner's Guide, Creative Writing for Teens, About.com, http://teenwriting.about.com/library/weekly/aa111102k.htm.

28. Sterling, Cynthia, Fifteen pointers for polishing your prose, Writing Articles, http://members.aol.com/_ht_a/CySterling/articlepolish.htm.
29. Simon, Rachel, The Writer's Writing Guide: Revision, http://www.rachelsimon.com/wg_revision.htm.

Appendix: Grammar Tips

COMMA AND SEMICOLON USAGE

Lists

For most lists, use commas. Only use semicolons when commas create confusion. There is some debate as to whether or not a comma is required before the conjunction. However, I suggest using the comma to prevent confusion.

- *Commas.* The breakfast menu included ham, eggs, pancakes, omelets, and French toast.
- *Commas and Semicolons.* The breakfast menu included a choice of fried, scrambled, or hard-boiled eggs; ham, bacon, or sausage; and potatoes, grits, or gravy.[1]

Nonessential and Essential Clauses

Nonessential Clauses

Nonessential clauses should be set off by commas.

- *Incorrect.* My window *as dirty as it is* reveals the beauty of nature on a snowy morning.
- *Correct.* My window, *as dirty as it is,* reveals the beauty of

nature on a snowy morning.

The clause "as dirty as it is" is not essential to the meaning of the sentence, and therefore should be set off by commas.[2]

Essential Clauses

Essential clauses should not be set off by commas.

- **Incorrect.** A man, *who is married*, has a date every night, whether he wants it or not.
- **Correct.** A man *who is married* has a date every night whether he wants it or not.

The clause "who is married" is essential to the meaning of the sentence; therefore, it is not set off by commas.[2]

COMMONLY CONFUSED WORDS

Affect/Effect

Affect is a verb meaning "to have an influence on" or "to cause a change in," except in psychiatry where it is used as a noun to characterize mood. *Effect* i s a noun meaning "something brought about by a cause or agent; a result."

- **Verb.** Bad weather will adversely *affect* the flight schedule.
- **Noun (Psychiatry).** The patient has a flat *affect*.
- **Noun.** The *effect* of bad weather is to alter the flight schedule.[3,4]

Backward/Backwards

Either adverb, *backward* or *backwards*, may be used when meaning "in reverse order of direction," although backward is preferred.

- **In Reverse Order of Direction.** Tony is good at skating *backward* (or *backwards*).[4]

Between/Among

Between should be used for two people or things and *among* for three or more people or things.

- **Two.** The choice is *between* the red sweater and the yellow sweater. He called his wife *between* the third and fourth quarters of the football game.
- **Three or More.** The choice is *among* the red sweater, the yellow sweater, or the green sweater. He ran *among* the trees in the forest.

Similarly, *each other* should be used with two people or things; *one another* should be used with three or more people or things.

- **Two.** My daughters love *each other*.
- **Three or More.** The three of us will see *one another* at the next ballgame.[3]

Bimonthly/Semimonthly

Bimonthly is an adjective that means "every two months" or "twice a month"—take your choice. Because of the confusion, the best choice is to avoid the term and say exactly what you mean. *Semimonthly* is an adjective that means "happening twice a month."

- **Bimonthly (Avoid).** We get paid *bimonthly*. **(Use).** We get paid every two months. We get paid twice a month.
- **Semimonthly.** We have *semimonthly* meetings on the 1st and the 15th.[3,4]

Blonde/ Blond

Blonde is feminine and *blond* is masculine. However, in recent years, as an adjective, *blond* has been used for either sex. As a noun, *blonde* is preferred when referring to a female.

- *Adjective.* The girl has *blonde* (or *blond*) hair.
- *Adjective.* The boy has *blond* hair.
- *Noun.* The *blonde* crossed her legs and winked.[3]

Capital/Capitol

The "city or town that is the seat of government" is called the *capital*; the "building in which the legislative assembly meets" is the *capitol*. The term capital can also refer to an "accumulation of wealth."[3]

- *City or Town.* The *capital* of Mississippi is Jackson.
- *Wealth.* The company has built up a great deal of *capital*.
- *Building.* The legislature meets in the *capitol*.[4]

Cite/Site/Sight

Cite is a verb that means "to quote as an authority or example." It also means "to recognize formally" or "to summon before a court of law." *Site* is a noun meaning "location." *Sight* has to do with vision.

- *Quote as an Authority.* I *cited* many research studies in my dissertation.
- *Recognize Formally.* The mayor was *cited* for service to the community.
- *Summon before a Court.* The company was *cited* for cooking the books.
- *Location.* They chose a *site* for the new hospital near the lake.
- *Vision.* His *sight* is not what it used to be.[3]

Complement/Compliment

Complement is a noun or verb that means "something that completes or makes up a whole." *Compliment* is a noun or verb that means an "expression of praise or admiration."

- **To Complete.** Her earrings are a perfect *complement* to the blouse.
- **Expression of Praise.** I received a *compliment* about my new jacket.[3,4]

Convince/Persuade

Strictly speaking, one *convinces* a person that something is true, but *persuades* a person to do something. Following this rule, convince should not be used with an infinitive.

- **Something is True.** Jack *convinced* his son he needed a haircut.
- **To Do Something.** Bill *persuaded* me to ask Charlotte for a date.[3,4]

Discreet/Discrete

Discreet is an adjective that means "prudent," "circumspect," or "modest." It applies only to people. *Discrete* is an adjective that means "separate" or "individually distinct." It applies only to objects.

- **Prudent, Circumspect, Modest.** Her *discreet* handling of the touchy situation put him at ease.
- **Separate, Individually Distinct.** Light is made up of *discrete* particles called photons.[3,4]

Elicit/Illicit

Elicit is a verb that means "to draw out." *Illicit* is an adjective meaning "unlawful" or "prohibited."

- **To Draw Out.** I tried to *elicit* a few scandalous stories from her.
- **Unlawful or prohibited.** She kept knowledge of the *illicit* activity from the police. Jack admitted he had an *illicit* love affair.[3,4]

Emigrant/Immigrant

Emigrant is a noun that means "one who leaves one's native country to settle in another." *Immigrant* is a noun that means "one who enters and settles in a new country."

- **Leaves Native Country.** The *emigrants* left their country on board a ship.
- **Enters New Country.** Most of the *immigrants* easily found jobs.[3]

Especially/Specially

Especially means "particularly," "more than others," or "to a marked degree." *Specially* means "for a specific purpose" or "for a designated reason."

- **More than Others.** Sam is an *especially* capable teacher.
- **Specific Purpose.** The house was designed *specially* for an invalid.[3]

Farther/Further

Farther is an adjective and adverb that means "at a more distant point." *Further* is an adjective and adverb that means "to a greater extent or degree." It can also mean "in addition" or "moreover."

- **More Distant Point.** We drove 50 miles today; tomorrow, we will drive 100 miles *farther*.
- **To a Greater Extent.** We won't be able to suggest a solution until we are *further* along in our evaluation of the problem.
- **In Addition.** They stated *further* that they would not change the policy.[3]

Figuratively/Literally

Figuratively is an adverb that means "metaphorically" or "symbolically." *Literally* is an adverb that means "actually." It also means "according to the exact meaning of the words."

- **Symbolically.** When the large man jumped out of the shadows, we *figuratively* jumped out of our shoes.
- **Actually.** I'm not exaggerating when I say I *literally* fell off my chair.
- **Exact Meaning.** I translated the Latin passage *literally*.[3,4]

Flammable/Inflammable

Flammable and *inflammable* are synonyms, both meaning "easily set on fire." You should use *nonflammable* to mean "not flammable."

- **Can Burn.** The highly *flammable* (or *inflammable*) fuel was stored in a specially built tank.
- **Cannot Burn.** The contents of the truck were *nonflammable*.[3]

Flaunt/Flout

To *flaunt* means "to show off shamelessly" or "to boast." To *flout* means "to show scorn or contempt for."

- **Show Off.** John *flaunted* his wealth by bedecking his wife with jewelry and expensive clothes.
- **Show Contempt.** Women in the 1930s who openly smoked *flouted* convention.[3,4]

Foreword/Forward

Foreword is a noun that means "an introductory note or preface." *Forward* is an adjective or adverb that means "toward the front." Forward is also a verb that means "to send on."

- **Introductory Note.** In my *foreword* I explained my reasons for writing the book.
- **Toward the Front.** I sat in the *forward* section of the plane.
- **To Send On.** *Forward* the e-mail to everyone in your address book.[3]

Founder/Flounder

In its primary sense, *founder* means "to sink below the surface of the water." By extension, founder means "to fail utterly." *Flounder* means "to move about clumsily" or "to act with confusion."

- **Sink below the Surface, Fail Utterly.** The ship *foundered* after colliding with an iceberg. The president *foundered* in his attempt to bring peace to the country.
- **Act with Confusion.** After *floundering* through the first half of the course, Amy finally passed American History with the help of a tutor.[3]

Good/Well

Good is an adjective referring to "quality" or "appearance;" *well* is an adjective and an adverb.

- **Quality, Appearance.** I had a *good* meal. The tangerines look *good.*
- **Health, Verb Modifier.** My brother looks *well* (healthy). Tom runs *well* (how he runs).[3,4]

Hanged/Hung

Hanged is the past tense and past participle of *hang* when the meaning is "to execute by suspending by the neck." *Hung* is the past tense and participle of *hang* when the meaning is "to suspend from above with no support from below," not referring to a person.

- **Hung by the Neck.** They *hanged* the convicted killer at dawn.
- **Suspend from Above.** I *hung* the painting on the wall. The painting *was hung* at a crooked angle.[3,4]

Infer/Imply

To *infer* is "to draw a conclusion from what someone has said or from circumstances." To *imply* is "to suggest or to hint."

- **Draw Conclusion.** From the facts I *infer* you are guilty.
- **Suggest, Hint.** Do you mean to *imply* I stole the money?[4]

It's/Its

It's is a verb contraction for "*it is*" and requires an apostrophe. *Its* is used to indicate possession and lacks an apostrophe.

- **Verb Contraction.** *It's* the plane Lindberg flew across the Atlantic.
- **Possession.** The boat slipped *its* moorings.[3,4,5]

Laid/Lain/Lay

Laid is the past tense and the past participle of the verb *lay* and not the past tense of *lie*. The parts of speech of lay are *lie, laid, laid*. *Lay* is the past tense of the verb *lie* and *lain* is the past participle. The parts of speech for lie are *lie, lay, lain*.

- **Past Tense of Lay.** Tom *laid* his books down.
- **Past Participle of Lay.** Tom *has laid* his books in the same place for months.
- **Past Tense of Lie.** Tom *lay* down on the couch.
- **Past Participle of Lie.** Tom has *lain* on the couch for an hour.[3,4]

Principal/Principle

Principal is a noun that means "a person who holds a high position" or "plays an important role." It is also an adjective that means "chief or leading cause." *Principle* is a noun that means "a rule or standard."

- **Hold a High Position.** Our school *principal* is an excellent administrator.
- **Chief or Leading.** The necessity of moving to another city was the *principal* reason I turned down the job offer.

- ***Rule or Standard.*** He refused to compromise his *principles.*[3]

Stationary/Stationery

Stationary is an adjective that means "fixed position." *Stationery* is a noun that means "writing materials."

- ***Fixed Position.*** They maneuvered around the *stationary* barrier in the road.
- ***Writing Material.*** We printed the letters on company *stationery.*[3,4]

Than/Then/To

Than is a conjunction used for comparisons. *Then* is an adverb indicating "when."

- ***Comparison.*** He is better in math *than* I.
- ***When.*** We studied for an hour; *then* we went to the movies.

Confusion sometimes occurs between the use of *than* and *to.*

- ***Incorrect.*** The athlete is much superior *than* all the rest. Red is preferable *than* blue.
- ***Correct.*** The athlete is much superior *to* all the rest. Red is preferable *to* blue.[3,5]

That/Which

The key to determining when to use *that* and when to use *which* is in deciding whether the clause or phrase that follows is essential to defining what you mean or is simply parenthetical information. Use *that* with essential phrases or clauses and *which* with nonessential phrases or clauses.

- ***Holding up one book.*** "I'll give you this book, *which* explains grammatical rules."
- ***Holding up more than one book.*** "I'll give you the book *that* explains grammatical rules."

In the first example, you don't need to know the book is about grammar to know which book is meant. There's only one book. In the second example, if a history book and a grammar book are held up, you need to know the book referred to is the one that explains grammatical rules to know which book is meant.

Rule: When the information that follows is nonessential to the meaning of the sentence, use *which* and set the phrase or clause off by a comma. When the information that follows is essential to the meaning of the sentence, use *that* and don't set your phrase or clause off by a comma.[6]

Toward/Towards

Both words, *toward* and *towards*, are acceptable in writing.

• I ran *toward* the wall. I ran *towards* the wall. [4,5]

Many more examples of the correct use of words are found in Morton S. Freeman's book *The Wordwatcher's guide to Good Writing and Grammar* (1990).[3,5]

DOUBLE NEGATIVES

Unfortunately, double negatives occur in daily conversation and are carried over into narrative by some writers. Characters of course are allowed to use double negatives or any other breach of good grammar rules.

• ***Incorrect.*** He *doesn't* know *nothing* about nuclear physics.
• ***Correct.*** He *doesn't* know *anything* about nuclear physics. He *knows nothing* about nuclear physics.

The proper constructions is to use either the negative adverb or a noun of negation, but not both.[1]

MODIFIERS

A modifier is a word, phrase, or clause that limits or qualifies the sense of another word or word group.

Dangling Modifiers

A *dangling modifier* is a phrase or clause that because of its proximity seems to modify a word it could not logically modify. One of the most common dangling modifiers occurs in the following sentence:

- *Incorrect.* Hopefully, the novel will be interesting.
- *Correct.* I hope the novel will be interesting.

In the incorrect example, "hopefully" is an adverb that appears to modify the noun "novel," the subject of the sentence. But how can a novel be hopeful? To fix the sentence, you need to show who's really doing the hoping, as in the second example.

Now, consider the following example:

- *Incorrect. Screaming all the way, the roller coaster thrilled us.*
- *Correct. Screaming all the way, we were thrilled by the roller coaster.*[1]

The incorrect example implies that the roller coaster was screaming, resulting in a thrill for the riders. It should be made clear that the riders were screaming not the roller coaster, as in the correct example.[1,7,8]

Nearly, Almost, and Only

Pay special attention to the modifiers "nearly," "almost," and "only." They must appear adjacent to the word they are intended to modify. The placement of these words can change the meaning of a sentence. For example, consider the following:

- *Joe **nearly** passed the test with 100 percent.* (means he nearly passed the test, but failed despite his great grade)
- ***Only** Joe was accused of theft.* (no one else was accused)
- *Joe was **only** accused of theft.* (accused but not convicted)

- *Joe was accused of theft **only**.* (accused of nothing else)[1,6,9,]

ONE WORD OR TWO?

Alright/All Right

All right means "okay." *Alright* is not a word. Don't use it.

- *It's not **all right** to use **alright**.*[3]

Altogether/All together

Altogether is an intensifying adverb meaning "wholly," "completely," or "entirely." *All together* is applied to people or things that are being treated as a group. All together is the form that must be used if the sentence can be reworded so that "all" and "together" are separated by other words

- **Entirely.** I am *altogether* pleased to be receiving this honor.
- **Group.** We put the knives, forks, and spoons *all together* in the drawer. We put *all* the knives, forks, and spoons *together* in the drawer.[3,10]

Anyone/Anybody/Any One

Anyone is a pronoun meaning "any person at all." *Anybody* is a less formal form of anyone. *Any one* is a paired adjective and noun meaning a "specific item in a group;" usually used with "of."

- **Any Person at All.** *Anyone* who can solve this problem deserves an award.
- **Specific Item in a Group.** We looked at all the cars in the lot, but we didn't like *any one* of them.[4,10]

Anyway/Any Way

Anyway is an adverb meaning "in any case" or "nonetheless." *Any way* is a paired adjective and noun meaning "any particular course, "direction, or manner."

- **Nonetheless.** He objected, but she went *anyway*.
- **Any Manner.** You may dress *any way* you choose. [4,10]

Awhile/A While

Awhile is an adverb meaning "for a short time." It usually does not need a preposition. *A while* is a paired article and noun meaning "a period of time."

- **For a Short Time.** Won't you stay *awhile*?
- **A Period of Time.** We chatted for *a while*, and then we went to sleep. [10]

Cannot/Can Not

Cannot means "is unable to do," while *can not* is an awkward way to say "is able to refrain from." In general, it's best to avoid *can not* altogether.

- **Unable to Do.** I have a paralyzed arm. I *cannot* move it.
- **Unable to Refrain From.** I bet you can't move your arm. I understand that I *can not* move my arm. If I do I lose the bet. [3]

However/How Ever

However is used to mean "in which manner" or "nevertheless." *How ever* is used to emphasize.

- **In Which Manner, Nevertheless.** *However* we decide, we must decide soon.
- **Emphasis.** *How ever* did you make such a big mess in your room? [4]

Maybe/May Be

Maybe is an adverb meaning "perhaps." *May be* is a form of the verb "be."

- **Perhaps.** *Maybe* we should wait until the crowd clears.
- **Form of Be.** This *may be* our best chance to win the lottery.

Many more examples of the correct use of words are found in Morton S. Freeman's book *The Wordwatcher's guide to Good Writing and Grammar* (1990).[10]

POSSESSIVES

Add an apostrophe and an "s" to singular nouns to indicate possession. Add the apostrophe after the letter "s" to indicate a plural possessive, unless the dual "s" sounds are pronounced, then add apostrophe and "s." The following are all correct or preferred:

- **Singular Possessive.** We located the *cat's* toy under the chair.
- **Plural Possessive.** The two *cats'* toys were tattered.
- **Plural Possessive.** The *Smiths'* cat chased the dog.
- **Plural Possessive.** The *Jones's* cat chased the dog.[1]

PRONOUNS

Case

Pronoun *case* refers to the pronoun's status as a *subject*, *indirect object*, or *direct object* as shown in the following table.

Subject	I	we	you	he	she	it	they	who	thou
Object	me	us	you	him	her	it	them	whom	thee

There is a tendency by some to use the subjective case when the objective case should be used.

- **Incorrect.** He threw the book at Jane and *I*.
- **Correct.** He threw the book at Jane and *me*.

This mistake is so common that even news commentators, who should know better, sometimes make it. Needless to say, it is

333

a common error made by sports commentators.[1,8]

Noun-Pronoun Agreement

The form of the noun and the pronoun must be equal in number, person, and gender. To determine correct noun-pronoun agreement, determine if the noun that the pronoun is referring to is singular or plural.

"Person," a singular noun, requires a singular pronoun, "his" or "her." "People" is a plural noun and requires the plural pronoun "their."

- **Incorrect.** A *person* should see *their* doctor yearly.
- **Correct.** A *person* should see *his* doctor yearly.
- **Correct.** *People* should see *their* doctor yearly.
- **Correct.** Ed and Sarah should see *their* doctors yearly.[9]

Antecedent Agreement

Pronouns should agree with their antecedents. "He," "she," "his," "her," and "their" are confused by many writers. When you see "their" in a sentence about "each" or "every," it is probably incorrect.

- **Incorrect.** *Each* student is asked to bring *their* supplies to class.
- **Correct.** *Each* student is asked to bring *his* supplies to class.

"Each" is a singular pronoun antecedent and therefore requires a singular mate.[1]

SENTENCE STRUCTURE

Comma Splice

Comma splices are independent sentences that are run together into a single sentence, joined by a comma. Comma splices often can be corrected by a semi-colon, a conjunction (and, or, nor, yet, but, so, for), or a period.

- *Incorrect.* Smith's arguments in favor of investing the money are quite effective, they are very similar to those of many financial advisors.
- *Correct.* Smith's arguments in favor of investing the money are quite effective; they are very similar to those of many financial advisors.
- *Correct.* Smith's arguments in favor of investing the money are quite effective *and* they are very similar to those of many financial advisors.
- *Correct.* Smith's arguments in favor of investing the money are quite effective. They are very similar to those of many financial advisors.[1,5, 6,9]

Run-On (Fused) Sentences

Run-on or *Fused sentences* are two independent clauses joined without punctuation or without a conjunction. When connecting two independent clauses, some form of punctuation is required.

- *Incorrect.* Mary walked through the meadow she liked the smell of the wild flowers.
- *Correct.* Mary walked through the meadow; she liked the smell of the wild flowers.
- *Correct.* Mary walked through the meadow *and* liked the smell of the wild flowers.
- *Correct.* Mary walked through the meadow. She liked the smell of the wild flowers.[1,6]

SPLIT INFINITIVES

Americans tend to insert adverbs between "to" and the verb in an infinitive. Because this tendency has existed for a long time, it sounds correct to most people. Unfortunately, writers are guilty of perpetuating the error. When writing dialogue, a writer must create believable characters, which most of the time means letting them use split infinitives when they speak. But you shouldn't use split infinitives in those sections of text that are not dialogue. Common split infinitives include:

- **Incorrect.** *to* quickly *go*
- **Incorrect.** *to* angrily *say*
- **Incorrect.** *to* impatiently *wait*

The most famous splint infinitive in American literature, which includes movie and TV scripts, is "to boldly go" from the *Star Trek* opening. The adverb in infinitives should follow the verb:

- **Correct.** *to go* quickly
- **Correct.** *to say* angrily
- **Correct.** *to wait* impatiently

And of course, "to go boldly."[1]

SUBJECT-VERB AGREEMENT

A singular verb must be used with a singular subject and a plural verb with a plural subject. Many singular verbs end with the letter "*s*" while plural nouns end in "*s*" as well.

- **Singular.** The *cat dreams* about chasing mice.
- **Plural.** The *cats dream* about chasing mice.[1]

Subject and Verb Separated by Dependent Clauses.

- **Incorrect.** *Conflicts* within the group *interferes* with the ability to reach a consensus.
- **Correct.** *Conflicts* within the group *interfere* with the ability to reach a consensus.

"Conflicts" and not "group" is the subject of this sentence. Therefore, the verb should be plural not singular because it is "conflicts" that "interfere" with the ability to reach a consensus.[11]

Singular Words Assumed to be Plural

- *Incorrect.* The problem of delivery is due to a number of factors. *Each are* interrelated.
- *Correct.* The problem of delivery is due to a number of factors. *Each is* interrelated.

"Each" is a singular word and so requires the singular verb "is."[11]

Joining Two Subjects with Connecting Words or Phrases

Joining two subjects with some connecting words or phrases often causes a problem. The verb must agree with the subject closest to it.

- *Incorrect.* Maps or a *diagram help* find the location of the mall.
- *Correct.* Maps or a *diagram helps* find the location of the mall.[11]

All/Most

The indefinite pronouns "all" and "most" can be singular or plural depending on the phrase that follows the pronoun.

- *Singular Verb.* All of the *pie* was *eaten.* Most of the *pie* was eaten.
- *Pleural Verb.* All of the *women were pleased.* Most of the women *were pleased.*[9]

Fractions

If the subject of the sentence is a fraction, look at the phrase that follows the fraction to determine whether the verb should be singular or plural.

- *Singular Verb.* Half of the *candy bar was* eaten.

- *Plural Verb.* Half of the *candy bars were* eaten.[9]

Either/neither

If the correlatives "either ... or" or "neither... nor" are present in the sentence, the verb must agree with the subject closest to it.

- *Pleural Verb.* Either Sam or his *friends drive* to the arena.
- *Singular Verb.* Sam's friends or *he drives* to the arena.[9]

Group Nouns

Group nouns such as "team," "class," "committee," and "jury" are considered singular when they are acting as one unit and plural if the members are acting as individuals.

- *Singular.* The *team celebrates* by eating steaks after every victory.
- *Plural.* The *team* (members) *argue* over where to eat steaks after each victory.
- *Singular.* The *committee was formed* to nominate a candidate.
- *Plural.* The *committee* (members) *were voting* on which person to nominate.[9]

You

The pronoun "you" requires a plural verb whether it is referring to one person or a group of people.

- *One Person. You were* the first one I ever dated
- *Group of People.* Do all of *you have* proper identification?[9]

VERBALS

A *verbal* is the form of a verb that is used as another part of speech. The term *verbal* indicates that it is based on a verb and therefore expresses action or a state of being. There are three verbals: (1) Participles, (2) gerunds, and (3) infinitives. In addition, each can be used in a phrase.

Participles

A *participle* is a verbal that is used as an adjective. Since it functions as an adjective, it modifies a noun or a pronoun. There are two types of participles: present participles and past participles. Present participles end in "ing." Past participles usually end in "ed."

- **Present Participle.** The *crying* baby was hungry.
- **Past Participle.** The *overstuffed* sofa sat in the den.

A *participial phrase* is formed by taking a verb's "ing" form (present participle) or its "ed" form (past participle) and adding a prepositional phrase.

- **Present Participle Phrase.** *Listening to her sing* he was impressed by her vocal range.
- **Past Participle Phrase.** Children *introduced to music early* develop a strong interest in the type of music they heard.[12,13]

Gerunds

A *gerund* is a verb that ends in "ing" and is used as a noun. Since a gerund functions as a noun, it occupies positions in a sentence that a noun ordinarily would—subject, direct object, subject complement, and object of preposition.

- **Subject.** *Reading* is an intellectual pursuit.
- **Direct Object.** They don't appreciate my *singing*.
- **Subject Complement.** My dog's favorite activity is *lying* in my lap.
- **Object of Preposition.** The Principal kicked him out of school for *cheating*.

A *Gerund Phrase* is a group of words consisting of a gerund and a modifier, noun, pronoun, or noun phrase that functions as the direct object, indirect object, or complement of the action or state expressed in the gerund.

- **Subject.** *Writing fiction* is a skill most people don't possess.
- **Direct Object.** I hope you appreciate *my offering you this job.*
- **Subject Complement.** His technique has been *lying to his wife.*
- **Object of Preposition.** You will probably get in trouble *for faking an illness* to avoid school.[12,13]

Infinitives

An infinitive is a verbal consisting of the word "to" plus a "verb" and functioning as a noun, adjective, or adverb.

- **Subject.** *To flee* seemed dumb since there was no place to hide.
- **Direct Object.** I want *to sing* at the Super Bowl.
- **Adjective.** He lacked the strength *to resist.*
- **Adverb.** You must study *to learn.*

An *infinitive phrase* consists of an infinitive combined with a noun object or a modifying word or phrase.

- **Direct Object.** Sam agreed *to share his food.*
- **Adjective.** I have a lot *to do before the game.*[12,13]

When to Use Verbals

Verbals can be used to change the emphasis or to eliminate some wordage.

To Change the Emphasis

In the following paragraph from Rich Hamper notice how the reader's attention is called to the noises.

- *He couldn't concentrate; the noises were just too distracting. Children quarreled shrilly in the street. Car horns blared as tires squealed. Dogs barked. A vacuum cleaner hummed. Someone beat on a set of drums, trying to pound them into submission.*[12]

Now notice how a little reworking using verbals changes the focus by putting less emphasis on the noises:

- *His concentration was broken by too many distractions—the shrill quarrelling of children in the street, the blaring of car horns as tires squealed, the barking of dogs, and the beating of drums by someone trying to pound them into submission.*[12]

To Eliminate Some Wordage

Again an example from Hamper:

- *The siren shrieked and jolted Sam out of a sound sleep. He rolled out of bed and stumbled into the bathroom. He tried to remember what day it was.*[12]

The above can be shortened somewhat to read:

- *The shrieking siren jolted Sam out of a sound sleep. Rolling out of bed and stumbling into the bathroom, he tried to remember what day it was.*[12]

WHETHER OR NOT

Whether or not should be used only to mean "if or even if not." It is a contraction of "whether it will or will not."

- I'm going shopping *whether or not* you go (I'm going shopping whether you go or do not go).
- You should fire him *whether or not* he is late again. (You should fire him whether he will or will not be late again).

Whether or not is sometimes used incorrectly when *whether* alone is indicated.

- **Incorrect.** *Whether or not* you watch the game on TV or go in person, it should be exciting to watch.
- **Correct.** *Whether* you watch the game on TV or go in person,

it should be exciting to watch.[14,15]

References

1. Schnelbach, Susan D. and Wyatt, Christopher Scott, Tameri Guide for Writers, http://www.tameri.com/edit/gramerrors.html, June 15, 2005.
2. 11 rules of writing, Junket Studies, http://junketstudies.com/rulesofw/frules.html.
3. Easily confused or misused words, Infoplease, http://www.infoplease.com/ipa/A0200807.html.
4. Freeman, Morton, S., The WordWatcher's Guide to Good Writing & Grammar, Writer's Digest Books, Cincinnati, 1990.
5. Grammar, Illinois Wesleyan University, http://www.iwu.edu/~mcriley/papers/grammar.html.
6. Common grammatical errors, http://www.sunysuffolk.edu/Web/Selden/OWL/grammaticalerrors.htm.
7. Common grammatical errors and how to fix them, Academic Resource Center, Sweet Briar College, http://www.arc.sbc.edu/grammar.html.
8. Thompson, A.J. and A.V. Martinet, A Practical English Grammar, Oxford University Press, Oxford, 2003.
9. Grammar Tips, Writing Corner, http://homepages.cambrianc.on.ca/tutorial/thetutorialcentre/writing/Grammar%20Tips.html.
10. Spelling: Common words that sound alike, Purdue Online Writing Lab, http://owl.english.purdue.edu/handouts/print/grammar/g_spelhomo.html.
11. Organization and editing at sentence level, Steps to improving your writing (3), http://www2.umist.ac.uk/eltc/gpdp/Contents/unit7.htm, December 10, 2005.
12. Hamper, Rich, Verbals and what they're good for, http://home.comcast.net/~rthamper/html/body_verbals.htm, 1998.
13. Verbals: Verbals, Participles, and Infinitives, Purdue Online Writing Lab, http://owl.english.purdue.edu/handouts/grammar/g_verbals.html#participles.
14. Fowler, H.W., A Dictionary of Modern English Usage (*2nd ed.*) Oxford University Press, Oxford, 1984.
15. Writing Tips, Writer's Block, "Whether or not," http://www.writersblock.ca/tips/monthtip/tipapr96.htm.

INDEX

Allegory, 112-113
Backstory, 43-52
  direct methods, 43-50
    exposition, 44-46
    flashback, 46-50
  indirect methods, 50-51
    implied past expectation,
      51
    implied past network, 51
    past as present event, 50-51
  length, 51-52
Body language, 283-294
  examples of, 293-294
  facial expression, 284-285
  gestures, 285-286
  groups, 288
  posture, 286-287
  spatial relationships, 287-288
  table of, 289-283
  types of, 284-288
Characterization, 213-244
Character attributes, 236-238
Character chart, 239-242
Character classification, 213-223
  major characters, 214-218
    antagonist, 217-218
    main character, 216-217
    protagonist, 215-216
  major or minor characters, 219-
    223
    eccentrics, 220
    foil, 219
    memorable, 221
    off-beat, 219-220

    phobic, 221-223
    psychos, 220-221
  minor characters, 218-219
    bit players, 218
    sacrificial characters, 218-
      219
    stock characters, 218
Character description, 223-
  229
  compensation, 228-229
  desires and goals, 228
  dominant characteristics, 223-
    223
  involvement, 227-228
  self image, 229
  tags, 224-225
  uniqueness, 225-227
Character development, 229-231
  character change, 230-231
  methods of creating, 230
Character, how to bring in, 238
Character names, 231-233
Clichés, 52-56
  cliché characters, 54-55
  cliché phrases, 52-54
  cliché situations, 55-56
Coincidence, 134-135
Comma splice, 334-335
Commonly confused words, 320-
  329
Conflict and suspense, 128-134
  conflict, 128-132
    external, 128-131
    internal, 131-132

suspense, 132-134
  creating, 133
  mechanisms for creating, 134
Copyright, 297-298
  infringement penalty, 298-299
  notice, 298
Crisis and challenge, 127
  challenge, 127
  crisis, 127
Description, 56-59
  blending, 56-57
  brand names, 57
  the words to use, 57-58
    adjective-based, 59
    noun- based, 58
    verb-based, 59
Dialogue, 245-280
  conventions, 255-259
    bits and pieces versus chunks, 256
    cursing, 259
    emphasis, 257
    individuality, 257
    internal, 257
    men talking to men, 255
    situational, 256
    sounds, 257-258
    speeches, 258-259
  dialect, 263-264
  direct, 246
  jargon, 264-265
  indirect, 246
  punctuation, 265-267
    nested quotation marks, 266-267
    new speaker, 266
    statements, questions, and exclamations, 265-266
  rules for good, 259-260
  slang, 263
  slang and jargon websites, 265
  tags, 260-262
    action, 261

creative dialogue tag syndrome, 261-262
    excessive direct address, 262
  speech, 260-261
  techniques, 253-255
  types of 249-255
    directed, 249-250
    interpolated, 250
    misdirected, 250-252
    modulated, 252-253
  uses of, 246-249
  versus conversation, 245-246
Double negatives, 329
Emotions, 269-280
  and body language, 271
  characteristics, 269-270
  descriptive phrases, 276-277
  etiology, 269-270
  examples of, 276-280
  levels, 270
  mixed, 270
  range, 270
  situations, 277-280
  table of, 271-276
Essential clauses, 320
Fiction, literary, 2
  length, 3-4
  novel, 3-4
  novelette, 3
  novella, 3
  novella, 3
  short story, 3
  Key elements, 4-15
    characters, 7-10
    plot, story, and structure, 4-6
    point of view, 11-12
    prose, 12-13
    setting, 6-7
    theme and subject, 14-15
Figurative language, 63-65
  analogy, 63-64
  apostrophe, 65

hyperbole, 64
irony, 65
metaphor, 64
metonymy, 65
onomatopoeia, 64
oxymoron, 65
paradox, 65
periphrasis, 64
personification, 64
pun, 65
sarcasm, 65
simile, 64
synecdoche, 64
wordplay, 65
Flash forward, 67-68
Form, 68
Foreshadowing, 66-67
Genre, 2, 19-39
    action/adventure, 20
    Christian, 21
    fantasy, 21-23
    gay/lesbian, 23-24
    historical, 24
    horror, 24-25
    mystery/detective, 25-29
    romance, 29-31
    science fiction, 31-35
    spy/espionage, 35-36
    thriller, 36-38
    western, 38-39
    young adult, 39
Ideas, getting, 300-302
    record your, 302
    sources of ideas, 301-302
Imagery, 69-71
    levels of, 70
    suggestions for using, 71
Information, 71
Interlocking episodes, 71-72
Introspection, 72
Insight, 73
Linking episodes, 77-78
Literary fiction vs genre fiction, 2
    genre fiction, 2

literary fiction, 2
Manuscript,
    format, 302-304
    revision, 304-308
        steps for, 305-308
        types of, 304-305
Modifiers, 78-81, 329-331
    adjectives, 78-79
    adverbs, 79-80
        nonspecific, 79-80
    dangling, 330
    nearly, almost, and only, 330-331
    overuse of, 80, 262-263
    valueless, 80
Narrative, 81-82
Nonessential clauses, 319-320
One word or two?, 331-333
Pacing, 210-213
Perception, 73-74
Personality components, 233-236
Plagiarism, 299-300
    famous examples of 299-300
    steps to avoid, 300
Plot, 123-148
    outlining, 147-148
    parallel, 125-126
    structure, 125-127
    subplots, 126-127
    twenty basic, 137-146
    summary, 146-147
Point of view, 82-86
    first-person, 82-83
    multiple, 86
    second-person, 86
    third person, 83-86
Possessives, 333
Pronouns, 333-334
    antecedent agreement, 334
    case, 333-334
    noun-pronoun agreement, 334
Query letter, 309-312
Run on (fused) sentences, 335
Scene, 194-200

cause and effect, 196-197
  length, 200
  questions to answer, 194-196
  stages, 197-200
Scene and sequel, 193-212
Scene-sequel structure, variation, 208-209
Semicolon and comma usage, 319-320
  lists, 319
Sentences, 87-88
  fragments, 87
  variety, 87-88
Sequel, 200-208
  length, 208
  purposes, 201-203
  stages, 203-208
Series novels, 88-89
Setting, 91-96
  experience, 95
  place, 92-95
    fictitious, 94-95
    real, 92-94
    single versus multiple, 95
  mood, 95-99
    five senses, 97
    weather, 98-99
  time, 92
Simultaneity, 99-100
Special scenes, 100-109
  action, 100-102
  crowd/battle, 102-105
  death, 105
    off scene, 105
    on scene, 105
  love, 105-109
    effective, 106-108
    ineffective, 108-109
Split infinitives, 335-336
Story focus, 135-137
  character driven, 136-137
  idea-driven, 136
  plot-driven, 135-136
Structure, 69, 151-190

beginning, 157-174
  beginnings to avoid, 173-174
  big event, 171-172
  complications, 177-179
  components, 161-172
  hook, 162-170
  main character, 170-171
  questions readers ask, 159-161
  setting, 171
  story question, 159
  wide and narrow, 172-273
chart, 188-190
end, 181-187
  circular, 183-184
  climax, 182
  dues ex machine, 186-187
  happy, sad, and satisfying, 184-185
  linear, 184
  no, 185
  resolution, 182-183
  stated goal versus true goal, 185-186
  symbolic event, 187
epilogue, 188
middle, 174-181
  complications, 175-177
  crisis, 177-178
  disaster, 176-177
  sagging, 178-181
prologue, 154-157
  test, 157
  types, 155-156
title, 152-154
  categories, 152-153
  importance, 153-154
Style, 111-112
Subject-verb agreement, 336-338
Symbolism, 112
Synopsis, 312-316
Telling versus showing, 113-115
  showing, 114-115

telling, 113-114
Time, 115
Tone, 112
Transitions, 115-129
    chapter breaks, 119
    jump-cut, 117-118
       120-121
    simple, 116-117
Verbals, 338-341
    Gerunds, 339-340
    Infinitives, 340
    Participles, 339
    When to use verbals, 340-341

Verb strength, 119-121
    active versus passive voice,
       119-120
    strong verbs versus weak verbs,
       120-121
Ways to keep the reader worried,
    209-210
    scene ways, 209
    sequel ways, 210
Whether or not, 341-342
Withholding information, 135
Writing fiction, craft 1
    talent, 1

CPSIA information can be obtained at www.ICGtesting.com
Printed in the USA
238235LV00001B/125/A